What people are saying about Skill Wars: Winning the Battle for Productivity and Profit

"*Skill Wars* truly drives home one of the most serious problems we face as a nation today. Where are we going to get our workforce for the 21st century? Clearly, if we don't change our collective behavior, what is in for us in the next century is the proverbial economic 'train wreck'. Ed Gordon's book is a call to arms. I hope we are up to it."

—**Ronald Gidwitz**, Former President and CEO, Helene Curtis Industries

"Ed Gordon's research demonstrates that investment in people pays off. Training and development improves earnings. [Ed's] writing provides a practical way to managing the investment in these activities."

—**Andrew J. McKenna, Jr.,** President, Schwarz

"I think that *Skill Wars* has great potential to move corporate America to action! Dr. Gordon has very cogently presented the case for investing in all forms of training and education, and clearly presented the consequences of continuing the paradigm of over-reliance on the short-run (quarterly) bottom-line."

—**Kevin Hollenbeck**, Senior Economist, The W.E. Upjohn Institute for Employment Research

"*Skill Wars* is ambitious in scope, covering not only the need for work force education in the workplace but also career education, technical education, computer literacy, and teacher technology education . . . Dr. Gordon masterfully frame[s] school reform in terms of the revolution going on in the workplace. Congratulations on a job well done!"

—**Eunice N. Askov**, Ph.D., Professor of Education, Head, Department of Adult Education, Director, Institute for the Study of Adult Literacy, the Pennsylvania State University

"*Skill Wars* is a must read for anyone who is managing people. Frequently "on the job training" consists of a new employee learning from an experienced co-worker how to perform the specific tasks for which the person was hired. All too often the training, and if you will, communications aspect of the job ends with that brief training period. We have found that a more productive employee is one who is not only better trained but also is one who provides suggestions on how different jobs can be performed more efficiently and effectively. Problem-solving skills and the ability to create a positive work force environment rather than reacting to the marketplace are needed in this age of incredible technological opportunities."

—**James E. Baumhart**, President and CEO, Better Business Bureau, Chicago, Northern Illinois

"*Skill Wars* is a wake-up call to all American businesses, large and small. Quick fix education and training programs will come back to haunt businesses later. Only a long term investment in human capital—in current and future employees—will allow businesses to prosper, grow and maintain competitive . . . My hope is that Skill Wars will cause everyone to act now."

—**Deborah Lenchard**, Senior Director, Education and Training Programs, Chicago Mercantile Exchange

"*Skill Wars* will help to fully awaken all levels and sectors of our society to the full depth of the educational crisis facing our nation, and its corporations. The current wave of down-sizings, mergers and other reconfigurations of today's corporations does nothing to alter the depth of the educational pool all must draw upon—only fundamental steps, like those discussed by Dr. Gordon, can improve this dimension of the competitive landscape."

—**Ronald R. Shepps**, Ph.D, Organizational Development Specialist, and Chief Learning Officer, Lima Chemicals, B.P./Amaco

"In *Skill Wars*, Ed. Gordon offers a wake up call to educators, training professionals, and CEOs as he demonstrates through extensive research and case studies that workforce education is a lifelong activity. High-level learning and critical thinking skills should be the ultimate goal of the American educational system as well as business and industry. Gordon describes and often challenges current educational and training practices. He suggests a huge, long-term human capital investment—and more partnering—is needed if America is to develop a competitive edge. He operationalizes this premise by offering a practical strategy to measure training's return on investment. His arguments should be heard by everyone."

—**Bridget O'Connor**, Ph.D., Associate Professor and Director, Business Education Program, New York University

"*Skill Wars* is a call "to get with the program" and make a dramatic change in investing in education and training at a time when the vast majority of the business leadership doesn't fully understand the scope and enormity of the problem confronting them. Dr. Gordon's ROI is a powerful message."

—**Don Clark**, President, National Association for Industry-Education Cooperation

"American business managers need to stop wringing their hands over the shortage of skilled workers and pick up this book. It has what we've been missing: real world models and tools for building the knowledge-based workforce every company must have to compete in the Information Age. Take heed—and take heart!"

—**Lynn Densford**, Editor, Corporate University Review

"Whatever your product or service, a trained work force is a key to victory. If you need convincing, read Ed Gordon's *Skill Wars*. If you're already convinced, read it for the new tools it gives you to measure the impact of your training efforts on the bottom-line."

—**Paul J. Miller**, Senior Partner, Sonneschein, Nath and Rosenthal

"Once again, Ed Gordon is ahead of the curve. In *Skill Wars* he cuts to the basics of increasing the productivity of this nation through better education. His analysis is thorough, his answer simple—invest in people and believe in people."

—**John M. McLaughlin**, Ph.D, President, The Education Industry Group, LLC

"*Skill Wars* is one of the few books I would call a "must read" for leaders moving toward the 21st century. Dr. Gordon's research and insights on the needs, development, and implementation of a highly trained and skilled workforce are practical and effective. It is a call to arms for our future."

—**Charles E. Fish**, Vice President of Human Resources, Wabash National

"It is indeed the most comprehensive documentation of the fact—FACT!, not assumption or theory—that investment in education and training DOES PAY!"

—**Dr. Hans Schieser**, International Business Consultant, Professor Emeritus, De Paul University, Chicago

"Chapter 8 of *Skill Wars* is a "must read" for leaders from education, business, community, and families. Dr. Gordon provides a "no holds barred," pragmatic discussion focused both on problems and concrete solutions—that must be addressed collaboratively by community stakeholders—to improve the education and skills of America's future workforce."

—**Susan D, Otterbourg**, Ed.D., President, Delham Educational Communications, Durham, North Carolina

"In short, I regard *Skill Wars* as a major contribution to problems involved in education/work relationships in the emerging information society. It deserves careful study by leaders both in business and in education."

—**Kenneth B. Hoyt**, Ph.D, University Distinguished Professor, Kansas State University

Skill Wars

Skill Wars
Winning the Battle
for Productivity and Profit

By

Edward E. Gordon

Butterworth-Heinemann
Boston • Oxford • Auckland • Johannesburg • Melbourne • New Delhi

♾ Recognizing the importance of preserving what has been written,
Butterworth–Heinemann prints its books on acid-free paper whenever possible.

 Butterworth–Heinemann supports the efforts of American Forests and
the Global ReLeaf program in its campaign for the betterment of trees,
forests, and our environment.

Library of Congress Cataloging-in-Publication Data

Gordon, Edward E.
   Skill wars : winning the battle for productivity and profit /
by Edward E. Gordon.
     p. cm.
   Includes bibliographical references and index.
   ISBN 0-7506-7207-2 (pbk. : alk. paper)
   I. Employees—Training of—United States.   2. Occupational
training—United States.   3. Skilled labor—United States.   I. Title.
HF5549.5.T7 G5474   1999
658.3'124—dc21   99-29526
                                                CIP

British Library Cataloguing-in-Publication Data
A catalogue record for this book is available from the British Library.

The publisher offers special discounts on bulk orders of this book.
For information, please contact:

Manager of Special Sales
Butterworth–Heinemann
225 Wildwood Avenue
Woburn, MA 01801–2041
Tel: 781-904-2500
Fax: 781-904-2620

For information on all Butterworth–Heinemann publications available,
contact our World Wide Web home page at: http://www.bh.com

10 9 8 7 6 5 4 3 2 1

Printed in the United States of America

Dedication

In memory of my beloved sister Marilyn, who always encouraged her brother to do his very best in helping other people.

Table of Contents

List of Figures

Boxes

Tables

Foreword

In one sense, it is a sad commentary on American business that a book such as the one you are about to read must be written. As we approach the twenty-first century in the midst of a knowledge economy that everyone admits is in full bloom, it would seem unnecessary for anyone to have to justify investments in education and training. One would think that the value of such investments would be a given. Sadly, they aren't. Too many CEOs and small business owners still just don't get it. They see education and training as something nice to do, but of questionable bottom-line benefit. They need measures of the value of the training and education they are providing, they say, but there aren't any that are truly reliable. Well, thanks to Ed Gordon, they now have them right here in this book.

In the pages that follow, Ed Gordon clearly and succinctly outlines why the skills of the American workforce have become the single most important factor in the competitiveness not only of individual companies, but of national economies. He documents the widening gap between the need for highly skilled workers and their availability, and he points out the chilling consequences that may occur if the skill gap continues to widen. As Ed points out, we face the worst of all possible worlds in which high-tech jobs go unfilled while millions of unskilled workers languish without jobs. Unfilled jobs lead to unfulfilled potential for companies and workers. Economies grind to a stop. The social consequences alone are horrible to contemplate. And all of this happens because we fail to invest in education and training.

Ed makes the case plainly. Education and training are needed on a massive scale. But what should we teach, and how can we evaluate the results of our efforts? Ed offers provocative answers to both questions in the pages that follow. Ed provides us with a Workforce

Education Triad that lays out the basic building blocks for a new business learning system. He also provides us with an interdisciplinary Human Capital ROI Worksheet to calculate an accurate return on investment (ROI) for education and training.

A Workforce Education Triad and a Human Capital ROI Worksheet—these are just two of the new tools Ed Gordon offers us. As you read what follows, you may not agree with everything Ed says, but we are certain you will be challenged by his ideas and insights. If you are a trainer or educator, you already know the need for increasing our investment in education and training. This book will provide you with invaluable new tools for making the case to upper management for the investment. If you are a member of upper management, we predict you will find Ed's insight and precise methodology enormously enlightening. If you are an average working American, once you read this book you will more fully understand the crisis we face, what we must and can do about it, and how we can and should measure our progress. Read on—there is much to be learned here.

Joseph H. Boyett & Jimmie T. Boyett
Co-authors of *Beyond Workplace 2000* and
The Guru Guide

Introduction

In an age of technology, people make the difference.

AMERITECH

During the twentieth century, America won the three great wars that largely defined her democratic existence and prosperity: World War I, World War II, and the Cold War. At the beginning of the third millennium America is again locked in global conflict that will again define her prosperity and decide if the United States is to continue to be a world leader in the twenty-first century. *Skill Wars* demonstrates the vital nature of this new struggle and clearly depicts the forces that must be marshalled for a successful outcome.

The new "weapons" in this twenty-first-century war are not tanks, planes, or ships, but the minds and creativity of all our people. The battleground has shifted from distant foreign lands to our local offices, production facilities, and classrooms in the workplace, school, or home. The "enemy" is much more difficult to see. For it is the ignorance inside each of us, the fear of the unknown, of admitting "we just don't get it." In past centuries, workers had a shortage of information to do their jobs. Now they have a glut. Employees and students need to develop a better framework through which they can learn to understand and turn all this information into useable knowledge. In other words, they must learn "critical thinking" or "critical competencies," meaning moving knowledge from the abstract to new concrete applications. In the new high-tech global economy skills have become the "new currency."

For the business person, *Skill Wars* is a policy book about managing and measuring workplace performance and profit. For the union leader and employee, *Skill Wars* is about employability and personal growth. For parents, *Skill Wars* is about their children's future careers and guaranteed participation in "the American dream." For politicians and government leaders, *Skill Wars* is a blueprint for what voters are beginning to demand in every state across America: new laws to create a more knowledgeable workforce. For educators and trainers, *Skill Wars* offers new ideas on how to better collaborate with all these groups and create innovative, diverse curricula, whether in a schoolroom or a corporate classroom.

Understanding the *Skill Wars* means changing your perspective. One recent morning in a typical downtown high-rise office building, a group of people gathered around the office coffee machine. It was a cold, windy, January day. Across from their office a new building was rising. As usual, the iron workers were going about their jobs. However, on this particular morning one office worker took a big piece of white cardboard and wrote "72°" on it in big, bold, red numbers and held it up to the window. In a few minutes some of the iron workers noticed the message. One grabbed a nearby piece of plywood, and scrawled his response: "$200 PER HOUR!" Winning the *Skill Wars* means altering our twentieth-century perspectives with a wider view of the skills people will need for productive work in the twenty-first century.

The Business Message

American business is underplaying the significance of their employees' knowledge and skills. Top management at companies large and small talk about developing their human capital, but in fact, they largely do not. Though senior management may pay lip service to "the learning organization" as a broad policy, training is largely dismissed for most employees as a burdensome cost that must be cut. In a contemporary American workplace fixated on technological change and short-term profit, this shortsightedness is threatening the long-term bottom line of American businesses.

Since the 1970s, the driving force behind the new industrial/technological revolution has been the explosive growth of computers, robots, "digital factories," and team/quality management systems.

Yet by education and training, only 20 percent of all American workers can fit well into this demanding new high-tech workplace. The poor fit between available jobs and available workers is the people paradox that's been emerging in this last decade of the twentieth century. Blizzards of business, government, and think-tank reports contend that the other 80 percent of the nation's workforce lack the required skills and problem-solving abilities to participate fully in this revolution.

In this new race between advanced technology investment and human resource investment, both American companies and American workers are becoming the losers. Four-fifths of all the people employed by our economy today—a figure that includes many managers as well as production and technical workers—are in danger of turning into the "new techno-peasants of the information age" because they lack appropriate skills.

The simple fact is that America has run out of adequate numbers of well-educated, problem-solving, technically astute workers. As U.S. unemployment continues to fall, every business sector is screaming that it cannot find "skilled" workers. Even though a slowdown is expected by many in the overall U.S. economy, when it happens employers don't see that translating into significant layoffs of skilled workers. That's because many organizations have told me they're already operating on too-lean staffs because of the lack of skilled people. Why? Today entry-level back-office personnel need to have computer skills. Even maintenance people need to be literate to handle dangerous chemicals. According to a 1994 U.S. Department of Education study, more than 90 million employees in the United States today lack the education/business skills to perform their jobs adequately. Yet advancing technology requires ever-increasing education levels on the job. As David Birch, CEO of Cognetics, Inc., states, "It is no longer the production of technology, but its application that creates growth opportunities."

Presidents of companies that have tried to address these workforce-performance issues report that their quality programs too often fail because "my people don't comprehend the message." Those few companies that do offer comprehensive in-house training/education programs too often consider abandoning them, citing high costs and saying "they haven't found the right training programs yet."

According to a 1994 survey conducted by Price Waterhouse, despite these unsatisfactory experiences 64 percent of senior managers report that they expect their training needs to increase over the next five years.

The fact that the learning organization has largely flunked out in the boardroom can be traced to two causes: first, presidents, CEOs, and small-business owners still see no connection between company profit and investing in their human capital, because they believe you can't measure it; and second, current training programs often don't improve employee performance because they aren't based on the most recent advances in teaching critical-competency/problem-solving skills.

Mention "lifelong learning" to the typical group of managers and you will most likely hear a groan or see blank stares of disbelief. It's just too damn intellectual! Let's face it—many people still talk about the year they "got out," not of prison, but of school. For most people schooling was not a very pleasant experience. It was a life phase to get through. Yet talk to these same people about systems and productivity applications, complex issues though they may be, and you will get all their attention.

What's the Difference?

Complex and multilayered workplace performance-learning issues need to be stated in a language and format that will move more business leaders and the public to give them their personal support. A good example of how this was done is the environmental movement, a very complex set of scientific–economic issues. Back in the 1970s only an extreme fringe group talked about a global environmental-pollution threat. However, over the next two decades these issues were presented in understandable, compelling ways so that today few people do not support the concept of a cleaner environment for all. Even though most American business people and the public support the concept of better education in general, it is in the particular (i.e., in my business, in my community) that support falls apart. Winning the *Skill Wars* challenge means accomplishing for lifelong learning what was done for the environment across America.

Though U.S. business as a whole hasn't gotten the connection between productivity and a well-prepared workforce, our competitors in Germany and Japan have. The era of exclusive American domination in advanced technologies has ended, but all the reasons for this aren't so widely understood. Many of America's chief competitors are beating us at our own game because they understand that knowledge equals profit. Rather than ignoring the relationships, they are acting on the critical interactions among technology, smarter employees, and return on investment. They invest extensively both in student career-education and employee retraining programs and reap the short-term and long-term profits. How can we profitably apply the same strategy in America?

The Human Capital Scoreboard

Skill Wars introduces a Human Capital Scoreboard™ that gives managers a new tool kit to quantify the results for practically any training/education program. These five tools include a Managed Performance Matrix, a Knowledge Economic Model, the Workforce Education Triad™, planning maps, and a Human Capital Return-on-Investment Worksheet™, addressing serious pitfalls that have compromised previous efforts at making this a standard business calculation. Over a four year period, this author worked with an interdisciplinary team of an economist, a CPA/tax attorney, and a quality engineer to prepare a nine-step human capital ROI worksheet that quantifies people performance to the bottom line.

Business case studies offer examples of how to use this worksheet for different training/education/performance/productivity improvement programs. We will also discuss the adoption of accounting/bookkeeping procedures that make human capital investment a more attractive alternative for management.

Skill Wars offers business leaders sophisticated systems of measurement, concrete benchmarks, and the key policy concepts they need to prepare their employees successfully for the future of work. The key is high-quality reeducation programs that encourage employees to take charge of their own learning, leading them to see how they can increase personal performance, better their lifetime careers, and, in turn, give business a higher ROI. The case studies in this book offer management action plans that can be applied to any high-quality employee-education program and/or career-education program with local schools preparing the next generation of workers to enter a fast-paced business environment.

U.S. business demands leadership, and *Skill Wars* shows how it can be developed throughout any business. The key is providing appropriate education and training that enables employees to learn how to think and innovate on-the-job. A well-educated workforce, Joseph Stiglitz, chair of the Council of Economic Advisors, agrees, "can implement new ideas and innovations more quickly, generating technological advancements that are the key to raising productivity and enhancing long-term growth." *Skill Wars* outlines straightforward, real-world management models for workforce-education programs that can be immediately adopted by companies both large and small in any business or industry.

Answers to the Fundamental Question

Skill Wars centers around one fundamental question—"What is the least understood and most underrated asset in American business today?" I contend that in today's stripped-down, outsourced, reengineered, high-tech workplace, each employee's contribution assumes ever greater importance. Yet, the development of this key resource through training and education lags far behind our major foreign competitors.

Skill Wars aims to convince managers across America that knowledge equals profit by drawing upon case studies from the United States, Europe, and Asia. It provides management with a realistic business plan that begins to point out the way to reengineer an organization's human capital investment for greater productivity and profit.

I wish to acknowledge the hundreds of people who have contributed their invaluable information and ideas to *Skill Wars*. These include Eunice Askov, Professor and Department Head of the Adult Education Program, The Pennsylvania State University; Chad E. Cook, Director of Human Resources, Rubbermaid; Lynn Densford, Editor of *Corporate University Review*; John J. Ferrandino, President of the National Academy Foundation; Kevin Hollenbeck, Senior Economist at the W.E. Upjohn Institute for Employment Research; Ken

Hoyt, University Distinguished Professor, Kansas State University; Suzanne Knell, Executive Director of the Illinois Literacy Resources Development Center (ILRDC); Peggy Luce, Education and Training Manager of the Chicagoland Chamber of Commerce; Donna Manley, Outreach Specialist at the Center on Education and Work, University of Wisconsin; Ronald R. Morgan, Professor of Educational Psychology, Loyola University, Chicago; Robert M. Naiman, CPA and Tax Attorney; Charles J. O'Malley, educational consultant and former Director of Private Education, U.S. Department of Education; Susan Otterbourg, Education Conference Chair of the Conference Board; Boyd Owens, Production Supervisor at Equimetre, Division of BTR; Philip A. Pagano, Executive Director of the Northeast Illinois Metropolitan Transit Railroad Authority (Metra); Jack Phillips, President of the Performance Resources Organization; Judith A. Ponticell, Associate Professor, Educational Psychology and Leadership, Texas Tech University; Rick Quinn, Rick Quinn & Associates and former Executive Vice President for Quality, Sears Roebuck and Company; Hans Schieser, Professor Emeritus, DePaul University; Florence Stone, Group Editor, American Management Association; and Kenneth P. Voytek, Chief Economist, National Alliance of Business.

Most of all I thank all of my colleagues at Imperial Consulting Corporation. They provided invaluable assistance in preparing business case studies for this book.

Once again Sandy Gula-Gleason provided her great expertise in preparing the final manuscript after wading through many, many revisions.

I also thank my publishing agent, John Willig, for his many suggestions and perseverance in making this book a reality.

Finally, above all else I wish to acknowledge my wife, Elaine Gordon. This book would have never been completed without her constant expert research and insightful editorial assistance. For any factual errors contained herein, I take sole responsibility.

Edward E. Gordon
Chicago, Illinois
February 28, 1999

The Quality Journey Becomes a Short Trip

Business is moved by both the big shoves of its leaders, and by the tiny pushes of its "knowledge workers."

The Techno "Wind-Chill"

The winds of change are blowing from Chicago. As a world-class convention city, it played host to the International Manufacturing Technology Show. This annual techno-blowout gathers a whopping 120,000 industrialists, engineers, and machinists from around the world.

Robert McGowan was standing in McCormick Place beside a computer-numerical-controlled milling and turning machine. A behemoth, it cuts metal or plastic in any way you can think—milled, drilled, bored, or shaped. He was worrying out loud, the *Chicago Tribune* reported, about the future of American business and the future of the United States.

"Trouble is, we have a hard time recruiting enough people to operate it these days. We're not a country that's into building things anymore. We're a country into flipping hamburgers." But machine-tool firms remain critical to the overall U.S. economy because they traditionally produce a higher degree of innovation, and that is often transferred to other parts of industry.

American management and its workers are struggling anew to find an understandable bridge between the myths and the hard truths of how the U.S. economy really works. Perhaps the classic Yankee knack for tinkering is retro and unhip in a looming service economy.

"I guess this just isn't glamorous enough," said Jerry Biggs of Cincinnati Milacron, Inc., a leading tooling and manufacturing firm. "It's a shame because producing something tangible is what makes nations work. It's made us what we are." However, the good news for this industry is that the most startling technical innovations in the past few years have been American.

Not long ago the typical machine shop was a gritty place. Big guys loaded chunks of metal into huge machines that drilled, cut, and ground out parts for everything from washing machines to doorknobs.

Things have changed. High-precision, high-tech, high-speed equipment now dominates the industry. "I predict that in 2000," says Patrick F. Cherone, CEO of Wisconsin Machine Tool Corp., "there will not be single machine tool that doesn't communicate. They all will or they'll be history."

The people who run these machines have also changed. They use more mental tools, such as knowledge of computer software, and earn up to $70,000 a year.[1]

The once besieged U.S. machine-tool business has struck back after years of domination by Japanese and German competitors. In the past 10 years, machine tool exports have jumped 30 percent according to the Association for Manufacturing Technology (ATM).

The Chicago show displays look more like science-fiction sets than the grungy metal shops that in the past typified this industry. Now computers and robotics are everywhere. ATM spokesman Charles Pollock explains, "This field's full of creative energy. Your average machinist doesn't wear blue jeans and stop by at the bar for a beer anymore. He's a computer expert, a math expert."

The high-tech irony this creates is that businesses now need fewer people because of these technical advances, but they need far better educated people. The Chicago area alone suffers from a shortage of 450 precision, high-tech, high-pay metal workers every year. Why? Because few parents want to see their children in an apprenticeship program even if they have the aptitude and interest.

Robert McGowan is not hopeful that this is about to change. "We're a nation of button-pushers. We don't care how things work." Looking at these icy winds of change, his Yankee company has entered into a partnership with a high-tech Italian firm. Sounds familiar, doesn't it? But another company, Wabash National in Lafayette,

Indiana, has discovered an alternative to moving business offshore. It has gone into the "knowledge business" at home.[2]

People Make a Business

In 1985, working from a card table and three folding chairs in a downtown office, Donald J. Ehrlich began Wabash National to build truck trailers. This company's managers, besides calling on suppliers they already knew for orders, also called on Purdue University's management department for training. "The philosophy was that the people at Wabash were either going to make it or break it," explained Chuck Fish, vice president of human relations, in a front-page *Wall Street Journal* story.

They began classes for workers who wanted to be welders and for recent immigrants to learn English. A worker complained to Ehrlich that he was wasting his profit-sharing (part of the company's participatory motivational culture) on parking lot improvements. Ehrlich added a course in business basics. Now everyone can learn the difference between a capitalized expense (paving parking lots), and an operating expense (a load of parts). This formed part of a series of classes in business economics, statistical process control, the just-in-time inventory system, and team building.

All workers and managers have the opportunity to improve their skills, to receive training in basic business systems, and to be educated in the problem-solving, decision-making, and team-building processes. Wabash depends on its workers learning how a company makes a profit and how rapid growth and constant change will keep it profitable. Ehrlich says at Wabash, "We're trying to get workers to think about building trailers."

Over the last two years, workers have participated in 164 practical teams, such as the air brake stroke and free-play adjustment team. These groups have saved the company hundreds of thousands of dollars through practical, thoughtful production innovations.

Does Wabash support a more knowledgeable workforce? At Wabash, Jerry Ehrlich says, "Three Einsteins would be no match for a factory full of workers attending classes and contributing ideas." This is the essence of the so-called "learning organization" concept.

American business is at the end of an era in which only managers control people, information, and ideas. Victor Hugo was right:

"Nothing in the world is as powerful as an idea whose time has come." A new economic world order is now being organized around knowledge, speed, and technology defined by the capabilities of each employee.[3]

The Quality Road to Nowhere

Remember the old saying, "What's good for General Motors is good for America?" That adage is about to change. The percentage of gross domestic product (GDP) stemming from computers, semiconductors, and electronic instrumentation already equals the auto industry's share of 3.5 percent. It should exceed it by the century's end (*Wall Street Journal*, September 30, 1996). High tech's contribution to the U.S. economy has doubled during the past 10 years. We're moving into a new era where people will say, "What's good for Microsoft and Intel is good for America!"

On the eve of the twenty-first century, a tidal wave of technological advances and the expansion of international trade are transforming the business landscape. The U.S. economy remains the strongest in the world. The American Management Association (AMA) ranks U.S. firms number one (in sales volume) in 13 major industries: aerospace, apparel, beverages, chemicals, computers, food products, motor vehicles, paper products, petroleum, pharmaceuticals, photographic and scientific equipment, soap and cosmetics, and tobacco.[4]

Yet the U.S. economy's two weak spots threaten this continued world dominance. The trade deficit continued to widen throughout the 1990s, and growth in productivity remained sluggish. For the first 70 years of this century, nonfarming productivity rose at an average annual rate of 2.2 percent. But from 1973 through 1995, the increases have averaged just 1 percent.

This is hardly news. In the 1980s and 90s the rise of Total Quality Management (TQM) made it the preferred American management process to address this decline in productivity. According to A.T. Kearney, in the late 1980s poor quality cost the average U.S. company 10 to 20 percent of its sales dollars or two to four times its profits. Manufacturers spent 25 percent of their sales dollars fixing quality problems. The service industry saw 40 percent of its operating costs eaten up on nonconformance issues.

Yet although there have been some successes with TQM, by and large it has struggled to live up to its reputation.

So why has U.S. management struggled in applying TQM? The experience of a midsized Illinois industrial parts manufacturer is typical. As part of an ISO-9000 certification effort (a European quality standard), the company initiated a quality management program. They hired a vice president of quality assurance and established a management/union committee to implement employee involvement teams. A team facilitator was appointed, and a problem-solving process and training package presented throughout the company.

After a first-year program expenditure of $500,000, the measured result showed no change. Business productivity and quality measures had not budged. The CEO walked the plant during the course of several months to find out why. He had informal conversations with scores of production and supervisory employees. What he found out was disturbing. People enthusiastically attended the quality training seminars. They had heard the quality message. They had believed in the quality concept. But the president dejectedly told us, "My people didn't comprehend what we were saying." American management has typically underestimated the long-term education effort with all employees needed to make TQM a success. Many companies mistook it for a one-shot program, an event, or a short-term campaign. But far from being short-term, TQM is a long-term way of thinking that stresses change over the status quo.

In spite of this, the United States continues to receive the highest leadership marks for competitiveness. We still come out on top in economic strength, new technology, and financial services compared to 46 other developed countries. An international agency, The Organization for Economic Co-operation and Development (OECD), sees America's success resulting from bold economic reforms, deregulation and privatization, and renewed leadership in new technology.

But a major underlying weakness remains in people skills—education and training—in which the United States scored 15th (OECD, May 1996). This body described the low quality of American education at work and in the schoolhouse as "a major threat to America's future economic well-being, its productivity and competitiveness." This has been accentuated by globalization that has fundamentally transformed or displaced jobs across the United States in every economic sector, permanently altering labor/management relations.

"More and more, we see that competition in the international marketplace is in reality a battle of the classrooms," says Norman R. Augustine, CEO at Lockheed Martin Corporation and chair of the education task force at the Business Roundtable, a Washington association of more than 200 corporate CEOs (*Education Week*, November 27, 1996).

Globalization is fundamentally reorganizing the U.S. job market. According to the *Chicago Tribune's* R.C. Longworth, globalization is a handy term for the revolution that enables any entrepreneur to use money, technology, communication, management, and labor located anywhere in the world, to make things anywhere he wants, and sell them anywhere he wants. The productivity of America's industry is enhanced by exposure to this international competition, making America stronger, not weaker. According to the World Trade Organization, the United States increased its exports by 10 percent to $513 billion in 1994, more than any other country.[5]

What has changed is that jobs aren't being temporarily lost because of any downturn, but are being permanently wiped out by technology and new ways of organizing work. Merrill Lynch reported (1992) that 70 percent of the manufacturing jobs lost in the 1990s were white-collar, not blue-collar jobs. Hordes of educated middle managers are unable to find any work similar to their past occupations. Add in the undereducated workers incapable of handling almost any job in a high-performance economy, and America could face serious future social and political repercussions.

The People Paradox

These techno-competitive forces have the potential to improve our standard of living, if American management wakes up to the new economic realities. One of the new ideas that has yet to be fully understood by the business community is that the U.S. economy throughout the twentieth century rested largely on the exponential expansion of human knowledge and workforce education.

We predict that it will be in the twenty-first century that management realizes that the so-called "knowledge worker" (someone whose head is more important than his hands) has become a key business asset that links jobs–knowledge–profit in every organization. What we mean by "knowledge" is simply "finding a better way to do things." This has been the main source of long-term economic growth from the early industrial revolution until today. (In the past some people have called this American personality trait "Yankee Ingenuity.")

"All this means there's been a breaking of the mold economically," comments TRW's CEO Joseph Gorman about this change in the marketplace. "The old paradigms are no longer very helpful, very useful" (*Wall Street Journal*, November 22, 1995). This new "workforce education" is still a poorly understood management concept; it places people and innovation, not things, at the center of commercial success. Whether a company is making a world-class car, a world-class razor, or a world-class software program, well-educated people are now the defining element for business success. Ideas come from people, not machines.

Using this new approach in ranking the value of each country's natural resources, the World Bank (1995) ranked the top 15 industrial countries' per capita wealth—their machinery, buildings, and people. U.S. wealth amounted to $421,000 per person, nearly 60 percent of which reflected human resources, the value represented by people's productive thinking capacity. Human capital is the glue that holds society together.[6]

The new high-performance workplace has begun a transformation of what business values, because science and technology now drive the world's marketplace. The vital force in high-tech offices or factories is not mechanical force, but the human mental force that manipulates these material assets. Humans put machines in place. Machines do not replace human thought. "Computers are useless. They can only give you answers." (Pablo Picasso).[7]

However, for many executives talking about increasing performance means adding technology, not improving human performance. This is the thinking behind a popular story about the "factory of the future" entitled "A Man and a Dog." The man is there to feed the dog, and the dog is there to keep the man away from the equipment. The moral to the story is that future technology will be so powerful that people will only get in the way.

I have toured many such production facilities run by computers and robots. A few people in white lab coats were there only to monitor the equipment. But when the equipment broke down the entire production line was idled, costing in some cases millions of dollars in lost productivity, until a skilled technician, who was often many miles and hours away, could be called to fix the technology.

The real moral to "A Man and a Dog" is that "we cannot turn technology into our new god," thinks Paulo Freire. Technology was meant to serve people, and not to become an end unto itself. Those managers who make it so are bound to be disappointed with the final results.

A "people paradox" exists because, as these technological breakthroughs have multiplied throughout the U.S economy, the "education bar" has risen faster than the supply of knowledge workers. About half of the CEO's of America's fastest growing companies report (see Figure 1-1) that finding skilled, trained workers is a problem that threatens to slow company growth.

Andre Miles applied for a job at Lincoln Electric Co. (makers of motors and welding products) in Euclid, Ohio, three times in three years. He never got past a first interview, and he wasn't alone. More than

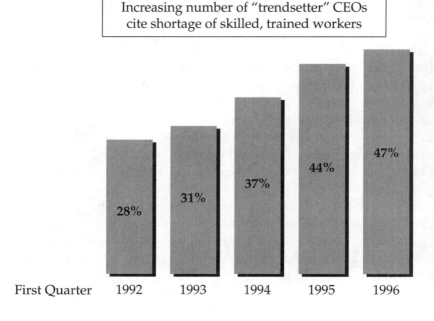

Figure 1-1 Worker Shortage
Source: Courtesy of *Corporate University Review,* July/August 1996.

20,000 applications were submitted over an 18-month period. Most job seekers were rejected. Yet Lincoln still had positions to fill and couldn't find the educated workers it needed. These were not low-wage jobs. Average worker pay was $19,800. But because the company did well, so did the employees. With bonuses, their average compensation came to $55,614.

To command these wages, today's technology employee needs to use advanced math, have good communication skills, and understand the use of computers. Most high-school students with these educational abilities have gone to college. So Lincoln is now getting more poorly educated students who apply to operate computer-controlled machines. The lack of knowledge workers stymies Lincoln's change-management plans. Nor is Lincoln alone in facing this dilemma (see Figure 1-2). How much lost productivity and profit does this account for?

The company won't specify how much it has spent on recruiting efforts, but it says it has spent more in the past 2 years than it had in all of the previous 98 years. This coincides with a significant continued annual rise across the United States in recruiting costs for both exempt and nonexempt employees (see Figure 1-3).[8]

In a national survey of major U.S. companies (May 1996), the American Management Association (AMA) reported that 40 percent of job applicants flunked basic math tests and 32 percent lacked the reading skills needed to do the jobs they sought. An earlier (1994) national literacy audit by the U.S. Labor/Education Departments contained the disquieting statistic that only about 20 percent of the current American workforce will fit well into the next century's demanding new workplace. These same government agencies (1994) also estimate that 80 percent of all U.S. jobs will require 12th- or 13th-grade reading comprehension levels. At present more than 90 million American workers (including 20 percent of all managers) fall below this benchmark. From a practical standpoint this means that one out of five Americans do not understand the directions on an aspirin bottle. Almost one-quarter cannot work out a newspaper weather chart (OECD, 1995). Eighty percent of these employees will still be in the workforce in the year 2010. It appears that a staggering number of younger and older workers alike are so poorly educated that they are now in real danger of permanently becoming the new "techno-peasants" of the information age.

Percentage of Surveyed Executives that Reported by Areas of Difficulty Change Management Issues Due to Employee Skill Deficiencies

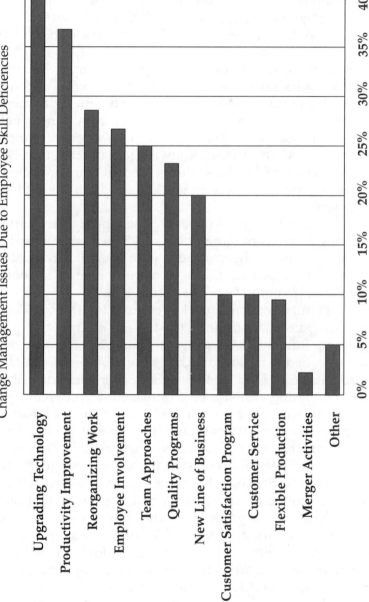

Figure 1-2 Employee Education Deficiencies Stymie Best-Laid Management Plans
Source: Adapted from NAM/Towers Perrin, *Today's Dilemma: Tomorrow's Competitive Edge,* November 1991.

Number of Interviews/Cost per Hire, Exempt Employees

**Companies interviewing
substantially more candidates . . .**   **. . . driving up cost per hire**

Candidates Interviewed
for Exempt-Level

Cost per Hire–Exempt
Employees
(20,000+ companies)

| 36% increase | | 13% increase |

Figure 1-3 Need for Better Talent Drying Up Exempt Recruiting Costs
Source: 1992 Cost per Hire Survey, Adapted from Saratoga Institute.

What does this cost American business? The Commerce Department (1993) estimates that the U.S. economy loses over $300 billion each year in reduced worker productivity because of the people paradox. And with each passing year, this number will continue to rise.

In the face of these devastating facts, most business managers seem strangely detached, largely indifferent to organizing a knowledge workforce. If we discount all the inflated business rhetoric concerning the support of workplace learning, it appears that most top management does not believe so much in "the learning organization," as in "the cheap organization." In 1998 the American Society for Training and Development estimated that business invested over $60 billion in formal education and training. This represents a decline in real terms, because the size of the U.S. workforce has expanded.

Between 1986 to 1998 actual employee growth was 24 percent, while during the same period training and development budgets increased by only 20 percent. These are the bottom-line facts: U.S. employees are now receiving less rather than more education at work (see Figure 1-4). Managers see training as a cost to be cut like any other HR function. Training on the cheap is now the accepted street wisdom for most corporate policymakers. A 1996 task force of the Twentieth Century Fund forecast that the private sector will need to invest $160 billion annually if all U.S. companies are to duplicate those firms that already place a high priority on creating a knowledge workforce (September 1996). This sounds like a lot, but is only a fraction of America's annual investment in capital hardware, which runs over $400 billion each year. Why should any business make a heavy capital investment in the latest technology if it does not have enough knowledge workers to properly use it to increase productivity and profit? Something has to change.

The workforce education our employees must have is much more sophisticated than "skills" training. Math, science, communication, and computer skills are critical for today's employees. Even professionals, such as engineers, need to be comfortable operating in teams

Although the 1998 budget pie is bigger than in the past, the percentage of training dollars dedicated to various types of employees has remained constant. While the number of workers continues to increase, training aimed at managers and professionals absorbs the lion's share of resources—especially relative to their numbers in the work force.

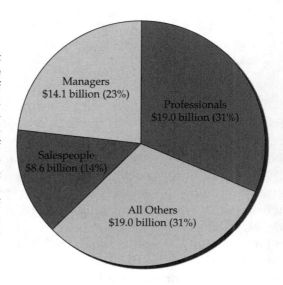

Total: $60.7 billion

Figure 1-4 Who Benefits from Training
Source: Adapted from ASTD/*Training,* 1998

and communicating with earthlings who know nothing about circuit-board design or quantum mechanics. With technology changing so rapidly, employers will want all employees to continuously update their technical and people-management skills.

When we discuss "training," we mean the information that changes all the time. But all employees will also need some additional "education." These are the foundational building blocks they need to better process (i.e., comprehend) the explosion in work-related knowledge.

A world-class education standard for the high-performance workplace is now emerging. Over the next decade this standard will probably evolve to require at least one month of workforce education annually for every employee just to keep up. This will be accomplished through a wide variety of educational options occurring on both company and employee time. In the early 1990s Motorola began as a company practice the participation of each employee in at least 40 hours of training each year. However, even this may not be enough. By 1997 Motorola reported that to keep their products competitive, some workers received more than 400 hours of training. For any business to remain competitive and its people to remain employable, both employers and employees will have to focus much more time on the concept of lifelong education.

At present most U.S. organizations are light-years away from this concept. The American Society for Training and Development reports (1996) that 90 percent of all U.S. workplace education is done by the top 5 percent of American companies. Eighty percent of these education programs are only for managers. Other employees receive little or nothing. While most employers offer technical training or on-the-job training (OJT), few managers see any reason to upgrade educational skills or problem-solving, critical-thinking abilities (Society for Human Resource Management, 1996). Survey after survey shows a credibility gap between how many executives acknowledge a need for more education (37 percent) and how many are willing to provide it (10 percent) (Olsten Staffing Services, October 1996).

Most employers provide no opportunity at work or outside work to develop the skills, training, and education that might increase employee productivity and long-term company earnings. Many believe it is not in management's interests to provide all employees with ample workforce education. Seeking alternative solutions, a growing number of companies have relocated or outsourced production and service activities overseas.

In a recent trip to Scotland, the author toured a 70-mile industrial corridor between Glasgow and Edinburgh. Here, 300 American companies have set up shop. Motorola, Hewlett-Packard, and other high-tech, industrial giants are planning major new capital investments in even more plants. Why? If you read the "Locate in Scotland" ads carried in *The Wall Street Journal*, you will learn of the Scots' "high priority on education . . . with a particular focus on science and mathematics. And instead of learning how to memorize, they learn how to think." Is it any wonder that so many U.S. companies think Scotland is a very intelligent place to locate their business? But the availability of these knowledge workers is even beginning to fall behind U.S. business requirements in parts of in Europe and the Pacific Rim. We must find alternative solutions located in America.

Joseph Boyett in *Beyond Workplace 2000* pictures an ideal future in the way American companies will employ more highly educated workers. They will work in new, high-performance workplaces and create high-value-adding products and services at extremely low costs. However, this will only happen by leveraging employee skills through internal and external workforce education programs. [9]

In this book we will explore shaping new business policies for strategic improvements that align information technologies (IT), and other new high-tech demands, with the measurement of innovative people productivity/performance programs. *Skill Wars* offers a new policy primer about the future of jobs and work. We will learn what must be done for the current workforce to handle the globalization of the world's economy successfully and how to ensure the next generation's fuller participation in a high-performance workplace.

You Get What You Pay For

About 100 years ago our current structure of public–private schooling took shape (1890–1920). America was then entering a mass-production, assembly-line economy that required many low-skill-level workers. The American educational system was organized on the premise that we need to educate only 20 to 25 percent of the entire population for professional/managerial careers. Since then, although almost everyone goes to school, many receive at best a minimal education.

For most of the twentieth century, through two world wars, the rise of the American middle class, and the collapse of the Soviet Union ending the Cold War, this educational arrangement worked very well. It transformed America from a rural, agricultural nation into the world's number one political–economic superpower. Here's how it worked: about 25 percent of the population graduated from college; 40 percent graduated from high school, some going on to additional technical or postsecondary education; the bottom 35 to 40 percent had a hard time in school, and more dropped out with each passing decade of the century. (These are approximate ranges.)

Because this U.S. educational game plan worked for so long, for so many, most Americans came to believe that only a fraction of the population (particularly future managers and professionals) were capable of really benefiting from quality education programs. So why spend more money on the rest?

Today and into the foreseeable future, because of the historic rate of human technological progress, business is becoming more and more dependent on jobs that call for the majority of all employees to exercise their brains rather than their brawn. Human knowledge doubled between 1750 and 1900. In the first 50 years of the twentieth century, it doubled again. Since 1960 each decade has seen a further acceleration in the pace of change. For many centuries workers had a shortage of information to do their jobs. Now they have a glut. People need to develop a framework through which they can understand and judge information. Some have called this process "critical competencies."

Unlike the last 50 or even 70 years, during which U.S. business had an almost unquenchable thirst for men and women with minimal education, 1990s technology has less and less use for them. In every type of business there is a demand for "knowledge workers" (i.e., persons with certain amounts of specialized training, based on prior, sound basic education). With job content changing so often in every field, greater mental dexterity is a necessity for almost every worker.

The "catch-22" is that the United States has outstripped the human resources supported by the business community in general, and by local public/private schools in particular. We simply lack enough people who have developed the successful critical thinking and technical skills required by a worldwide, high-performance workplace.

As Americans we need to recognize that the U.S. population pos-sesses a wide diversity of untapped talents and capacities. Business has a natural leadership role to play in every community to help plan and deliver workforce education through both student career educa-tion and employee lifelong learning. For those local economies that choose to participate, this will mean that a larger number of well-educated Americans will qualify for high-skill/high-wage jobs that yield business greater productivity and profit in the competitive, high-performance workplace.

What Is a "High-Performance Workplace?"

Most management gurus agree that organizations need to develop a high-performance workplace (HPW) as mass-production jobs disap-pear or migrate to other nations, and older industrial nations are forced to compete on quality rather than price; variety over volume; or after-sales service over quantity. But exactly what is an HPW? And why is worker education such a critical component of it?

In the HPW, manufacturing has been transformed. Layers of man-agers have been eliminated so that the production work team now monitor, control, and troubleshoot the manufacturing process.

These same high-performance work processes are also happening in service and professional organizations. Fewer people are doing the actual work, but more of them are being called on to think, analyze, solve, decide issues—in other words, to become critical thinkers—even if this has never before been their traditional work role.

In the early 1990s a National Job Analysis Study was sponsored by the U.S. Departments of Labor and Education to identify the charac-teristics of an HPW. Executives at 3,000 organizations were asked to identify the essential traits of an HPW through a sample of 6,000 jobs in which they provided their own definitions.

The eight characteristics shown in Box 1-1 were derived from this survey.

Workforce education stands at the center of every HPW and makes it happen. This HPW Model has three essential elements:

1. Technology—machinery, software

2. Process—systems, structures

3. People—knowledge workers

Profitability—The organization makes increasingly more money over time. Public/not-for-profit organizations work within budget constraints by being below budget or providing greater services.

Productivity—The organization is committed to achieving productive outcomes through work-output-per-resource allocations that capitalize on employee input and technologies.

Information sharing—Information is shared quickly in the business through top-down and bottom-up channels and across organizational levels/divisions using integrated information systems and technologies. The organization shares information and employees' ideas and concerns are communicated throughout the organization.

Workforce education—The organization invests in and actively supports training and continuous learning at all levels of the organization. Education through classroom and on-the-job instruction is ongoing. A culture that values employee development exists within the organization.

Leadership with clear vision/commitment—Corporate leaders convey through sustained action a vision of the company's purpose and value. Leaders articulate their vision for the future and provide a climate that engages employees in contributing to the vision.

Flexible culture/openness to change—The organization views change as positive. Changes often reflect a quick and deliberate response to feedback from customers and employees. The company culture builds and reinforces the recognition that change is essential to the organization's renewal and vitality.

Focus on customer satisfaction/input—Customer feedback is valued and sought by the organization. Employees are focused on meeting customer needs. Customer recommendations about products or service improvements are incorporated into decisions made by the organization.

Focus on quality—The business strives for continuous improvements in all processes, products, and services. Quality standards are built into product and service development and delivery systems.

Box 1-1 Characteristics of High-Performance Workplaces
Adapted from National Job Analysis Study, U.S. Department of Labor and Education

Both the technology and process elements can now be found worldwide. Technological advantages are now seldom held for very long by any one country or business. New management processes are also quickly replicated. American higher education is well populated by foreign business students who take their new knowledge back home. The only controllable variable is the number of people that are considered "knowledge workers" and capable of working in this fast-paced environment. How can business increase the supply of these people for all kinds of organizations?

We must not blindly cling to the old myths of "doing business by the numbers" using a military command and control system of multi-tiered layers of management. The features of today's and tomorrow's workplace are shifting over from this traditional model to a twenty-first-century, high-performance model (see Box 1-2). The essential organizational features of strategy, production/service, hiring/human resources, and job opportunities are all contingent on the use of work-force education to leverage the current employees and prepare future knowledge workers. This means a significant business investment over time to transform any organization into a successful HPW. However, the U.S. business community's serious lack of commitment to workforce education remains the major obstacle to the success of the high-performance workplace and our future competitiveness as a nation.

Workers of the World Compete

The National Alliance of Business believes that the evidence of the past 15 years demonstrates the following points conclusively:

- To increase our standard of living, U.S. firms must be globally competitive.

- To be globally competitive, firms must adopt modern operating technologies and quality-driving processes—which require a more highly skilled workforce.

However, most people still see no real payoff from learning. To them, running a business isn't about education or skills, but about products, markets, and profit. Many in top management have no appreciation of the need to acquire, maintain, and build company-wide skills, so their companies make no investment in workforce education.

FEATURES OF TODAY'S AND TOMORROW'S WORKPLACES

Traditional Model 20th Century	*High-Performance Model* 21st Century
STRATEGY	
• Mass production • Long production runs • Centralized control	• Flexible production • Customized production • Decentralized control
PRODUCTION/SERVICE	
• Fixed automation • End-of-line quality control • Fragmentation of tasks • Authority vested in supervisor	• Flexible automation • On-line quality control • Work teams, multiskilled workers • Authority delegated to worker
HIRING AND HUMAN RESOURCES	
• Labor-management confrontation • Minimal qualifications accepted • Workers as a cost	• Labor-management cooperation • Screening for basic skills abilities • Workforce as an investment
OPPORTUNITIES	
• Internal labor market • Advancement by seniority	• Limited internal labor market • Advancement by certified skills
WORKFORCE EDUCATION	
• Minimal for production workers • Specialized for craft workers	• Education sessions for everyone • Broader education programs • Career education (internships, apprenticeships)

Source: Adapted from K. Haigler and S. Stein, *Workplace Literacy Training is Modernizing Manufacturing Environments,* Washington, D.C.: National Governor's Association, 1994.

Box 1-2 Features of Today's and Tomorrow's Workplaces

With this dominant business mindset, John Rennie, CEO of Pacer Systems, Inc., sees a growing risk that more and more better-paying techno-jobs will go overseas where there are far more skilled, unemployed people who will work at a competitive wage. Business is global now, and location is not so important (*Business Week*, June 15, 1996).

The Wall Street Journal reported (May 23, 1995) that the technological revolution increased the need for skilled workers, but at a faster pace than the supply of these workers, bidding up wages. This was a compelling reason for American firms to move production abroad. Marina Whitman, a professor in the School of Business at the University of Michigan, estimates that in 1995 11 percent of those goods and services produced overseas by American business were imported back into the United States.

Companies such as Boeing, Intel, Motorola, and Hewlett-Packard (HP) are among hundreds, perhaps thousands, of high-tech multinational corporations searching the globe for the "knowledge workers" they cannot find in the United States.

Frances Cross, a 28-year-old native of Limerick, Ireland, has risen from the clerical pool to become a technician who tests computer chips. Analog Devices, Inc., a U.S. specialty-chip maker, sent her to a local technical college at night. She now earns a decent salary and has valuable skills. This expanding pool of educated workers is driving a big expansion in services and technology business sectors. Government analysts expected 115,000 jobs to be created between 1991 and 1998. Many of these jobs are at international banks (Citicorp), investment houses, or high-technology companies (Analog Devices) that are moving into Ireland or expanding existing Irish operations with the large available pool of knowledge workers (*Wall Street Journal*, December 5, 1996).

In a survey of the world economy *The Economist* (1996) reported that, after years of heavy investment in education, the availability of knowledge workers in Asia is catching up to that in the United States. Hewlett-Packard came to Malaysia mainly for low wages. But since 1974 this firm has begun employing a fast-growing class of professionals and thousands of well-educated factory hands who have the kind of high-skilled, well-paid jobs Americans covet.

As early as 1994 this shift was sending billions of dollars of capital from the United States to countries such as Malaysia, fueling the growth of high-paying jobs overseas. According to the United Nations

Investment Report, in the early 1990s American companies doubled their annual foreign investment to a record $50 billion. These operations are doing more and more sophisticated work.

In 1991 Motorola refused to let its Penang, Malaysia, plant design new software for cellular phones. However, by 1994 the company gave its approval. The plant began to hire a permanent software team.

To create these skilled workers, multinational corporations offer elaborate training programs, some far more generous than those back in the United States. In the corporate quest for more knowledge workers, "They have made a virtue out of necessity," says Mr. R. Meganathan, a World Bank economist. Motorola pays for the college education of promising Malaysian high-school students and in return gets first crack at hiring them. Advanced Micro is sending dozens of workers to school full-time to learn new skills. The employees get better jobs and Advanced Micro gets knowledge workers for a high-performance workplace (*Wall Street Journal*, September 30, 1994).

Global Productivity Check

Where physical contact with customers is not essential, there also is increasing scope for outsourcing service business to countries with well-educated workforces. People linked by computer networks or satellites to the home office can be employed anywhere to carry out labor-intensive computer programming and data processing.

Around the globe, workers are now processing data for companies on insurance claims, hospital patients' records, consumer credit reports, and more. Computer centers in Ireland work on the backroom activities of U.S. banks and stock brokers. Swissair has transferred all of its revenue accounting to Bombay. *The Economist* reports that most American computer firms now subcontract labor-intensive programming to Bangalore, India (October 1, 1994). It is not only blue-collar manufacturing workers who face this competition; other occupations higher up the earnings ladder will also feel the pain of lost jobs unless American business can be persuaded to create more knowledge workers at home.

Perhaps the most forceful argument for relocating are the potential mouthwatering labor-cost savings. But it depends where. Germany has the world's highest labor costs $32.10 (1995) for one hour of work (see Figure 1-5). Compared with other major industrial powers, the

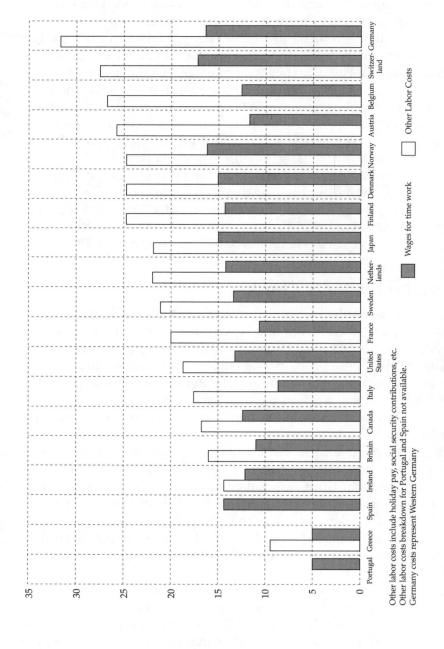

Figure 1-5 Manufacturing Labor Costs 1995 $ per Hour
Source: Swedish Employers' Confederation 1996

Other labor costs include holiday pay, social security contributions, etc.
Other labor costs breakdown for Portugal and Spain not available.
Germany costs represent Western Germany

■ Wages for time work   □ Other Labor Costs

United States is in the bottom half. However, in select industries such as the textiles industry, America's costs are far ahead of Mexico, Eastern Europe, or China (see Figure 1-6). But low wages alone do not give the full competitive picture.

Economist Stephen Golub of Swarthmore College explains how U.S. workers can compete successfully with low-wage workers. Low

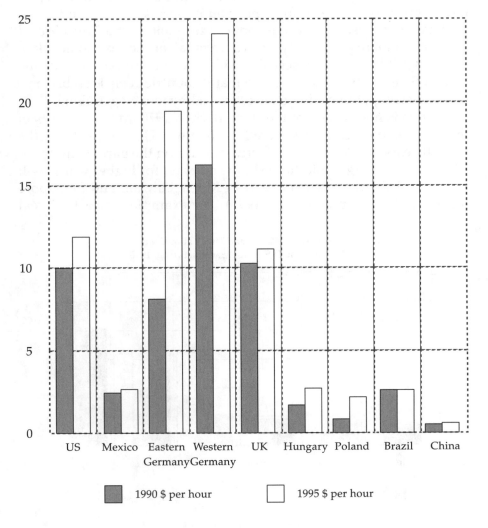

1990 $ per hour   1995 $ per hour

Figure 1-6 Wage Warp
Source: Adapted from *Werner International* 1995

wages in foreign countries usually go hand in hand with low productivity, so that labor costs per unit of output are closer to U.S. levels (see Figure 1-7). Although 1990 factory wages and other compensation in these countries were only 10 to 32 percent of U.S. pay, unit labor costs were 71 percent in South Korea, 68 percent in Mexico, and actually above U.S. levels in India, the Philippines, and Malaysia. Other factors can hold down productivity in poor countries, such as low levels of general education, poor public infrastructure, and transportation services. What use is modern technology if a Third-World worker cannot read a quality-process manual, or the road to his plant is inaccessible due to miserable roads? When compared with the United States, low productivity in many countries considerably narrows any competitive advantage conferred by low wages alone.

But this is not the end of the story. Back in 1970 unit labor costs in these developing countries were less than half U.S. levels. Over the next 20 years, workers' wages increased, closing the gap. As these societies create a larger middle class, the demand for higher wages will continue. This trend has emerged in Korea, Taiwan, and Singapore (*Business Week*, September 11, 1995). For example, since 1977 real

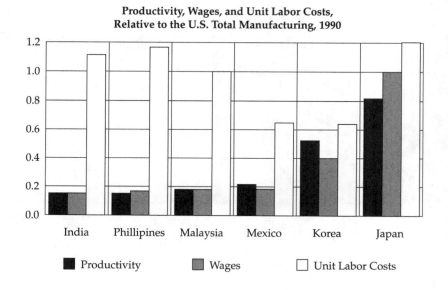

Figure 1-7 Output Matters, Too
Source: Adapted from *Stephen S. Golub*

wages in South Korea have risen eightfold (*The Economist*, September 28, 1996).

Grim Reality

Business could choose a high-performance strategy that requires high-skill/high-wage employees. Or business can continue to largely follow the current low-cost/low-wage option, while still shopping the world for available well-educated knowledge workers who can handle the latest technologies in select high-performance workplaces. For the United States the long-term economic consequences of this latter scenario are chilling. If business continues to ignore the work-force education gap, the jobs may be there, but where will the qualified workers come from?

Some business leaders with a big stake in the outcome are speaking strongly for systemic change. George Daniel, president of United Technologies, in a speech at the National Press Club drew a stark picture of what lies ahead for the U.S. workforce. Since 1990 his company eliminated 33,000 jobs in the United States (one in three), while adding 15,000 jobs abroad. Of the 120 million Americans at work, he sees "as many as 30 million will be at risk: 10 million people in administrative support jobs prone to automation, 10 million in manufacturing jobs susceptible to foreign competition, and 2 million additional white-collar jobs that medium and large companies like ours, under the pressure of competition, will learn to live without."

But he rejected the notion that market forces alone will provide an answer for those threatened workers. Instead he called on companies "to expand greatly their education programs for their employees" (*Chicago Tribune*, February 14, 1996). In taking this stand Daniel acts like a maverick because he perceives a business competitive advantage from the fact that the world of business as we have known it is rapidly passing away. He sees education as a core business policy, not an external issue.

In the Beginning Was the Chip . . .

In 1970 about 25,000 computers existed worldwide. By the latter half of the 1990s more than 140,000,000 computers are leading us into the "third wave of technological change."

The early eighteenth and nineteenth centuries saw "the first wave," brought on by the industrial revolution. Between 1890 and 1920 Henry Ford and others perfected the concepts of mass production, creating "the second wave," which transformed America into the greatest superpower of the twentieth century.

An ever more pervasive computer began "the third wave," led by the PC (personal computer) that is now everywhere. But it is the computer chip that is such a commonplace component today. It makes everything work from computers to cars, cameras, heavy machinery, and the cash card. The ever more powerful memory chip is the most productivity-enhancing, life-changing technology since the harnessing of steam power and the taming of electricity.

According to "Moore's Law" (named after Gordon Moore, cofounder of Intel), computer power is doubling every 18 months. The laptop computer of today is many times more powerful than a $10 million dollar mainframe of the mid-1970s, and far cheaper. Over the past two decades, as computer memory power has skyrocketed, prices have fallen dramatically at about 30 percent each year. This has encouraged many new innovations for chip applications, and it is inventing the techno-jobs of the future.

Who in the 1970s used videocassette recorders, cell phones, Sony Walkmen, or soft contact lenses? Today's consumers wear more computing power on their wrists than existed in the entire world before 1961. They make widespread use of the new products that chip technology helped create, along with new jobs.

The new wave in this techno-revolution is the application of microelectronics to communication. The birth of "cyberspace" is transforming communication by making it universal, quick, and cheap. In 1930 a three-minute call between New York and London cost $200. By 1996 the price tag had been slashed to $2.00. Some predict that by 2005 a trans-Atlantic videophone call will be made for a few cents an hour. A whole new generation of computer processors made from a crystalline ferroelectric material may replace the silicon chip to make this possible. This new wonder chip (from Australia) is 100 times more efficient than state-of-the-art silicon versions.

Computer researcher Raymond Kurzweil notes that if "Moore's Law of computer power continues to improve at its current rate, by 2030 a computer will be able to process data at quadrillions of operations per second, or 'pedaflops'—about the same speed of the human brain" (*Los Angeles Times*, January 7, 1997). This may be done by new "quantum computers"—devices that could outperform conventional computers. Today's computer is little more than a sped-up abacus. It stores and shuffles numbers by remembering the "on" or "off" positions of tiny switches or "bits." The next generation of quantum computers, with even tinier bits and few other operating components, could solve vast problems that today's conventional computers can't begin to solve.

French researchers also have developed a paper-thin plastic transistor that contains no metal parts. This development, they believe, may lead to computer screens that roll up like window shades. What host of new products and services might this create?

This third wave of technological change will transform life more radically and more quickly than the introduction of the automobile, electricity, and the telephone in the early twentieth century. What is different in the current "knowledge revolution" is that information technology (IT) has sped up the shift toward a knowledge-based economy. How? We can transmit more information in digital form over long distances than ever before. What we are now producing through IT are "intangibles" based on new "ideas" rather than "things." Today in the workplace we are experiencing a "knowledge undertow" from this third wave of technology. Education will help adjust this growing mismatch between the old knowledge needed for twentieth-century jobs, and the new knowledge needed for twenty-first-century employment.

During the second wave of technological development (1890–1920), there was a lag time of between 30 to 40 years between the introduction and initial investment in new technology and productivity growth. An example of this was the introduction of electricity, which at first depressed labor productivity.

The same pattern is being repeated. According to Kenneth Voytek at the National Alliance of Business, between 1973 and 1995 investment in computers and technology rose from $200 million to $91.6 billion. Yet the rate of productivity growth in business began to decline from 2.9 percent annually in 1973 to only 1 percent in 1995. Why?

Martin Baily and Robert Gordon at the Brookings Institution report that investment in technology may not show immediate returns to a business, "before employees are educated to learn how to incorporate these applications of new technologies efficiently in applications that

Industry	Transportation	Energy	Agro-Business	Manufacturing	Construction	Communication	Hospitality Industry
	"Fastship" Jet-Propulsion Sen Freighter	"Super Conducting" 2/3 reduction in power transmission loss	"Electronic Cows" Cow computer chip activated robotics milking machine	"Cimline" Integrates Manufacturing Software for Product Variation	Robotics/Automated Hi-Rise Building Assembly	Universal Satellite Personal Cellular Community Worldwide	Fully Automated Fast-Food Restaurants Operated by 2–3 Employees
	"Mag-Lev Trains" +200 MPH Passenger Trains	"Super-Battery" Technology Allows cars to operate for 300 miles at up to 70 MPH before 2–3 minute recharge.	"Precision Farming" Satellite Crop Yield Management	"HVM 600 Milling Machine" Use of Magnetic Energy to Produce Engine Blocks	Satellite-Assisted Construction Systems	Voice Activated Computers	Computer-Assisted Hotel Self Check-In
	"Smart Cars" • Dash Board Navigation Maps • Power Train Diagnostic Sensors • Collision Safety Radar			"'A' Transfer Press" 49 foot Machine-Tool operated by one person stamps out 3,000 car parts per day		Plain English Software Commands	
	"Statosonic Aircraft" High-Speed, High-Altitude Aircraft (1,800 MPH 90,000 ALT 100,000)						

Source: Edward E. Gordon, 1999.

Figure 1-8 Third Wave Technological Applications

produce innovations." Business techno-leaders, such as David Birch, president of Cognetics, Inc., agree: "It is no longer the production of technology, but its application that creates growth opportunities."

Further investigation by Paul David (Stanford University) and Jeremy Greenwood (University of Rochester) tells us that the interrelationship between technology and productivity goes something like this. Productivity slumps as new technology comes on-line, and then surges once it is distributed throughout the economy. Simultaneously, the premium for education increases rapidly as better-educated people have a competitive advantage in using the new technology.

David and Greenwood reached these conclusions after studying the earlier industrial revolutions in the United Kingdom and the United States. They found compelling similarities between that period (1890–1920) and the situation facing America today.

According to the U.S. Labor Department (1995), 20 million tech jobs are now in the American workplace. In 1996, 25 percent of all the jobs created centered on technology. The government and others believe that by 2010 this will rise to possibly 50 percent of all new jobs. Where will all these techno-jobs come from? Computers and chips are only one of the many new innovations that are being introduced today or will emerge over the next 10 to 20 years (see Figure 1-8). Who will work in these new industries? How will we educate people to prepare for these third-wave careers? With the unemployment rate at a thirty-year low (4.2 percent, May 1999), a severe shortage of knowledge workers won't go away anytime soon according to Jerry Jasinowski, president of the National Association of Manufacturers. "The fundamental problem is that long-term, we are not providing enough high-skill, labor-force entrants to meet the demand" (*Wall Street Journal*, November 27, 1996). This is now emerging as a major national problem.

Educate Who?—To Do What?

A central problem of the people paradox is that the great American "education machine" of elementary/secondary schools is not up to this revolutionary task. Its curriculum and priorities are geared to college preparatory education alone, not techno-education, and most U.S. students today never will finish college. In addition, economists and labor experts assert that 70 percent of future jobs will not require a four-year college education.

There is a desperate need for businesses to publicize this mismatch by providing information on their current and future techno-jobs to students, parents, and high-school counselors. A good example of this situation is in Nogales, Arizona, where as a consequence of NAFTA (the North American Free Trade Agreement), new employers have boosted the growth of manufacturing jobs by 5.6 percent (1997). But something was seriously out of whack. The city's overall unemployment rate was 22.6 percent and still rising.

American factories in Texas, Arizona, and California supply nearby Mexican plants with auto parts, plastics, and other materials. The U.S. plants make the complex components that Mexican factories need, but their poorly educated workers can't produce.

In order to make these high-tech components, plants in Nogales need more knowledge workers. However, the region has neglected tech-prep, science, and math, and has even failed to make sure that their largely Hispanic residents are able to read, write, and speak English. Most technology instructions and training are in the English language. Duke Petty, the Nogales economic-development director, complains, "I've hollered about vocational training for 30 years. Maybe now somebody will listen."

In 1996, 46 new plants and businesses were started in the Arizona county that includes Nogales. To find adequate numbers of knowledge workers, companies have begun importing people from the Midwest. Carpenters, mechanics, plumbers, and electricians are being sought by help-wanted ads placed in Cleveland, Milwaukee, and Pittsburgh to fill this local labor mismatch (*The Wall Street Journal*, March 21, 1997).

Because the demand for knowledge workers in many other areas of the United States is growing so fast, importing them from other states may only be a short-term solution. This author addressed 250 California AFL–CIO apprenticeship directors (1996) to help them come up with new recruitment strategies. California has a chronic shortage of young adults interested in technical apprenticeships. The state government has begun many new initiatives to foster the collaboration of business, unions, schools, and parents to fill this ever-increasing knowledge-worker gap for traditional skilled trades and other high-tech occupations.

In the Midwest a large, new high-performance information-technology (IT) plant stood idle for two years. The problem was that the plant required a high-tech workforce of 4,000. However, 1,000 people couldn't be found from the local communities. This international IT corporation responded by investing billions for new high-performance plants in Scotland, China, and elsewhere.

If businesses cannot find knowledge workers at home, they will search the world for them. The long-term educational solutions for Nogales, Arizona; the state of California; and this Midwest IT manufacturer are yet to be determined. Today these business case studies can be repeated in far too many communities all across the United States.

Hedrick Smith in *Rethinking America* (1995) believed that the biggest obstacle to bringing this about was changing the public mindset on who is responsible. The former Republican governor of New Jersey, Tom Kean, told him, "The American public doesn't really understand what's going on in schools. They don't recognize it's their child who isn't getting the kind of education which would enable him or her to earn the kind of living that they deserve. I don't think we've yet really energized ourselves to understand that this is a national priority. This is really a crisis." When will American parents begin to understand that the future of work means proportionally fewer and fewer managers/professionals, and more and more well-educated, well-paid technicians?

Rumblings for change are now beginning to appear on the corporate horizon. The chiefs of more than 200 major technological companies desperately pleaded at the White House in Washington, D.C. (April 2, 1997), for the rebuilding of a stronger educational system across America. These executives admitted that our schools are failing to provide enough skilled workers to fill thousands of high-tech jobs.

Without skilled workers, they warned, American leadership in technology and the economic growth that it brings is threatened. They related how their high-tech companies are forced to look overseas for knowledge workers who must understand statistics.

"What this is really about is about the new economy and what our kids, our companies, and society have got to do to compete and prosper," says John Doerr, a venture capitalist. These executives believe that neither schools nor businesses are teaching enough people the proper skills in reading, math, science, engineering, or computer programming to allow them to work in computer or biotechnology jobs.

"People in the high-tech sector bang their heads against each other trying to hire enough people," states Marc Andreessen, cofounder of Netscape Communications in Mountain View, California (*Chicago Tribune*, April 3, 1997). There is a whole series of things that have to happen to educate more knowledge workers. Where can a business start?

Instead of corporate charity to local schools, communities need business-education collaboration in career education at the local community level. Here's a "to do" list for management to consider:

1. Increase both junior-high and high-school counselor and student knowledge regarding the variety of careers within local businesses.

2. Help high schools establish meaningful internship/apprenticeship opportunities for a specific career with both classroom instruction and work experiences.

3. Help community groups and parents realistically accept a variety of career education options for their children other than four-year colleges, and have parents encourage their children to evaluate these education options.

4. Help students, parents, and the general public learn to understand the question, "Which is the best occupational choice for this specific student?"

Some business leaders are showing an increasing understanding that business–education collaboration is not charity. It is their company's survival that compels them to become involved in local career education as a necessary part of their strategic workforce education plan. As some companies bid up wages for skilled employees, others are led to invest more in training and education.[10]

Twentieth-Century Knowledge Economic Model

According to Joseph and Jimmie Boyett in *Beyond Workplace 2000*, the problem we face in creating and sustaining this new "learning organization" is an American business-culture legacy of half-hearted learning efforts. Today most U.S. companies have chronic learning deficiencies. Throughout the twentieth century, Americans have pursued a "Knowledge Economic Model" (see Figure 1-9) that has

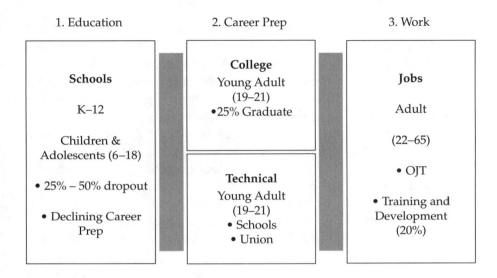

1. Education

2. Career Prep

3. Work

Schools

K–12

Children & Adolescents (6–18)

• 25% – 50% dropout

• Declining Career Prep

College
Young Adult
(19–21)
•25% Graduate

Technical
Young Adult
(19–21)
• Schools
• Union

Jobs

Adult

(22–65)

• OJT

• Training and Development (20%)

Figure 1-9 The Twentieth-Century Knowledge Economic Model

tended to compartmentalize their lives. Education was one compartment; career preparation was placed in a second compartment; business/work in a third. We have treated the various arenas of American life as separate pieces.

All children (ages 6–18) received a basic education, with higher school drop-out rates and a declining number of high-school career-preparation programs as the century progressed. We inserted a filter between basic education and career preparation. Through it passed only about 25 percent of our population who ultimately graduated from college. We also filtered technical preparation of young adults through a disjointed system of postsecondary vocational education and union programs of uneven quality.

The bastions of business were even more isolated. America built an artificial wall between education and business that insulated both worlds from the needs of the other. On one side stood the practical world of business—how to make a buck. One the other side existed a larger theoretical "world of ideas." To mix the two was considered dangerous, almost "un-American," by most business and education leaders.

Managers do receive some postcollege training and development, but this is limited mostly to about 20 percent of employees found in larger organizations. The rest get only on-the-job training (OJT), if that. For most people in the workplace, formal learning has stopped. The Council on Competitiveness reports (1995) that U.S. business spends less on workplace learning than the 11 other top industrial nations (see Figure 1-10). For example, German workers receive five times as much training as their U.S. counterparts.

There is almost an arrogance about learning. It definitely is not a lifelong need. Most American executives see no real payoff from learning, other than from their own college careers. To them, running the business isn't about improving employee competencies or skills, but about end products and markets. Companies make little or no investment because knowledge is static and America is in control.

This Twentieth-Century Knowledge Economic Model rejects the very basic notion that any organization could fundamentally profit from an organized business learning culture. As a result, except for acts of corporate charity, the "real world" of business and the "theoretical world" of education disdain each other.

The 1990s' move toward globalization has meant that corporations have begun altering these arrangements. The current American Human Capital Development business policy (see Figure 1-11) selectively uses employees and world markets to enhance business competitiveness. To achieve this goal, business has implemented three solutions.

1. *Limited Schooling Focus.* Business continues to encourage the current system of elite career preparation for the top 25 percent of American society. Organizations collaborate heavily with higher education, donating money and time to increase a tie-in of more realistically applied classroom curriculum to the workplace. In general individual, scattershot, company pilot programs are just beginning to attempt to overcome lukewarm, even fierce opposition from corporate ranks, parents who remain rooted in a college-preparatory school system, and unions that maintain near total control over most techno-job education preparation.

2. *International Corporate Selectivity.* Business now shops the world for knowledge workers and high-performance workplaces.

3. *Economic Value Strategies.* The chief objective of business is maximum short-term return-on-investment programs, regardless of short-term/long-term effects on human resources.

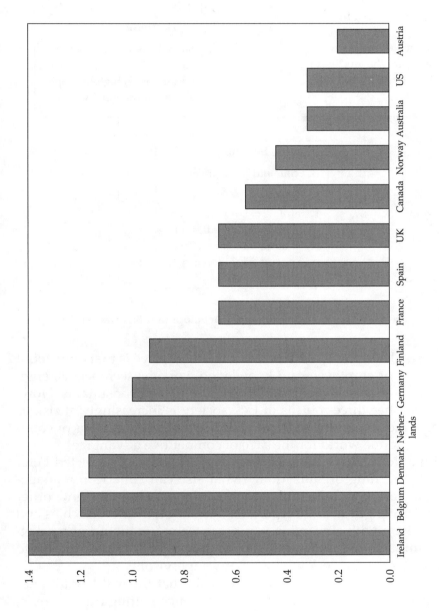

Figure 1-10 Percent of GDP Invested in Job Training
Source: Adapted from *Council on Competitiveness* 1995

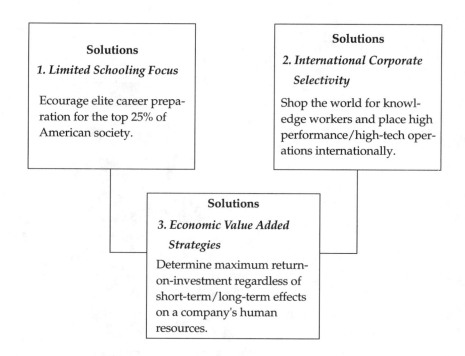

Solutions

1. Limited Schooling Focus

Ecourage elite career preparation for the top 25% of American society.

Solutions

2. International Corporate Selectivity

Shop the world for knowledge workers and place high performance/high-tech operations internationally.

Solutions

3. Economic Value Added Strategies

Determine maximum return-on-investment regardless of short-term/long-term effects on a company's human resources.

Figure 1-11 Current Human Capital Development Business Policy

The results of this globalization of the workplace is that only about 25 percent of employees are knowledge workers: technicians, engineers, well-educated professionals, managers, and consultants. However, the other three-fourths of U.S. society is increasingly at risk as business moves service and production in and out of regions or countries around the world for the sake of competitive advantage.

With a dominant business culture that has basically rejected Peter Senge's "learning organization," what else can American management do to compete? Until recently Michael Hammer and other reengineering gurus told corporations to smash their hierarchies and replace them with streamlined "process teams" made up of marketing, manufacturing, sales, and service people who use computers to combine tasks and work without many supervisors.

But now business has found once again that the real key to long-term growth on the reverse side is not so much getting rid of people, as getting more out of people. What about the organization that lacks the training and educational programs to survive in an international

High-Tech High-Performance Workplace	+	Shortage of Knowledge Workers	=	Stagnating Productivity 1%

The Results:

    1. Movement to Offshore for Educated Workers

    2. Cheap Labor Used in Low-Tech Offshore Operation

Figure 1-12 America's Business Dilemma

business environment where management is minimal and employee tasks are complex? "America's Business Dilemma" (see Figure 1-12) is that we need a high-tech, high-performance workplace. However, a severe shortage of well-educated "knowledge workers" is helping to freeze U.S. productivity growth at an average of 1 percent (1996) (see Figure 1-13). The uncomfortable result for the American workforce is a one–two punch as business moves offshore in search of better-educated workers, or uses cheaper foreign labor but in low-tech operating environments. What is the United States to do?

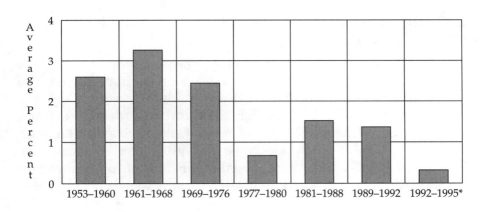

* 1st and 2nd quarters

Figure 1-13 Annual Productivity Growth per Period Slows
Source: Adapted from *Center for Economic Policy Research, Stanford University*

Paul Kennedy in *Preparing for the Twenty-First Century* draws a historical analogy between the current American dilemma and Britain 100 years ago. Britain then was a preeminent world power whose economic competitiveness was in decline. Britain's public schools, industrial efficiency, and pattern of personal career choice (too few technicians, too many lawyers and accountants) cried out for systemic change. However, Britain's leaders rejected the calls for change, and today British commerce and industry are largely owned by foreign investors. In 1995 Mercedes-Benz bought Rover, Britain's last domestic-owned car company.

Harvard University's Michael Porter (*The Competitive Advantage of Nations*) believes that the comparative economic advantage among countries in the twenty-first century will increasingly depend on how well workers apply knowledge. The deciding factor in standard of living differences among countries will be the relative availability of educated and uneducated people (i.e., knowledge workers versus grunt labor). During the twentieth century the United States rose to the top under favorable historical circumstances. As a synergistic society our dynamics rewarded leaders who fostered change and overcame reactionary vested interests. We need to do it again.[11]

Getting Commitment for "Workforce Education"

A 1995 CEO roundtable on "the learning organization" was held in New York's St. Regis Hotel. In attendance were an impressive list of corporate "top guns": Reginald K. Brack, Jr., chairman of Time; Frank V. Cahonet, president, CEO, Mellon Bank Corp.; Gordon E. Forward, president, CEO, Chaparral Steel; Steven D. Goldstein, chairman, president, CEO, American Express Bank; Richard F. Teerlink, president, CEO of Harley-Davidson; and 23 other CEOs from other forward-thinking American corporations (*Chief Executive*, March 1995). Here is what they said.

Nearly all agreed that a climate of risk-taking and experimentation is necessary if employees are to learn effectively. However, corporate experience with organizational learning is at an early stage. Transferring knowledge from one part of an organization to another remains problematic.

What seems to separate businesses that sustain workforce education from those that don't is what David Shanks of Arthur D. Little calls "purposeful intent." Does your company have a strategic performance learning system that creates, stores, and acts on new knowledge at either the procedural or the policy levels? Some already do.

Motorola invests close to $100 million in workforce education and reports a return-on-investment of $3.00 in product sales for each education dollar invested.

Chaparral Steel calls its education-for-life program "K through 90" (kindergarten through age 90). Their CEO Gordon Forward says this group learning for process improvement is tracked and tied to compensation.

Why do they do this now? "Because technological changes and shifting market demands make rapid learning essential," the CEO roundtable members believe. These winning CEOs have no choice but to encourage learning at all levels of their organizations. They even think that "perhaps companies soon will put intellectual capital on the balance sheet and trumpet it in annual reports"!

These comments make it seem that American business is about to place a classroom in every office—except this isn't happening. As we have already seen, workplace education is in actual decline. Why does corporate America not "walk the talk" when it comes to the reality of "the learning organization"?

Throughout the 1980s and 1990s there has only been paper-thin support for more training and education, and usually only in the ranks of top management. Establishing a "corporate university" has gained some business support, but for most managers it sounds too academic, too theoretical—far removed from the practical world of daily business give and take.

The jargon is a big turn-off. Many people in business found much of their own formal education painful. Their schooling was a time to be endured, not extended. As a result, they don't like learning. Concepts such as "the learning organization" and "lifelong learning" sound like a new definition of "purgatory at work." They are not popular.

America as a society embraces the idea of education in general, but rejects learning in particular. For too long training has been stalled at the level of programs offering "behavior tricks" that are quickly learned in a one- or two-day management program, and just as quickly forgotten. Instead, business must focus on education that moves people away from the past and facilitates new ways of learning and interacting in the workplace. High-performance workplaces require changing "management thinking," not just management behavior. Training is for dogs. Education is for people. It occurs over a lifetime.

How do we popularize "education"? A basic motivator for most adult workplace learning is for people to experience an immediate, quick use for new knowledge the next day, back on-the-job. "Workforce education" is an all encompassing, nonthreatening idea that conveys this utilitarian approach to all kinds of education activities, whether the learners are managers, professionals, technicians, secretaries, or factory workers.

American business needs "workforce education" not just because we have been doing so little adult training and development, but also because we have been doing it so badly. What business has done in the past just isn't good enough. A.T. Kearney estimated (1992) that 80 percent of all workplace training is lost and is never used back on-the-job. Broad and Newstrom in *Transfer of Training* (1992) concurred with these findings. Education is useless unless change results, and it is part of a management process that awakens people to their own strengths and weaknesses. The challenge now is to have not only universal, but also high-quality workforce education, not just for the top few but for everybody. The business challenge is to teach many more people the principles of managing others during today's "future shock" period of rapid globalization. In order to perform the elastic, evolutionary jobs of the future, more employees than in the past must develop leadership abilities for teams and self-management. Static jobs for life have become a relic of the historic past.

A Business Performance Learning System

The Workforce Education Triad™ is a new business performance learning system (see Figure 1-14) that addresses the people paradox by leveraging every organization's primary assets, its human capital—people. It features the new essential building blocks of learning in the information technology (IT) workplace for the development of employee skills, behaviors, and critical thinking abilities. These three components build on each other to reach the final goal of personal innovation.

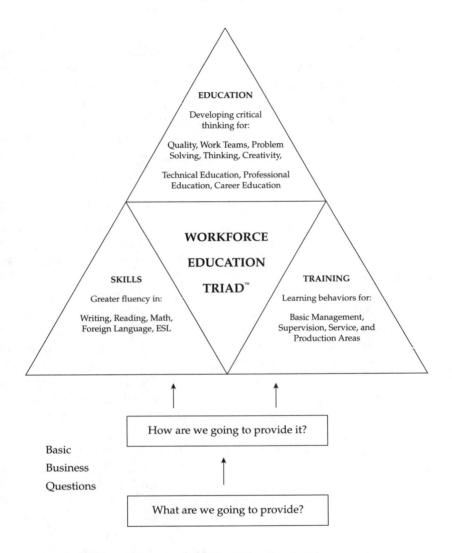

Figure 1-14 Business Performance Learning Systems
Source: Courtesy of Imperial Consulting Corporation

Most organizations need the first component of the Workforce Education Triad, "skills," to raise the overall comprehension or fluency of their people's abilities in reading, writing, math, foreign language, or English as a second language. For most employees the issue is no longer "basic skills" or literacy per se, but becoming more "fluent" in the building blocks of knowledge.

According to the U.S. Departments of Labor and Education (1992), by the year 2000 complex technologies will demand most employees to possess a 12th- or 13th-grade-level of reading and math comprehension for many essential business tasks. These include using many software packages, writing client letters in understandable business English, employing statistical process control (SPC) in most quality manufacturing organizations, preparing the latest wave of immigrants for productive employment, or sending a U.S. businessperson overseas prepared to better compete with at least minimal foreign-language skills.

"Training," the second component of the Workforce Education Triad, is needed in supervision, sales, project management, service, assembly techniques, and other business behaviors. This includes fundamental knowledge of how a business operates and makes a profit. The "training" component of the Workforce Education Triad is needed by most employees, rather than just by managers. Why? How can self-empowered employee work teams be expected to provide business solutions and solve work problems if they do not understand how the company operates and makes a profit? The American Management Association Executive Council (1993) believes that "When the workers get the picture, they are better prepared to solve the problem. And without teaching them the fundamentals of business management and decision making, don't expect them to understand what you are doing."

Employees must first meet the prerequisites of the Workforce Education Triad's two developmental components of "skills" and "training" before tackling the "education" component at the top of the triad. Education encompasses the abstract-reasoning abilities and critical-thinking skills for: problem solving, empowerment, decision making, personal creativity, quality programs, ISO-9000, advanced technical or professional education, and career education/apprenticeships for either school-age students or the present workforce.

The Workforce Education Triad begins the process that awakens people to their own strengths and weaknesses and gives them the means to grow by increasing skills, training, and education. The Triad helps to continue the management evolutionary process begun more than 30 years ago (see Figure 1-15). If you develop your employees' own unique talents, they will make a larger contribution to the competitive edge of present and future productivity and profit.

Management Development Trends
(1960–2020)

Audiences	Training Skills	Broaden Knowledge	Develop New Approaches/ Teams	Create Fundamental Change/ Empower Thinking
Employee Empowered Work Teams				
Supervisors/ Quality Circles				
Dept. Managers and Organizational Development (OD)				
Individual Managers	Traditional Behavioral "Training by Technique"			

1960's	1970's	1980's	1990–2020

Time Line

Figure 1-15 Management Evolutionary Process
Source: Courtesy of Imperial Consulting Corporation

The Workforce Education Triad also includes the collaboration of business with local schools through career-education programs. To become employable, all students must possess higher levels of basic education fluency in reading, writing, and math. They must know how to apply these skills with the use of a computer, and in written and oral communication. Through career education they will know how they can use this knowledge in or out of school for specific careers.

Unlike past generations, more students will understand that career education means that lifelong learning is a necessity once their formal schooling ends. Most importantly, career education will be done through joint collaboration with local unions and business, providing meaningful high school/college, intern/apprenticeships. These educational programs will integrate both theoretical and practical knowledge for broad lifelong personal career opportunities as technology and the job market continue to drive unrelenting change. This career education component of the Triad will also enhance the competitive edge of business and labor by providing the next generation of knowledge workers across America.[12]

Growing America's Productivity

Ask any economist what America can do to increase its productivity and you will hear at least two standard answers: increase investment in either (1) physical capital (i.e., plant, equipment), or (2) the educational level of the workforce. Business is doing the first; the second is a hard sell.

In *The End of Affluence* Jeffrey Madrick states that since the early 1970s productivity in this country has grown at an average rate of only 1 percent. This is a rate of increase that can be attributed just to adding more people each year to the workforce. This is not good enough when compared to the 3 percent U.S. annual growth rate achieved during the 1950–1970 era. Why has this productivity gap developed?

A provocative answer from Joseph Stiglitz, chair of the Council of Economic Advisors, is that during the past 30 years increasing American's personal education has added as much as three-tenths of a percent per year to the nation's growth (i.e., about 20 percent of the growth in personal incomes). He believes that a well-educated workforce "can implement new ideas and innovations more quickly, generating technological advancements that are key to raising productivity and enhancing long-term growth" (*Phi Delta Kappan*, March 1996). However, education has to catch up to technology for higher productivity increases to occur.

If this is true, it means that any business—from a multinational corporation, to a midsize company of 500 people, to a small family business—will measure its productivity potential not only by checking the last quarter's profits, but also by counting the brains it can bring to bear on the process today—its so-called "intellectual capital." How well does any organization develop its people and their capabilities to make a profit? Ernst & Young (1996) sees this as "knowledge management," an integral part of a growing trend by business to manage "institutional intelligence" as they would any other precious asset. Knowledge drives our third-wave economy. Knowledge is not scarce. What is a scarce business asset are the people who have the ability to understand and use knowledge. What is the vital link between knowledge and growth? A business will perform best that develops and manages its "knowledge assets" most effectively.

A Strategic Plan

We offer the following strategic plan to develop our intellectual capital for a "second American century" through universal workforce education that will enhance business competitiveness (see Figure 1-16).

1. *Redefine Schooling.* Increase the segment of well-educated Americans from 25 percent to at least 50 percent of the total population in order to provide business with an adequate number of "knowledge workers."

2. *Adopt "The Corporate University," "Learning Organization," "Lifelong Learning" Concepts.* This business policy shift will happen through a network of practices using:

   Computer-based training
   Distance learning
   In-house programs
   External consultants
   Degree/credit programs
   Local college/university/technical/secondary/elementary
      schools

3. *Return-on-Investment of Education.* What is the exact return-on investment (ROI) of each workforce education program supported by a business? Both publicly traded and closely held businesses can use realistic ROI models and updated accounting practices to create a new business revenue driver and profit center.

Policy—Practice—Profit

What this strategy translates into is a new Twenty-First-Century Knowledge Economic Model for America encompassing policy, practice, and profit (see Figure 1-17). The only long-term solution for America's twenty-first-century economic expansion is to ensure that the labor force is given an education that is not behind the times. But such basic education improvements could take a generation to become popular and show up in the U.S. labor market. America is now losing the international race to create a larger proportion of well-educated citizens.

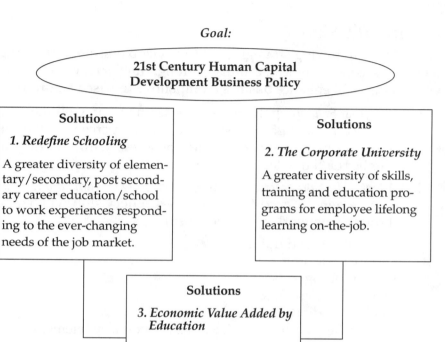

**Figure 1-16 Twenty-First-Century Human Capital
Development Business Policy**
Source: Courtesy of Imperial Consulting Corporation

The answer to the *Skill Wars* is for business to better leverage its intellectual capital by helping develop larger numbers of well-educated people who are capable of redesigning job and work processes. The policy, practice, and profit concepts of the Twenty-First-Century Knowledge Economic Model will begin driving labor costs out of the productivity equation by having fewer highly educated workers use more complex technologies that will increase overall productivity (see Figure 1-18). Thus, knowledge workers using third-wave technologies will be able to create more high-value-added products and

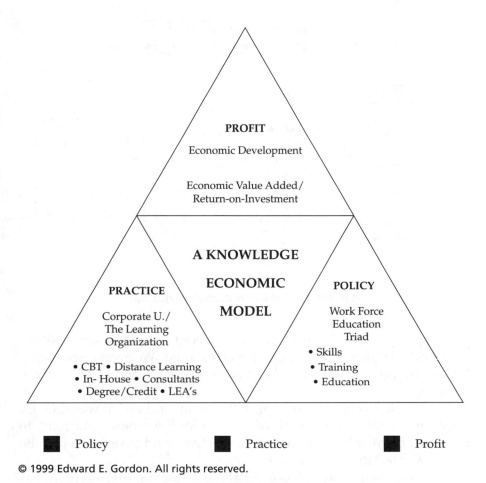

Figure 1-17 Twenty-First-Century Knowledge Economic Model

services at extremely low cost. Increasing knowledge will mean increasing profit.

The popularity of Sony camcorders, Mitsubishi VHS recorders, Lexus, Honda Civic, Canon, Mercedes—all point to lost American productivity. Where has our fabled "Yankee ingenuity" gone?

America has always prided itself as a "land of opportunity." Generations of Americans understood it as a matter more of intellectual enrichment rather than material enrichment. America offered immigrants a different "mindset" from the rest of the world.

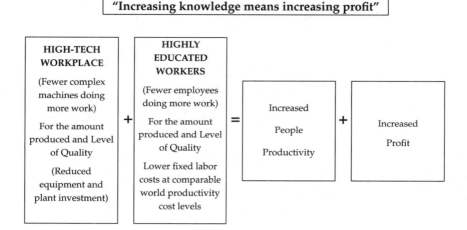

Figure 1-18 A New Productivity Equation

European visitors have often written about our restless curiosity—America's skeptical, iconoclastic frame of mind. We are a resourceful, self-reliant people, with an inborn capacity for invention and improvisation.

To instill in every person a spirit of "get up and go" at work, many must be taught a framework of how to look for new solutions, to think, problem-solve, become more creative. And people need to be well rewarded for their successes.

There are many ways of looking at the future: as fate, as chance, as an opponent to be outwitted, or as a force from which to hide. America treats it as a problem to be solved. Call it pride or pragmatism, upon this fundamental belief the United States was founded and still stands—that Americans need not be the victims of ignorance.

How Practical?

Heavy investment in employee education cannot compensate for poor management or misguided product strategies, as IBM found to its cost in the early 1990s. However, the best companies already understand that, if they are to remain flexible, they must also make their people as flexible as they can. Workforce education costs money, and the pioneering firms (such as Arthur Andersen, Motorola, McDonald's, Intel, and Xerox) that have taken this path run the risk of having their employees poached by rivals. But the organizational rewards are also greater—both in greater employee loyalty and in higher-quality services and products. Also, better people want to get inside a business that offers them not the illusion of lifelong job security, but a better opportunity to stay employable.

Rapid innovation and new service/product introductions require a creativity ("critical competencies") that is now lacking in many corporate bureaucracies. Throughout the workforce education process, people learn how to use critical thinking to flatten organizations, establish team-based management structures, and speed up the market responsiveness of any business.

In the minds of most managers there still is one basic problem with this system: it is too difficult to tie "knowledge-management" principles to bottom-line improvements. Many suspect that "critical competencies" is just another fad. Education and training represent "the soft side" of the business. To answer these skeptics, we will review in the next chapter return-on-investment (ROI) case studies from diverse business sectors that have successfully applied "knowledge management" principles that increase organizational profit. We will then go on to introduce a new nine-step ROI process as a realistic industry standard to measure human capital development.

SECTION

Measuring Human Capital Development

CHAPTER

2

Where's the Beef?
The Case for Measuring Training ROI

Training less to save money is like stopping the clock to save time.

JOHN TOBIN, SIEMENS CORPORATION

The management at Trident Precision Manufacturing would certainly agree with Tobin. They work for one of the smallest companies ever to win a Malcolm Baldrige National Quality Award (1996) thanks in large part to Trident's investment in its human capital. Over a period of six years, the company educated their employees in a big way, investing 4.7 percent of the payroll.

Trident is a custom-products sheet-metal company. Applications range from simple brackets to machines that sort X-rays. Six years ago, management realized that quality was being undermined because turnover was a crippling 41 percent a year. In many cases, employees quit within six months of learning their jobs.

Management decided to start concentrating on people and learning rather than technology and products. "We taught workers blueprint reading, trigonometry, and English as a second language," says Nicholas Jushiw, Trident's CEO. As the education program progressed, the company also worked to improve the problem-solving abilities of its employees by letting people make more decisions on the floor. A recognition program gave people feedback on their on-the-job results by giving the average worker some kind of public praise or reward nine times a year.

What has been the return on investment for Trident's training and development program? Where there was a 3 percent product-defect rate in 1988, 99.994 percent were defect-free in 1996. Employee turnover fell from 41 percent to 5 percent a year. Company revenue quadrupled from $5 million in 1988 to over $19 million in 1996. Finally, revenue per employee shot up 73 percent.

Can any doubt remain that Trident's investment in human capital yielded an impressive ROI? Unfortunately, the answer is yes! Considerable doubt prevails across the American business community that employee education is in any way a driver of business profit that can be measured by ROI. One of the most dismal, yet most consistent, research findings is that less than 20 percent of training transfers back to the employee's job. In a typical year (1998), more than $55 billion is invested in training; apparently, a great deal of that money is wasted on training that is ineffective![1]

Senior management currently is examining the cost–benefit ratio in every department. Many business sectors already have developed industrywide ROI measures used for benchmarking and decision-making on capital investments (plant and equipment). ROI defines evaluation methods and calculations used to determine the financial impact that a specific business investment has had on the organization's performance, productivity, and profit. But can ROI be applied to "human capital?"

What is human capital? It is the sum total of individual intelligence built upon the acquisition of skills, training, and educational experience over a lifetime. The application of this human knowledge to the workplace creates real value. The merging of three types of capital— human, organizational, and customer—creates the financial capital (value) of any business (see Figure 2-1).

In a 1997 American Management Association national survey, "increasing return on investment" was ranked as third out of 25 current corporate concerns. Certainly there exists great interest in ROI. However, most senior management and finance managers see training and education as an "ivory tower," the soft side of the business. Bookkeepers and accountants argue that it is not realistic to measure the long-term quantitative effects of training for a business. The truth is that sensible bosses have always valued the accumulation of skills by their workers.

In the 1930s Alfred Sloan, the pioneering manager of General Motors, created a category of general managers to gather information

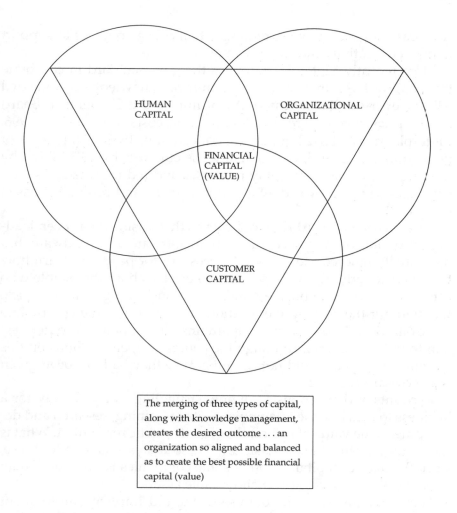

The merging of three types of capital, along with knowledge management, creates the desired outcome . . . an organization so aligned and balanced as to create the best possible financial capital (value)

Figure 2-1 Value Platform

Source: Hubert Saint-Onge, Charles Armstrong, Gordon Petrash, Leif Edvinsson

from the shop floor and consumers, and then to use it as a basis for allocating resources.

Lest we forget, IBM was the really first full-fledged "learning organization," which at one time adopted the word "Think" as its corporate motto, and modeled its headquarters after a university campus. By the 1980s IBM invested over $1 billion annually in its corporate university, even granting actual college degrees to support employee creativity through learning.

More recently Motorola, hailed as the gold standard in corporate training, declared that increasing employee knowledge has yielded $30 for every dollar invested. According to the Conference Board (1997) it has saved more than $3 billion in costs from 1987 to 1996. Motorola invested $120 million on education in 1992—3.6 percent of its payroll. Since 1987, the company has cut costs by $3.3 billion by training employees to simplify processes and reduce waste. As a result, sales per employee doubled in five years, and profits increased 47 percent.[2]

Career coach Richard Koonce believes that business has been loading up on information technology, both software and hardware, but has usually ignored the "how to" necessary for people to learn how to use it properly. Technology does not exist without the people who can make it work. In business there is no such thing as a "technical fix" without the employee education on how to use the equipment. For example, a Midwestern company installed a new computer system to track inventory. Although the company spent millions on this system, employees could not use it because they had not been given the necessary training.

Accounts and economists are now struggling to find a way for a business to measure the intangible assets of training, research and development, the value of its brands, even its public reputation. What is their "added value" to the business? These analysts have little choice, since the market capitalization of some companies is now more than ten times the book value of their tangible assets.

This coincides with the demise of the old implicit employment contract in which bigger company profits generally were followed by better wages, benefits, and job security for employees. The new employment contract of the 1990s gives employees the responsibility for increasing company profit, and the employer the responsibility for making their people as valuable as possible. Business creates "added value" by redefining jobs with more responsibility. They unlock personal creativity for workplace innovations by providing the training opportunities that increase the individual employees' self-actualization skills (i.e., critical thinking) that can improve products, processes, and quality. One unique "asset" in a company is its "human capital."

We need to accurately measure the economic results of its development through training and education.

The Rush on Knowledge

Business is trapped in and the beneficiary of an ever-upward technical spiral. On one hand, we are creating more wealth and productivity. On the other hand, it will take ever more education to realize the productive uses of current technology, not to mention the introduction of even more complex high-tech almost everyday.

A business cannot create long-term value that is sustainable, no matter how sophisticated the technology, without the successful constant development of its human capital. Karl Erik Sveiley has said, "The economy of our Knowledge Era offers unlimited resources, because the human capacity to create new knowledge is infinite." The new business strategy is to increase employee critical competencies, i.e., the capacity to understand all these billions of informational bits and pieces, and put them to work.

Developing human capital addresses a business's ability to learn and adapt. There is now taking place a shift in the center of economic gravity of the U.S. marketplace, from the management and measurement of physical and financial assets, to how knowledge workers are cultivated as the most significant act of value creation by any organization.

If you asked an executive at Microsoft, Motorola, Hewlett-Packard, or Intel what percentage of total company value is attributed to people knowledge assets—educational abilities; technical know-how of IT systems; basic and design skills; interpersonal relationships with suppliers and customers; trademarks and patents—you would get the same answer: upward of 80 percent. In many ways your business is the same.[3]

Should it then be any surprise that in a survey (1996) the Institute of Management Accounting found that 64 percent of corporate controllers across the United States were actively experimenting with new ways of measuring performance? Or, as *Fortune* magazine reported (1994), that Dow Chemical now has a Director of Intellectual Assets to create an intellectual capital report for that company?

Hughes Aircraft set up an intellectual capital (IC) program called the Knowledge Highway. The Canadian Bank of Commerce established a leadership development program around intellectual capital (IC). Using this educational program as a benchmark, the bank instituted a loan program to finance knowledge-based companies using IC valuations as a key criterion. At the core of all these programs is an attempt to foster and measure the commitment of a business and its employees to learn and renew over time their personal knowledge and understanding (critical competencies) through continuous education.

Scandia AFS, a Scandinavian-based insurance company, is a recognized leader in measuring the value of human resource contributions. Leif Edvinsson and Michael S. Malone in *Intellectual Capital* (Harper Business, 1997) discussed how in May 1995 Scandia released the first public human capital annual report, as a supplement to their financial report. It included how levels of employees' education and training influenced turnover and retention, the corporate culture, and bottom-line earnings.

Edvinsson and Malone wrote, "The rise of Intellectual Capital is inevitable given the irresistible historical and technological forces not to mention the investment flows that are sweeping across the modern world and driving us toward a knowledge economy."[4]

Gordon Petrash, Dow Chemical's V.P. of R & D, told Edvinsson that they knew that the business was underutilizing and underleveraging its vast collection of patents.

> *Question:* How do you convince management in a short time of the usefulness of human capital investment as part of their pursuit of long-term goals?
>
> *Answer:* You measure it. You must brief business people on human capital investment in terms they will understand. But keep it simple. You need to be able to tell the whole story on a single sheet of paper.

The first step is to assess the personal knowledge of employees across groups. This gives management benchmarks to understand its human capital strengths and weaknesses. Second, select from performance-development-program alternatives in skill, training, and educational areas that track directly to productivity improvement. Third, using a reliable human capital ROI measurement system, produce the numbers that will allow management to select from these alternatives programs that yield the best short-term/long-term return-on-investment. On a single sheet of paper, list the alternatives and their ROIs.

Question: Why does human capital investment produce better business returns?

Answer: Because it provides cost savings in investments by better identifying either the recycling of the organization and its structural capital (i.e., plant, equipment, technology), and/or the recycling of people, to address specific performance and productivity issues. Maybe this split is about 50/50.

Question: What does human capital investment do to encourage business innovation?

Answer: By leveraging structural capital and human capital in combination, the company benefits from a steeper learning curve at the cutting edge: between the organization's internal people business units and its operational productivity issues. Employee critical competencies are generated in-house that encourage new procedures, new services, new products, new intellectual properties—the very ideas that run a business and generate real added value.

Question: When will this give business "added value"?

Answer (Peter Drucker): From the beginning innovation must be the core competency at the heart of every organization continuously nurtured by investment and systematically transformed into value by "people development."

(Tom Peters): In the world of unpredictable change companies must construct, dynamic, creative environments driven by "people development" if they are to remain at the cutting edge of products and services that fully satisfy customers.

Both of the "people development" goals of these gurus can be realized only through long-term infrastructure human capital investments.

Question: What can happen if a business invests in only structured capital and not human capital?

Answer: In the 1980s General Motors (GM) did just that. They made massive open-ended investments in the application of computers and robotics to their auto assembly lines without management assessment of how their own employees could better apply this advanced technology to meet measurable performance goals. After that near-debacle, GM invested billions in human-capital-improvement programs to develop its people into a convergent system that linked the application of technology to employees learning how to innovate and apply it to precise performance goals.

Question: What are the critical questions for a business in developing such a convergent system?

Answer:

I. What is the average education level of your employees throughout the organization?
   (a) Benchmark this to your leading competitor(s).
   (b) Determine this level for each operational area of your business.
   (c) Are you competitive today?

II. What is the average amount in hours of employee knowledge given per month by your business? Answer the above (a), (b), (c) questions.

III. Break out, by operating unit, employee development hours into three prime categories:

YOU — COMPETITION

   (a) Skills:
   (b) Training:
   (c) Education:
   (d) Are you competitive today?

IV. In order to remain competitive, what will be your future human capital requirements (in hours) in:
   (a) 6 months?
   (b) 12 months?
   (c) 3 years?
   (d) 5 years?

Question: How do you make human capital investment part of a successful strategic business plan?

Answer: Any strategic business plan that tries to move from restructuring using information-technology integration to total business integration will fail to produce the desired long-term value unless it also integrates a third component. A human capital measurement system is needed to track the flow of a business's investments in people-development programs. This system converts debt (costs) into assets that appear on the balance sheet.

The notion behind creating such a human capital return-on-investment yardstick is simple: a company creates value only when the return on its capital is greater than the opportunity cost of it, or the rate that investors could earn by investing elsewhere. Companies have long used "hurdle" rates of return to judge individual investment projects. A human capital ROI extends this practice to the often-cited intangible side of the business. The problem is coming up with a reliable human capital ROI industry standard. Can it now be done?[5]

Case Studies

Jack Phillips has published extensive business case studies that measure training's return-on-investment (see Figure 2-2). Magnavox, Coca-Cola, Litton Industries, and Yellow Freight System were among 18 organizations studied, and they used a wide variety of ROI approaches. In some cases the results offer extremely high rates of return (2,000 percent). How credible are these measurements? Phillips does recognize that many other business variables can affect performance, making it more difficult to determine how much of a transfer to the bottom line is due to training. He still believes that these ROI figures are as accurate as many other estimates that organizations routinely use to make decisions for other parts of their business operations.[6]

Arthur Andersen

On the other hand, Arthur Andersen developed a cost–benefit analysis for a five-week accounting course on state and local tax affairs. Darryl Jinkerson, director of evaluation services, at Andersen's Center for

Setting	Target Group	Program Description	Evaluation Program	Results
Electric & Gas Utility	Managers & Supervisors	Applied Behavior Management which focused on achieving employee involvement to increase quality, productivity and profits	• Action Planning (Variety of Projects) • Performance Monitoring	• 400% ROI • Benefit/Cost Ratio 5:1
Oil Company	Dispatchers	Skills Training Program including customer interaction skills, problem solving, and teamwork	• Follow-up Observations • Performance Monitoring	• Customer complaints reduced by 85% • Absenteeism reduced by 77% • Reduction in pull-outs saved $283,800 • 383% ROI • Benefit/Cost Ratio 3.2:1
Bakery (Multi-Marques, Inc.)	Supervisors/Administration Services	15 hour Supervisory Skills Training including the role of training	• Action Plan (Work Process Analyses) • Performance Monitoring	• 215% ROI • Benefit/Cost Ratio 3.2:1
Avionics (Litton Industries)	All Employees	Self Directed Work Teams	• Action Plan • Performance Monitoring	• Productivity Increased 30% • Scrap Rate Reduction 50% • 700% ROI
Truck Leasing (Penske Truck Leasing)	All Supervisors	20 hour program in supervisory skills utilizing behavioral modeling	• Performance Monitoring	• Turnover reduction of 6% • Absenteeism Reduction of 16.7%

Figure 2-2 Actual Business Results from Training and Development

Source: These cases appear in *Measuring Return on Investment.* Published by the American Society for Training and Development, Alexandria, VA 1994. Jack J. Phillips, Ph.D., Editor.

Professional Education in St. Charles, Illinois, tracked the billable hours of 60 tax-accountant trainees after they completed the course. He found that they were spending more of their billable hours doing state and local tax work.

Andersen next compared these billable hours to 60 similar trainees who hadn't taken the course. Jinkerson found that the trained group produced more revenue than the untrained accountants. In addition, he discovered that they were much more willing to promote their greater expertise doing state and local tax work to clients.

Jinkerson stated that the bottom-line increase after 15 months offset the cost of the training program, and that the average increase in revenue per accountant was more than 10 percent. This was a good ROI for a continuing professional education program (*Training*, March 1995).

Nabisco

In 1996 Nabisco also utilized an ROI program. It compared 104 sales representatives who completed a new "Professional Selling Program" to a similar sales group that was not trained. Robert Klein, Nabisco's sales education manager, says that the trained reps increased store sales by 8 percent. This meant an annualized increase of over $122,000 per trainee. After deducting the cost of this training (about $1,000/person), Klein believes that the ratio of increased sales for each dollar invested in training was 122:1.[7]

Rubbermaid

Rubbermaid of Wooster, Ohio, a manufacturer of plastic household products, took a different approach to ROI with a company-wide time-management course. Chad Cook, director of Human Resources, mailed a survey to 674 program participants at 12 company sites. This audience included executives, managers, administrators, and professionals. About 70 percent responded, far greater than the normal survey return rate of 15 to 25 percent.

What they reported was an average personal increase in productivity of 9.3 percent. Cook calculated that the productivity gain reported by these 422 employees, minus the cost of the program (including salaries, hotels, meals, and training), returned an estimated dollar benefit to Rubbermaid of over $1.1 million, or a 17.32 percent return-on-investment.

This program's time-management procedures have continued to be so useful at Rubbermaid that Cook now sees them as "part of the organization's culture." Rubbermaid is now considering repeating the program for new employees.

Iams University

In 1946 Paul Iams started the Iams Company in Dayton, Ohio, as a producer of cat and dog foods. It is now a $500 million company distributing pet products on three continents.

According to Jack Tootson, former director of Iams University, management invests approximately 3 percent of payroll in employee-education programs. More than 30 courses are offered through Iams University at company locations around the world. This is supported by an annual budget of $2 million. Tootson reports that Iams has now achieved (1996) a 7:1 ROI through its corporate education program. Because of this success, Iams has been referred to as the "Motorola University" of small companies.

Garfield Electric/Siemens

Gary Hartman, president of Garfield Electric Co. in Cincinnati, Ohio, a $27 million electrical contractor with 250 employees, has recently become involved in career education/apprentice programs with local high schools and postsecondary institutions. "Too many contractors look at training as an expense. It's not, it's an investment," he says, "and it's an investment that repays itself many, many times over."

Hartman points out that training workers reduces the cost of lost productivity, accidents, warranty callbacks, and redoing previous work. "It's people that make your business work. Unless you train them well, you're not going to have a high-quality, productive workforce."

For that reason Hartman helped found the four-year electrical apprentice program for the Associated Builders and Contractors Association in southwest Ohio 20 years ago.

ROI—LESSONS LEARNED

Cost per Skill/Set

- Least expensive model—Public High School
- More expensive model—Public Post Secondary
- Most expensive model—Incumbent Worker Training

Some Annual Costs to Employer

Public High Schools	$1,500 to $2,000 per annum
Community Colleges	$10,000 to 12,000 per annum
Incumbent Worker	$30,000 to $50,000+ per annum

Box 2-1 ROI Lessons Learned

The program has been expanded to a total of five trades and currently has 400 apprentices (1998). Twenty-nine of them are electrical apprentices who work for Garfield. His staff recruits these apprentices from local schools. Garfield then hires them part-time during the school year or full-time during the summer. The firm also participates in local preapprenticeship programs to help increase students' math and reading abilities. "We've been doing this for about two years and it's working out well," says Hartman.

John Tobin, at Siemens, would agree. Siemens participated in a study of the ROI of career-education programs through the National Employers Leadership Council (1998). The ROI lesson these businesses learned was that the most efficient training model was to invest in high-school career-education programs, rather than at the community-college level or by retraining current workers (see Box 2-1).[8]

Walgreen and Others

When the drugstore chain Walgreen developed a new training program for its pharmacy technicians, senior executives wanted to measure the program's ROI. To do this Walgreen compared the sales of two groups in its pharmacies: technicians who received the formal training versus the technicians who received only on-the-job training. The store sales of formally educated technicians were almost $10,000 higher than technicians who received only informal training on-the-job.

Other companies such as AT&T, Allstate, Will-Burt, Pacific Bell, GTE, the United Auto Workers/Ford Education Development and Training Program, Corning, Inc., MacLean-Fogg Company, and Intel have created units within their training departments to evaluate and measure the ROI of human capital investment. John Bourdreau and Peter Ranstead of Cornell University studied how Sears, Roebuck and Company also created a system that measures and connects training investments to store outcomes.[9]

Otto Engineering

Located in Carpentersville, Illinois, a suburb of Chicago, Otto Engineering is a small manufacturer of snap-action switches and electrical assemblies for industrial and commercial applications. Otto is a supplier for Motorola products.

By the late 1980s globalization was beginning to take its toll. For Otto to compete with the more than 100 other switch companies worldwide, product quality had to improve.

In order to improve its products, Otto's senior management established a Workforce Education Program, including statistical process control (SPC), blueprint reading, English-as-a-second-language (ESL) classes for nonnative speakers, and other technical classes. Over a period of four years, 185 employees participated in these training and education classes. What did the company earn from this investment? ROI could be measured in several different ways.

1. *Field Returns:* Field returns dropped dramatically as the ESL education program progressed. Figure 2-3 shows the average dollar of field returns per year dropped as the employees read at higher and higher grade levels. It does not include those returns that were caused by poor machine capability or bad parts from Otto's suppliers. The bottom line was that Otto saved $923 per year in field returns for each grade level in reading gained by an employee through its workforce education program.

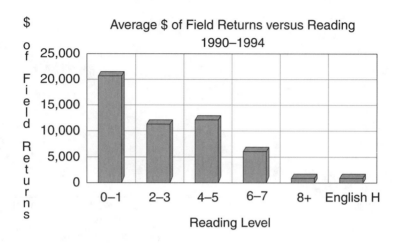

Figure 2-3 Field Return Results for Otto Engineering Workforce Education Program

2. *Scrap:* Over a five-year period, results showed that each dollar invested by Otto in this program reduced scrap caused by human error by $1.656. The company now believes that the improvement of employee educational skills is the main determinant for reducing scrap caused by worker errors.

3. *Productivity:* Otto Engineering experienced a large productivity improvement over the five-year period. Productivity results were measured as the dollars of product shipped per year, per person. Figure 2-4 shows the trend from 1990 to 1994. This productivity improvement resulted from training, capital investment, and management operational changes within the organization. In our statistical analysis of these productivity improvement dollars, the training costs and the capital investment costs indicate that 31 percent of the productivity improvement came from training, 32 percent came from capital investment, and 37 percent can be attributed to all other changes that were not specifically tracked. During this time period, Otto Engineering expended $556,000 in all training and $8.5 million in capital-equipment investment. These results seem to indicate a much higher payback from training than from capital investment. However, it is the author's belief

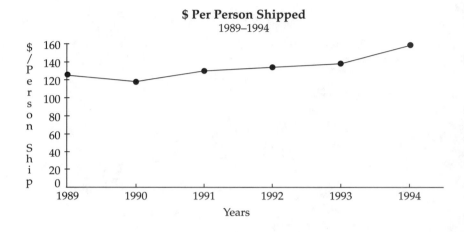

**Figure 2-4 Productivity Results for Otto Engineering
Workforce Education Program**

that only a careful simultaneous investment in both training
and capital improvements will yield the best results.

4.   *ROI:* The average productivity improvement of 31 percent was
     calculated to be $314 per person per year. Training costs for the
     Workforce Education Program were $1,877 per person per
     year. This results in an ROI of 16.7 percent.

Additional measurable financial benefits also included the following:

- Reduced injury claims ($625/person/year)
- Reduced field returns ($923/person/year)
- Reduced internal scrap ($3,097/person/year)

By adding these additional savings of $4,645 per person/year, the
total benefit rises to $4,959, or an ROI of 264 percent.

Also of interest to Otto was the fact that SPC, blueprint reading,
and other forms of technical training were successful largely because
of the immediate improvement of individual reading/math educational skills gained from the ESL classes. The long-term impact of
strong SPC and other technical skills will have the effect of adding to
ROI benefits for Otto as it continually introduces the latest advanced
manufacturing technologies of the switching industry.[10]

Dropping the "Other Shoe"

Corporate America has been on a diet. Businesses are now lean, and reengineering, outsourcing, and downsizing have contributed to record profits. A recent *Wall Street Journal* article suggests, however, that the shrinking corporation has gone too far, in many cases producing "corporate anorexia." There is a great danger here that companies can gradually lose their ability to grow. "You can't shrink to greatness" says Jim Stanford, president of Calgary-based Petro-Canada.

Training has been particularly hard hit during this present business cycle. Even though sales and profits have increased, corporate training and development often face a struggle merely to survive.

The German and Japanese track record for training expenditures during a genuine market downturn is the exact opposite of the United States'. Our chief foreign competitors increase training investment for employees as they reorganize/retool for the new services/products demanded by the subsequent business cycle. Employees have more time available to be trained. This business culture sees leveraging an organization's "intellectual capital" as a principal management strategy. Unlike the United States, neither Germany nor Japan possesses abundant natural resources. Businesses see people development as their most important national asset. They do not believe a company's competitiveness will be guaranteed by slicing, dicing, and chopping. Instead they seek to better manage by leveraging collective organizational knowledge. How do we modify senior American business culture to adopt this world-class standard for education investment in the workplace?[11]

New approaches to workforce education are beginning to influence American management to change its culture. The *Harvard Business Review* (July/August 1996) reported positive results from 19 California companies that developed those missing links. They cited economic benefits that included increased productivity, reduced costs due to less absenteeism, and lower worker's compensation claims. In using a workforce education investment approach, study director Frederick Kewin believes, "We would do well to remind ourselves that getting the job right the first time is not only cheaper, but always better business."[12]

Other companies have experienced the same success including Clorox, Marriott Hotels, Price-Waterhouse, Metra (Chicago's commuter railroad), and numerous others. More than a score of business case studies about workforce education for managers, secretaries, professionals, technicians, service workers, and industrial workers that improved performance are discussed in two of this writer's previous books, *FutureWork, The Revolution Reshaping American Business* (Praeger/Greenwood) and *Closing the Literacy Gap in American Business* (Quorum/Greenwood).

For the first time a growing number of national U.S. economic studies support the growing ROI evidence of companies such as Otto Engineering when they invest in human-capital development. As employee education increases, company income increases at a faster rate of return.

In 1995, the National Center on the Educational Quality of the Workforce at the University of Pennsylvania published results from its national survey, "The Other Shoe: Education's Contribution to the Productivity of Establishments," which was commissioned by the U.S. Census Bureau. This was the first detailed U.S. business survey of its kind, polling approximately 3,000 establishments with 20 or more employees.

The productivity results (see Figure 2-5) showed a direct connection between the level of training investment and the increase in company profit. A 10 percent increase in the average education of workers within an organization (equivalent to slightly more than one additional year of reading/math comprehension) is associated with an 8.6 percent increase in output for all industries. This rises to 11 percent for the nonmanufacturing sector, where nearly three times more productivity is gained by investing in human capital (training) than if the money were spent on plant and equipment.

In comparison, the study showed that a 10 percent increase in capital-equipment expenditure resulted in only a 3.4 percent increase in productivity. Some companies are not getting the bang for their buck from new technology, this report says, because they don't also invest in related human capital development. For example, U.S. business investment in computers has increased 55 percent since 1990; however, it has accounted for only 12 percent of the expected output growth. This is a major contributing factor to lower-than-expected productivity. One of the paradoxes is that, in spite of the billions of dollars that companies have spent on computers, aggregate productivity has not responded in kind.

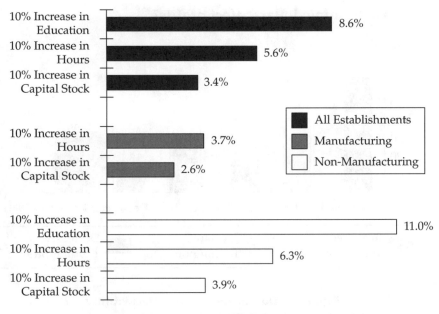

Percent Increase in Establishment Productivity

Figure 2-5 Factors for Increased Productivity
Source: 1995 Bureau of the Census

This survey concretely documented that investing more in improving the educational levels of a company's workforce has a major payoff in the form of increased employee productivity.

Cut Training, Cut Profits

The American Management Association (AMA) also found that training dollars affect productivity and profits. A well-publicized independent AMA study (1995) verified some of the same results from investments in training (see Figures 2-6 and 2-7).

- Of the companies that showed increased profits after downsizing or restructuring, 62.6 percent had increased their training budgets. Productivity also improved in the 45 percent of businesses that had increased their training investment.

Do training dollars affect profits?

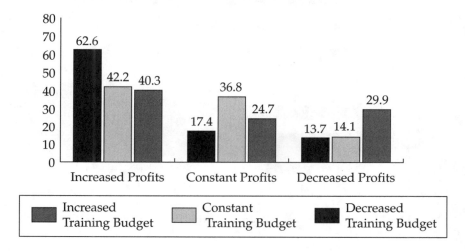

Figure 2-6 Do Training Dollars Affect Profits?
Source: AMA Research Reports

Do training dollars affect productivity?

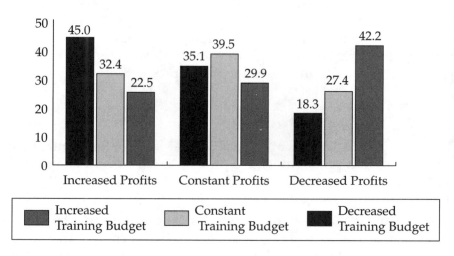

Figure 2-7 Do Training Dollars Affect Productivity?
Source: AMA Research Reports

- Of the companies that saw their profits decline after downsizing or restructuring, 29.9 percent had cut their training budget, and likewise, productivity declined for 42.4 percent of organizations that had decreased their training investment.

In a Conference Board survey (1995), 49 companies reported that they got better results by using a "performance enhancement" training model similar to the one created in 1989 at West Point. Cadets first used the critical competencies model to improve football skills, but it was then applied to enhance academic and leadership performance. The training program sought to improve stress management, self-image, team-building, positive thinking, and goal-setting, as well as attention skills and empowerment abilities.

The study found that 62 percent of the corporations that used four or more of these components appeared in the top 25 list of a Forbes ranking of companies. In comparison, only 18 percent of companies using three or fewer of these techniques even make the Forbes List. Conference Board Louis Csoka believes that this shows that overall employee performance can be improved when companies invest in systemic training programs for their people.

An international study, the 1996 "United Nations Human Development Report," confirmed these other reports. The key to national economic growth is investment in education. The U.N. found on a macroeconomic scale that raising employee education by one grade level increases gross domestic product by 9 percent. The bottom-line results from these four studies send the same message to management: The amount any organization invests or does not invest in training will have a positive or negative impact on both short-term and long-term profit.

Gary Becker, the noted University of Chicago economist, agrees. His book *Human Capital* (University of Chicago, 3rd ed., 1994) contains a "human capital theory." Becker believes that human capital investment should be based on the reality that employees, business, and society receive a direct economic benefit from investing in people. Do any successful executives doubt they would be where they are today without having first made an investment in their own education? Becker estimates that the ROI on personal education is between 12.5 and 25 percent.[13]

Kevin Hollenbeck, a senior economist at the Upjohn Institute, conducted a national study of work-based basic skills training programs.

He found that employee participation in these programs can increase productivity by 10 to 20 percent.[14]

One of the best known contemporary U.S. human-capital-theory economists, Jacob Mincer at Columbia University, concluded that a business receives a major economic benefit by raising their employees' skills. In a major study of U.S. job training, he estimated the profitability rate of employers' investments in training. Mincer found that the organization's productivity increase is more than twice that of any related employee wage increase caused by training.[15]

There is a strong demand from the American business community for a simple, flexible, precise way to measure human capital investment. Most businesses are not measuring for return-on-investment, and those that do will not share their process. Therefore, most executives believe that this "soft side of the business" cannot be expressed in precise dollar terms.

If human capital development is ever to be paid more than just lip service by management, it must be integrated into overall business strategies, and its value must be measured on the same terms that the business as a whole uses to measure its success. The Conference Board in its study of human capital development (1997) clearly stated the "catch-22" dilemma we must somehow solve. "On the one hand, the training function is under pressure to prove its exact value to the bottom line; on the other hand, such proofs are often inappropriate for types of training that are, intuitively, quite valuable."[16]

In the next chapter we will review our attempt to resolve this dilemma and find an acceptable answer to this training ROI mystery.

CHAPTER

3

Solving the ROI Mystery

Members of the accounting profession . . . have fretted openly about how to inform potential investors of the true worth of enterprises whose value results in the brains of employees.

ROBERT REICH, FORMER U.S. SECRETARY OF LABOR

Calculating an accurate return-on-investment (ROI) for human capital development is fraught with land mines. As we have seen, that doesn't mean companies aren't trying. Of 314 human resource directors surveyed by Brian Hackett of the Conference Board (1997), 44 percent reported that they do indeed "attempt to measure the value of training."

Two ROI systems widely in use are utility analysis (see Casio, *Training and Development in Organizations*, Jossey-Bass, 1989), and performance value (see Swanson and Gradous, *Forecasting Financial Benefits of Human Resource Development*, Jossey-Bass, 1988). Both economic evaluation programs offer a reasonably accurate ROI measurement; however, they fail to address three serious issues that compromise their final results:

1. *Training's Effectiveness versus Other Business Variables* Training is never done in a vacuum. A business may reorganize, buy new equipment, or introduce a new leading-edge product or service; a major competitor may go out of business; etc. To accurately measure what the training did to help the business, we must have a way to factor out all these other business variables. Otherwise, we will inflate training's ROI.

2. *Training Transfer* "Trainee A" completes a sales training program and as a result achieves X percent increase in sales (after

factoring in other variables). "Trainee B" completes the same training, as do 398 other sales people. Does the training transfer measure for "Trainee A" apply equally to the other 399 salespeople? The answer is no. Unless we have a way to calculate the "average" training transfer back on the job, we will inflate training's ROI.

3. *Depreciation of Training* How long will the training effects last and have a positive benefit for the business? Even the best training will not permanently improve a business. Unless we depreciate a training program's benefits over time, we will not offer an accurate business measurement.[1]

An accurate system for measuring human capital investment needs to address another problem: the lack of transparency in the costs of labor. More and more employees will need continuous education upgrades as a routine part of good management. This expands labor costs beyond pensions and benefits to include the direct costs of training (course costs, training materials), as well as the indirect costs such as the value of foregone production.

The main problem is the difficulty of measuring the productive capacities (skill, training, or educational abilities) that employees acquire from a specific performance-improvement program.[2]

An Interdisciplinary Approach

For the past four years, I've worked with an interdisciplinary team (the other team members are Kevin Hollenbeck, senior economist, W.E. Upjohn Institute for Employment Research; Robert M. Naiman, CPA and corporate tax attorney; and Boyd Owens, quality engineer at Equimeter Co.) to find an ROI program that would address these and other criticisms, be reasonably simple to use, and be acceptable to corporate management, accountants, and financial people. We produced the Human Capital ROI Worksheet™, as part of an overall productivity performance education tool kit we have entitled the Human Capital Scoreboard™ (see Chapter 5). The Human Capital ROI Worksheet is available as a software product that makes it possible to enter the data pertinent to most skill, training, and workplace-education programs, and then calculate the ROI for that program.

Why was it important to have an interdisciplinary team? Because it was essential to have a wide range of business information before we could begin to calculate a more accurate ROI for human capital performance. Human resources and training staffs need the cooperation of other people in their organization if they hope to use an ROI program. Whether you are in a service, manufacturing, industrial, or professional business, you will need information from engineering, accounting, marketing, and administration, as well as other departments, for your ROI model.

Don't let this intimidate you. Other business units that use an "ROI Industry Standard" (e.g., purchasing) already have access to proprietary business information on profit margins, diverse business operating benchmarks, etc. This information is essential for their calculations to make sense and be used for decision-making by senior management. Why should human capital investment be treated any differently? Many training industry executives have told me that senior management soon will require them to provide "ROI justification" for all their programs. Why should human capital investment's ROI be treated any differently than other parts of a business? Who, then, will do these ROI calculations? Probably the company's finance department, with input from operations, human resources, training, and other departments.

Nine Steps to Success

We have developed a nine-step ROI model for human capital investment (see Figure 3-1). To make these calculations we have developed a worksheet compatible with Lotus or Excel so that any financial manager can do the calculations. If you have excellent math skills, are familiar with formulas for linear regression and standard discount rate (depreciation), and can calculate a test's standard deviation, you also can use an advanced calculator.

We believe that this nine-step Human Capital ROI Worksheet will allow you to accurately estimate the monetary returns both before and after most training programs. It will allow any business to better calculate training cost as a business function. Every asset has a cost. Many in senior management envision a new policy of allocating "new assets" to solve priority problems and seize priority opportunities. By

Step One: Calculate all direct costs associated with the training program.	Step Four: Estimate expected hourly, weekly, or monthly productivity benefits per trainee. Methods may range from establishing control groups to using a standard linear regression formula.	Step Seven: Calculate profit per trainee.
Step Two: Calculate lost productivity while trainees are in the program.	Step Five: Estimate the actual quality benefit from the training.	Step Eight: Calculate benefits of the total training program.
Step Three: Calculate the total cost of the program.	Step Six: Using a standard discount rate formula, estimate the time length of the training's effect.	Step Nine: Calculate return on investment.

Figure 3-1 Human Capital ROI 9-Step Worksheet
Source: Courtesy of Imperial Consulting Corporation

using the Human Capital ROI Worksheet as a more accurate measurement system, we can begin to convert training and development into a new asset—human capital.

Business Background Data

Before you can begin the ROI calculations, you need to determine specific performance outcomes that will be reached by the proposed training, and to obtain related internal general business operating data. You will need to answer the following questions:

1. What is the employee performance area that you have targeted for improvement and for which you want an ROI measure? There are four basic business productivity issues around which you can organize your financial measurement: quality (rework), time, costs, and output.

You must be very careful to target a productivity issue that will respond to a performance improvement program involving skills, training, or education. Too often a business misapplies a proposed "training solution" to issues aligned with organizational structure, technology applications, or personal leadership issues. A good up-front management analysis of these areas can help you decide what areas will respond better to management consulting, counseling, or coaching than to the learnable aspects of performance improvement programs (see Chapter 5).

2. What is the productivity target? The skill, training or education program provider (internal/external) needs to give you his or her best estimate on the impact the specific program will have on this productivity issue. The provider should have enough prior experience to give you this estimate or run a trial pilot program to find out.

Not all skill, training, or education programs are equal. Some are definitely more powerful in terms of results than others. The whole purpose of running the numbers for a Human Capital ROI is to find out which program alternatives will give you the most bang for the buck. This is very healthy for your business because it forces education providers to give you their best effort and will better direct your investment capital to seek out and use realistic performance solutions.

3. How much gross revenue do the trainees now generate from their current work (in terms of the productivity area targeted)?

4. What is the value of outsourcing work in the area trained? (How much would it cost the firm to replace the target production?)

5. What are the total work hours for all employees being trained in the unit?

6. What is the company's or business unit's profit rate percentage on sales?

7. How many hours is the training program (work hours only)?

8. How many trainees are in the training program?

9. What is the trainee's productivity rate (percent) during the training? If training is done on employee time, the rate is 100 percent. If it is done entirely on company time, the rate is 0 percent.

After you have agreed on this information within your organization, the finance person can make the ROI computations for each program alternative. What follows is an outline of the nine steps found in our Human Capital ROI Worksheet.

Step 1: What are the training costs per trainee (excluding trainee wages)?

Calculate all the direct costs associated with the training program. These include training materials (books, software, tests), conference fees, trainer's compensation, consultant fees, travel, meals, hotel rooms, proportional capital expenditure for distance learning system, and computer hardware equipment.

Step 2: What is the trainee's lost productivity while in training?

This is an important calculation and is used instead of trainee salary, since productivity loss should be much larger than salary loss if the training is done on company time.

Step 3: What is the cost of the training program?

Computed by adding step 1 and step 2.

Step 4: What is the productivity benefit of the training?

The ROI is very sensitive to this estimate of the training effect on productivity. Here you will estimate the expected hourly, weekly, or monthly productivity benefits per trainee. We use several different methods, ranging from establishing control training groups to using a linear regression formula.

Step 5: What is the (posttraining) quality benefit from the training?

Step 6: What is the lifetime quality benefit from the training?

This is determined by deciding how long the training benefit will last (employee turnover, retooling schedule for a manufacturer, and other issues), and by using a discount rate formula to estimate the duration of the training's effect.

Step 7: What is the profit for each trainee?

Step 8: What are the benefits of the total training program?

Step 9: What is the Human Capital Return-on-Investment (ROI)?

Business Case Studies

I. Camshaft Production at XYZ Corporation

XYZ Corporation produces motors. Corporate managers have monitored production data and decided that there is a potential quality problem in the camshaft division. The division's gross production is 15,000 camshafts per week, and corporate engineers have set a production standard (with 95 percent quality) of 14,250. The last six weeks of production, however, were as follows: 13,000; 14,000; 13,300; 13,250; 14,100; 13,350. These average to 13,500. (The division was thus operating with a scrap rate of 10 percent, on average, instead of the 5 percent standard.)

When the division managers were asked about sources of this problem, they suggested that in their last two waves of hiring, several immigrants were hired. The managers indicated that the new employees were hard workers, but communication problems were noticeable. The Training Director suggested that the division could offer an English-as-a-second language (ESL) program for the 35 recent hires with limited English skills. The corporate Chief Financial Officer wanted to know what return on investment might be expected from this training.

To determine this, the Training Director investigated the ESL course and its potential effectiveness. The ESL course being considered involved 60 hours of classroom training over a 10-week period. The company offering the training suggested that the company should grant release time for half of the training (3 hours per week) and the employees should be expected to attend the other half of the training on their own time. Instructor time and materials would cost the corporation $6,000. The trainer indicated that the company should expect improved employee performance after the training, but of course, the worker's improved performance would probably decrease over time.

The managers of the camshaft division estimated that if the corporation had to purchase camshafts from their competition, the cost of each camshaft would be between $25 and $30. They told the Training Director that there were 120 total employees in the division who averaged 50 hours per week (10 hours of overtime). The average hourly wage without overtime premium is $10.00. The average tenure in the division is about 18 months. Furthermore, the latest annual financial report indicates that XYZ earns 17 percent before-tax profit on sales last year, but everyone believes that profit rates will be higher this year.

Assuming that the ESL training is sufficient to reduce the error rate to its production standard, what is the ROI on this training? The first worksheet uses the conservative (lower bound) estimates of effectiveness and impact. It assumes that the opportunity cost of a camshaft is $25. It assumes that the training effectiveness depreciates about half over the average (trained) worker's tenure, and it assumes a corporate gross profit rate of 17 percent. The second worksheet uses more optimistic estimates. It assumes an opportunity cost of a camshaft of $30, no depreciation of the training impact, and a gross profit rate of 19 percent.

These data result in an estimated ROI of 35.04 percent and 133.56 percent, respectively.

II. Room Preparations at the AAA Hotel

The AAA Hotel is a 500-room property located in a major metropolitan area. It employs a large number of recent immigrants in its housekeeping department. During an eight-hour shift, housekeepers have been given the goal of preparing 20 rooms for guest occupancy daily. The current average is 16 rooms.

In order to reach this goal, hotel management has identified what improved reading, writing, and oral communication skills are needed to achieve individual productivity improvements. Housekeepers will begin using portable computer terminals to list inventories of supplies and indicate room readiness for guest access. This technology requires far more knowledgeable workers; therefore, an English-as-a-second language program is an important part of the hotel's on-the-job training process.

Before or after each eight-hour shift, a group of five housekeepers received ESL training in a small-class setting. Employees were trained during a two-hour class that met twice each week over a period of 10 weeks. Results were then reviewed to determine if an individual needed additional training to reach the hotel's goal.

The results of the AAA Hotel's ESL training program resulted in an estimated ROI of 23 percent.

III. Kaizen Team Training at Equimeter Co.

Equimeter Co. in Pennsylvania applied a Kaizen-team-training program for a group of engineers to improve the quality/productivity of a gas meter assembly line. During one day of training the engineering team studied what it would take to rearrange the line to eliminate wasted effort. They achieved a 16 percent productivity improvement; a 22 percent space savings; reduced the work in process 10 percent; solved three safety issues; and reduced the walking distance to build one meter from 100 ft. to 44 ft.

The final result in an estimated ROI was over 31.6 percent.

How Practical?

We believe that most organization's training/education programs can use our Human Capital ROI Worksheet successfully to calculate a realistic business return. These programs include such areas as management; technical, skills, or professional education; and computer-based training. The key is access to essential business operational data and using widely accepted spreadsheet analysis that is embedded in our Human Capital ROI Worksheet. Following these practices substantially raises this model's credibility for business decision makers. This ROI model offers a far more credible and accurate measurement of training's effect on business productivity than previous attempts. Our model is an interdisciplinary effort to begin finally arriving at an "ROI training industry standard" that will remove employee education from the "soft side" of the business and provide a realistic business tool that drives corporate human capital development into the revenue side of the business. In the old employment contract, if the business made bigger profits, the employees could expect better wages, benefits, and job security. Today's new employment contract gives employers the responsibility for making their employees as valuable as possible.

Business can "add value" by redefining jobs that give more responsibility to each employee and by providing the education/training opportunities that develop the individual's "self-actualization abilities," unlocking creativity and workplace innovations that improve products, processes, and quality. A company's human capital is its unique asset.

In our next chapter we will consider a new way of looking at corporate accounting procedures for human capital investment. Is it possible to treat training and development as an amortized investment, rather than always as a cost that must be immediately written off?

CHAPTER

4

ROI Tax and Accounting Issues

Major business issues overhang the successful use of the Human Capital ROI Worksheet™. Even if people performance development programs provide a more accurate ROI estimate, senior management may still say, "Who cares about training's ROI? We can't capitalize training, so cut those training costs to improve our immediate earnings!"

The absence of a realistic business system that both manages and measures human capital investment heightens the risk in the eyes of most executives that precious resources will be misallocated. A human capital investment standard needs to be created that meets this condition and helps avoid overstating the results of skill, training, and education performance improvement programs. We also need to consider how corporate accounting now handles these issues. Only then can we plan the necessary policy changes that will gain strong management acceptance of the human capital investment concept.

Balance Sheet Issues

Talk to a company's accountants and you will find out that accounting principles have a real impact on how training costs are calculated. Generally training costs are "expensed"—that is, deducted against the current year's revenue—because training is considered a wage-related expense. In the current "corporate anorexia" mindset, training is viewed as an expense that should be minimized; any new costly training initiative should be avoided, since it would constitute a drain on the bottom line and quarterly shareholder earnings.

But times are changing. Lowell L. Bryan, a partner at McKinsey & Company, believes that historic accounting conventions understate both earnings and book capital when companies spend on "intangibles" such as training—which are increasingly the source of value to the U.S. economy. Why should these investments be "'expensed' even though as a by-product of this spending, intangible assets are being created that have value that will endure for years?"[1]

However, if depreciation accounting methods can be employed, training benefits (ROI) and costs could be spread out over time (amortized), making human capital investment more attractive to management. How can this be done?

Amortizing Human Capital

Those of us who took Accounting 101 learned that depreciation accounting is a system that aims to distribute the cost of tangible capital assets over the estimated useful life of the asset in a systematic and rational method. The depreciation for the year is the amount allocated to the year under the method. Companies review large expenditures to determine whether the expenditure benefits the company for more than one year. Thus, if a company buys equipment (such as computers, machines, trucks, or furniture), that equipment will depreciate over its useful life. The Internal Revenue Service publishes a list that indicates what it allows as the useful life of different types of equipment or other assets. The amount to depreciate is the actual price plus freight and the cost of setting up and training employees to operate the equipment.

Consider this example. A bank buys a new computer system for $5 million, which according to the IRS table has a useful life of 5 years. Technical training related to this new computer system is an additional cost associated with this purchase. In our extensive discussions with purchasing managers, we have discovered that adding the technical training costs to the purchase price of equipment is a commonly followed accounting procedure throughout much of American business. In our example the computer manufacturer told the bank that $200,000 of technical training for current and future employees will occur over the first 5 years. Thus, the amount to be depreciated would be $5.2 million. However, in the new high-performance workplace, this concept needs an updated, broader training application.

For hundreds of years workers had a shortage of information to do their jobs. Now they have a glut. What trainers are finding, much to their dismay, is that many employees never have developed an educational framework through which they understand and judge new information. Throughout the American workplace there is now a scarcity of these so-called "knowledge workers" who can comprehend the advanced technical training required by Information Technology (IT). A 12th-grade reading and math comprehension level is a commonly accepted IT benchmark. This technology also requires teams to employ "critical thinking" abilities in solving problems and personal communication skills to disseminate these solutions throughout a high-performance workplace. Additional employee training and education programs are essential throughout many organizations if each new generation of IT is to reach the targeted productivity and business-performance level. Otherwise, why bother making the purchase? The typical organization usually cannot find large numbers of people who can immediately use new IT because of this knowledge gap.

Business now has little choice but to begin offering more of these so-called "soft training" programs as prerequisites to technical training. In our bank case study, the business will need to offer $650,000 in training related to its new computers. This includes several new training programs related to mastering the new information technology (see Figure 4-1). Our Human Capital ROI Worksheet will provide an accurate calculation of monetary benefits to the business for each of these training programs. But does the company now have a choice to amortize them as part of the technical training required for their capital equipment purchase?

The Internal Revenue Service Ruling 96-62 states, "Training costs must be capitalized only in the unusual circumstances where training is intended primarily to obtain future benefits significantly beyond those traditionally associated with training provided in the ordinary course of a taxpayer's trade or business." It appears this favors only writing off all training as an expense for a tax deduction in the current year. However, it also seems possible to classify the $650,000 of new training programs provided to the bank's employees as an *unusual deduction*. This $450,000 represents *new* training never before offered to these individual workers and "is intended to obtain future benefits significantly beyond those traditionally associated with training provided (in the past by the bank)." The Human Capital ROI Worksheet will provide concrete monetary evidence of how significant those training programs benefits are to the bank.

Five-Year Depreciation Items

Item	Cost
(a) Computer and Software	$5,000,000
(b) Technical Training	$ 200,000
(c) Educational Skills (Reading, Math)	$ 200,000
(d) Team Training	$ 150,000
(e) Interpersonal Skill Training	$ 100,000
Total Depreciation	**$5,650,000**

Figure 4-1 Capitalized New Bank Computer and Related Training

For publicly traded corporations very concerned about quarterly earnings, this means that in some cases they may be able to capitalize training costs associated with new equipment or plant expenditures. In other instances the same business may wish to expense the training program and gain an immediate tax deduction of a related business cost.

Expensing Human Capital

For smaller, closely held companies (i.e., a family business, partnerships, etc.), this recent IRS ruling actually strengthens their ability to continue deducting their *full* training costs each year. As an added Human Capital development feature, we can now add ROI training benefits to the total income tax savings accrued from annual training expenditures. This will give businesses the total human capital performance benefit that can be derived from people-performance development or training activities.

How Practical?

To make the case for human capital investment, we believe that management needs the flexibility to determine if a particular training cost is to be capitalized or expensed. This approach adds to the benefits that ROI identifies for a specific training program (see Figure 4-2).

Proprietary business baseline measures are needed to calculate a training program's contribution toward solving realistic business problems. This means that interdepartmental collaboration (i.e., senior management, finance, operations, marketing training) is essential to gain agreement on how the ROI is to be calculated. It is probably best if the finance people make the final calculations.

Management must be very careful not to oversell the benefits that result from human capital investment. Poor overall quality in an organization's products or services cannot be remedied by any known training or education program. Also, know what results your people-performance-improvement programs are able to produce before applying an ROI measure. Not all training is equal. The more experience you have in using different training/education applications, the better you

Tax Alternatives	Capitalized	Expensed
Type of Business	Publicly Held Corporation	Closely Held Company
Cost Alternatives	Depreciated Human Capital over Time	Full Tax Deductions in the Current Year
Amortization Method	All Training Associated with Capital Expenditures • Technical • Nontechnical	(not applicable)
Performance Measures	ROI	ROI

Figure 4-2 Human Capital Tax Alternative

will be able to select the right training application that will yield a higher, yet realistic human capital ROI benefit.[2]

ROI Response: Lip Service or Reality?

We believe that our Human Capital ROI Worksheet will help you begin moving people-performance improvement to the strategic side of your organization. Since I first introduced an earlier version of this worksheet in *Corporate University Review* (1997), I have received a strong, positive response from businesses across America. Automotive, pharmaceutical, entertainment, industrial, and manufacturing businesses have expressed their interest in trying our new nine-step Human Capital ROI Worksheet.

In many public presentations across the United States on ROI, I also have encountered this same intense audience interest, and for good reasons. The U.S. economy roared ahead during 1997–98 at the fastest rate in about a decade. At the same time, news article after news article reported that many types of businesses across America were experiencing a rising shortage of skilled workers.

In view of low inflation, a plummeting unemployment rate, and Wall Street's frantic pace, the U.S. business community should be seeking to fill this shortage by expanding the learning organization and investing in human capital. The use of ROI measurements can help to determine which training and development programs work and which ones are a waste of time and money.

Skill Wars chronicles how this knowledge growth process is at work today within many, many U.S. organizations. But are they the rule or the exception? After many months of listening to managers, trainers, and consultants across the United States, it seems that too many businesses are only paying lip service to "the learning organization"; instead, they are often turning into "the anorexic organization."

During the past several years, I have interviewed a growing cadre of senior and middle managers who represent a wide range of U.S. businesses. They have seen training investment slashed or the entire training function outsourced to the cheapest possible providers. Also, in every geographic region of the United States, school-to-work initiatives have been very slow to start, in part because of the failure of business to sign on to this effort.

The continual rounds of mergers, restructuring, downsizing, and outsourcing has led to a rising tide of unemployed training professionals struggling to become consultants. High-quality talent, from recent executive vice presidents to top-notch graduate students, are now looking for employment. The temporary downturn in training across much of the nation has produced a buyer's market for this talent. The market will correct itself over time. However, unethical practices are increasingly exploiting the current labor market. Training executives have told me that a new management approach is to ask new training consultants to forego any fee, because the reference alone will be invaluable for their new consulting practice! Deflationary pressures also have caused consulting fees to plummet. For example, a large international manufacturer is now paying outside consultants only $250 per training day.

Because of these training practices, many knowledgeable training practitioners are leaving the field to seek employment elsewhere. Paradoxically, this is happening at the same time that U.S. business needs more experienced trainers to raise the "education bar" to help meet the skilled worker shortage.

The chairman of the board at Canon, Ryizaburo Kaku, spoke out about such practices in the *Harvard Business Review* (July/August 1997). He believes that some U.S. companies have taken the profit motive too far when they lay off workers to increase profits. "There is nothing wrong with the profit motive per se. . . . But making a profit is only the beginning of a company's obligations. As they mature, businesses need to understand that they play a role in a larger global context."

Kaku states that an important part of this context is developing people—training. "Management and labor start to see each other as vital to the company's success."

The pages of *Skill Wars* bear testimony that most companies believe in developing their own people for the long term. Today we know more ways to increase employee knowledge more rapidly than ever before. The diversity of America's response to doing business in the twenty-first century means there will remain organizations with short-sighted vision looking no further than the next quarterly dividend. By starving their investment in people, in the long term they increase their chances of appearing as a newspaper obituary. These businesses will always be left far behind by the agile entrepreneur who wants not just to survive but to thrive by sprinting ahead of the pack with new and better products and services and other innovations, not just cheaper mediocrity.

Much of life is illusion and desire. Americans need a new, fresh way of thinking about the workplace—a way of thinking not based on the illusion that maximizing short-term profit has no long-term consequences.

SECTION

Reports from the Firing Line: Improving Productivity and Performance

CHAPTER

5

Profit—Culture—Thinking:
An American Tale

*Your (U.S.) firms are built on the Taylor model, and even worse,
so are your heads. With your bosses doing the thinking while the
workers wield screwdrivers, you're convinced deep down that this
is the right way to run a business. For you the essence of management is getting the ideas out of the bosses and into the hands of
labor.*

*We (the Japanese) have gone beyond the Taylor model. We realize
that business has become so complex, the survival of firms so pre-
carious, and our environment increasingly competitive, and dangerous that firms' continued existence depends on their day-to-day
mobilzation of every ounce of intelligence.*

KANOSUKE MATSUSHITA,
FOUNDER OF MATSUSHITA
ELECTRIC INDUSTRIAL CORPORATION

What part of the above statement describes how your business is now
being managed? Some U.S. firms have broken out of the traditional
management box, but it has entailed a profound shift in business culture, in how to make a profit and how people think.

Rethinking an "American Icon"

What icon of American merchandising racked up 11 straight years of
losses, culminating with $2.98 billion of red ink in one year? Closed
more than 100 stores? Canceled its historic catalog?

You might think this depicts the plight of Montgomery Ward, the 125-year-old retail chain that filed for Chapter 11 bankruptcy in July, 1997. Or perhaps Woolworth, which closed all its stores after 117 years as part of the national fabric.

If so, you're wrong. This is a page from the recent history of Sears, Roebuck and Company, "the Big Store," which in 1997 reported their highest-ever quarterly earnings.

An important part of the Sears resurrection has been how this company transformed itself by moving organizational thinking away from a profit-first mentality to a focus on customer service. Sears has gradually changed employee thinking away from an old rigid military/industrial style to a new mindset based on meeting customer needs.

This new vision of "the softer side of Sears" required a profound culture change throughout the organization. For employees to learn to think innovatively, the change had to be driven down to the local store level. Here is the story of how "thinking for a living" became the essential element in the Sears transformation.

New Vision for 300,000

In 1992, Wal-Mart surpassed Sears as the nation's top retailer. Both the mall-based retail stores and the venerable Sears catalog had racked up 11 straight years of losses. Store outlets were generally run-down and sadly in need of renovation. Sears' "everyday low price" strategy had backfired. Customer-service ratings hovered around 58 percent compared to rival Wal-Mart's 78 percent.

That same year, the Sears board of directors named outsider Arthur Martinez as chief executive officer of the merchandise group. His job was to change Sears' organizational thinking. Through a series of management retreats and focus groups, top executives and managers started to dialogue about what it would take to get the company to world-class status. What Martinez learned was that unlike other organizations that had used reengineering, right-sizing, or other management reorganization strategies to "cut their way to greatness," a turnaround at Sears required a dynamic new vision of what the business was all about. This transformation needed to be based on fact, not just the "wisdom" of senior management or outside expert consultants.

Creating a new management paradigm was challenging enough. But an even greater problem would be changing the thinking of 300,000 employees on how to conduct day-to-day business all the way down to the sales floor. Unless they learned to "walk the talk" of the newly focused competitive Sears, any hopes at realizing a long-term success would remain only in the minds of upper management.

The Balanced Scorecard

To reach the new business objectives, Martinez introduced a powerful new assessment process, the balanced scorecard (BSC). It provided much of the content for one of the most massive employee-education programs undertaken by any business in the 1990s.

The BSC, developed by Robert S. Kaplan, a professor of accounting at Harvard, and David P. Norton, president of a consulting firm, was described in the January/February 1992 issue of the *Harvard Business Review*. It is a set of measures that can be used to help define an organization's business strategy. The BSC identifies critical success factors from four linked performance-model perspectives: customer, internal business process, learning and innovation, and financial.

For Sears, the BSC assessment process fell into three broad categories:

- Measuring customer service performance improvement
- Benchmarking competitors
- Building a new Sears culture paradigm through consensus-building activities (Box 5-1).

According to Rick Quinn, who was Sears' vice president for transformation and total performance indicators, the BSC assessment process helped the management team articulate three very powerful shared beliefs: *passion* for the customer, our *people* add value, *performance* leadership (the 3 Ps). These became the foundation for the 3 Ps Leadership Education Model—a new, ongoing education program that would reach each and every Sears employee (Figure 5-1).

Creating Front-Line Ownership

Sears' sales associates took ownership of the new 3Ps Leadership Education Model because they were treated like partners from the

---

SEARS ASSESSMENT TOOLS

Customer Service

- Customer-Service Teletests
- 60-Second Customer-Service Surveys
- Mystery Shoppers
- Daily Ready Meeting
- Observation
- 360-Degree Evaluation of Managers
- Customer-Service Surveys

Benchmarking the Competition

- Customer-Service Ratings
- Inventory Turnover
- Cost of Goods
- Profit Margin

Building a New Sears Paradigm

- Town Hall Meetings
- Learning Maps

Box 5-1 Sears Assessment Tools

beginning. A series of organization-wide town hall meetings were held for all employees as a kick-off program to gain their personal strategic commitment and belief. As a start to this process, the meetings were used to announce the elimination of 29,000 pages of prior procedures that historically had defined Sears' top-down military command-and-control business culture. Each town hall meeting focused on items that were actionable within the individual store and had impact on the customers. Associates were encouraged to become a member of a team to rewrite the rules and to help share in setting realistic goals that they could help reach in their local store.

To assure that this cultural revolution takes root and continues to grow at the grass-roots level, Sears provides customer service training to all their sales associates through a variety of learning venues:

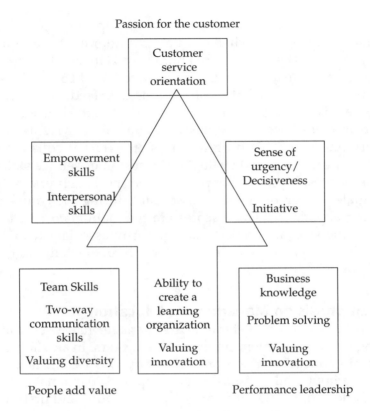

Figure 5-1 Leadership Skills Model

- An orientation program focusing on customer service and other retail issues

- Pure Selling Environment (PSE), an additional customer service training program

- Ready Meetings or Training in a Box, just-in-time training meant to cover important departmental issues and other training topics

- Sears Extension Institute, home-study courses on such topics as business math, business writing, and computer skills

How does Sears measure the success of these training programs? With the Sears Training and Tracking System (STTS). The automated dial-in 800 phone number is used to test all employees after they have completed any course, whether in a classroom or through a home-study program. The system's 800 number ensures that all employees company-wide are tested on the same material. STTS provides access to online data analysis that features immediate feedback on results to the trainee. This offers positive reinforcement to the learner.

Sears also employs another learning evaluation system—the Sears Mystery Shopper. This program uses an external consultant who shops at a Sears store and evaluates the customer-service skills of the sales associates. Mystery shoppers use the specific criteria of the 3 Ps to evaluate and grade the sales associates during the course of each shopping experience. These scores are then tabulated and feedback given to the sales associates' manager. Any associate who scores a perfect 100 percent score from a mystery-shopper evaluation receives a $100 bonus.

New Emphasis on Management Education

Prior to 1993, not one veteran Sears manager had been through a training and development program in five years. In an effort to foster leadership education, the Sears University was established. A "university without walls," it has enrolled up to 8,000 managers in more than 400 developmental programs. Upper, middle, and first-line managers participate in leadership, management-concepts, and customer-service education programs.

Approximately 200 new sales-management trainees are recruited from colleges each year to participate in one of the Sears Management Development Centers located in Chicago, Pittsburgh, Orlando, Washington, D.C., Dallas, Los Angeles, and Seattle. The scope of this 9- to 14-month education period includes developing interpersonal skills, product knowledge, the understanding of sales reports, personal motivation, and initiative. Trainees also work in all areas of the Sears store, with the emphasis being on learning superior customer-service skills.[1]

Revival or Revolution?

Montgomery Ward, Woolworth, and Sears all became victims of the retailing niche marketplace of the 1990s. A revived Sears has survived and flourished because the company reinvented itself by encouraging employees throughout the organization to rethink how Sears does business.

Gaining market share in modern retail marketing via distinctive products or service technology has become very difficult to accomplish. The only added value that management can leverage is in the people who can learn how to provide distinctive service. The sales staff must learn, and constantly be reinforced, on how to think creatively regarding the products they sell and the wants and needs of the customer. Management must provide employees with constant positive motivation and support throughout this thinking and doing process.

No business measurement system is worth a damn unless it constantly activates throughout the organization a meaningful learning–discovery process that challenges the status quo. The future of Sears, and for that matter most of American business, rests on how well we can teach people to work and perform in concert, to think creatively, and to invent new, ingenious ways to satisfy the customer.

"Our failure to develop our human resources not only harms individuals, it holds back the nation as a whole. America must have world-class education and training programs if we are to compete successfully in the twenty-first century," says Paul Allaire, chairman and CEO of Xerox Corporation and chairman of the Council on Competitiveness. "Competitiveness depends on lifelong learning."

At Ford, Breaking Habits is Job #1

Changing an ingrained management style isn't easy. In 1981 W. Edwards Deming was invited to help Ford begin a fundamental transformation process. He immediately took aim at the corporate mindset. Deming criticized those who blamed the company's problems on its workers. "The workers are handicapped by the system and the system belongs to management."

He told supervisors to stop screaming, "Do it and shut up!" and instead talk to people as if they were human beings. Ford needed to coach a new kind of manager who would listen to workers, understand their problems, and enlist their ideas to boost quality and productivity.

It took years of training courses at Ford to confront echelons of managers with their self-defeating attitudes. Ford taught them to rethink their management culture by breaking down old barriers and successfully trying out a new philosophy of teamwork and trust on the production floor. The company also invested billions in new worker-skills programs that continue to this day to raise the educational abilities of the average Ford worker.[2]

In the early 1980s General Motors faced the same problems as Ford. GM pursued an ambitious automation program. Ten years and $80 billion later, it had failed (see Figure 5-2). What GM eventually learned was it was not robots, but its own workforce that was its biggest and most valuable asset. It became apparent that the way workers were trained, managed and motivated, not high technology alone, was the real key to competitive car-making. As at Ford, "learning to learn" has become a major long-term investment in employee education at every level inside GM.

Motorola's Surprise

A new American technological standard is Motorola's ability to rapidly adapt to the changing conditions in the world economy. How do they do it? Considering the invention of the transistor in 1948, Motorola's Robert Galvin explains, "We didn't know that was coming in 1947. The laser is a surprise. The computer is a surprise. In 1940, I didn't know that there would be a computer. . . . Now those things are historical facts. They are events that took place, and they can be aggregated under the rubric of a surprise. . . . Historically, most institutions do not adapt to the next surprises. That's a lesson about human beings. . . . We did adapt. I think there's something special about that. I think that we had an orientation to 'renewal,' and every time something new happens, why can't we do it? It's a 'why not' versus 'why would anybody do that' or 'we're so satisfied'."[3]

To meet that next "surprise," Robert Galvin became a leading zealot for training at Motorola. When division managers complain that they can't afford either the cost of training or the employee-productivity loss during training, Galvin reminded them that, in reality, training costs them less than nothing. For example, "It just passes the common sense test that if you teach people how to engage in a statistical quality control analysis, and they're on a problem-solving team, and it costs maybe fifty to a hundred dollars to put them through that course, within three months they will have probably caused a ten- or twenty thousand-dollar savings as a results of their

NOT BY ROBOTS ALONE
Assembly plant characteristics*

	Japanese in Japan	Japanese in America	Americans in America	European Producers
Productivity (hours per vehicle)	16.8	21.2	25.1	36.2
Assembly defects per 100 vehicles	60	65	82	97
Repair area (% of assembly space)	4.1	4.9	12.9	14.4
Stocks (days) (for eight sample parts)	0.2	1.6	2.9	2.0
Workforce in a team (%)	69.3	71.3	17.3	0.6
Number of job classifications	12	9	67	15
Training of new workers (hours)	380	370	46	173
Abenteeism (%)	5.0	4.8	11.7	12.1
Automation (% of process automated)				
Welding	86.2	85.0	76.2	76.6
Painting	54.6	40.7	33.6	38.2
Assembly	1.7	1.1	1.2	3.1

*Average for plants in each region, 1989.

Source: Adapted from M.I.T.; J.D. Power and Associates

Figure 5-2 Not by Robots Alone: Assembly Plant Characteristics

better thinking process. . . . In general, we believe the ratio of the gain we get from training versus cost is about thirty to one.[4]

At Motorola fostering the growth of individual intelligence is viewed as enhancing its most precious economic resource. Four

percent of payroll is invested in training. This means that every employee participates in 40 hours of classroom learning each year, a figure the company hopes to quadruple to one month of training within
five years. Perhaps this might someday become a world standard?
The reason: "If knowledge is becoming antiquated at a faster rate, we
have no choice but to spend on education. How can that not be a competitive weapon?" says Gary Tooker, Motorola's CEO.[5]

Here Today—Gone Tomorrow?

In the 1980s and 1990s Sears, Ford/GM, and Motorola joined the
growing ranks of many companies that embraced the concepts of
workplace learning. However, American business is now experiencing a significant crisis of confidence in the so-called "learning organization." Perhaps this was bound to happen as a reaction to the
training industry's self-congratulatory proclamation that the 1990s
would begin an era of lifelong universal workforce education. Many
of us have been left behind at the boarding gate. What we thought
were first-class tickets on a nonstop flight turned out to be only
standby seats in the back of an overbooked plane.

Some might protest, "What crisis?" *Training* magazine's "1997 Industry Report" estimated that a 5 percent increase raised overall
training expenditures to $58.6 billion in organizations of 100 or more
employees. Yet, as the American Society for Training and Development (ASTD) recently noted, training expenditures for the past
decade have not kept pace with the rapidly rising number of Americans now working. In other words, more employees are actually receiving less and less training. This same survey also showed the
continued balkanization of training. Professionals, managers, and
salespeople gobbled up over 60 percent of the training pie. This
leaves the majority with slim pickings.

Finally, many organizations see investment confined solely to training technology (i.e., satellite distance-learning systems, computer-
based training (CBT), etc.) as investment in people development. Too
many of these training technology solutions feature cutbacks on
training staff or anyone else who might facilitate individual learning
in groups. Also, more businesses see personal learning as something
done on personal time through the Internet or some other learning
system delivered by a personal computer. This may work for some

learning applications, but it eliminates the vital social-group learning aspect essential for most training to stick. Overall, these trends hardly offer the picture of a thriving learning organization.

"Increasing shareholder equity" is the banner management employs when making cuts to "the soft side of the business," meaning any areas viewed as extraneous to profit-making operations. If you can't see it, touch it, or measure its profit potential, you should cut it, outsource it, or forget it. With each passing year in many organizations, more training and education programs seem to be meeting this description. However, the new management drive for maximum short-term profit has gone a step further.

In *Dangerous Company* (Time-Warner, 1997), James O'Shea and Charles Madigan spotlight the methods and practices of major management consulting firms. In their book and also in interviews with this author, they provide an archetype of the corporate productivity programs offered by these firms. Hordes of newly minted MBAs descend on a company and produce mountains of data. Charts, graphs, and statistics are then marshalled to convince senior executives that the road to corporate prosperity can be reduced to the following equation: Reengineer management systems + Employ information technology (IT) = Productivity improvement. The management consultants argue that there is no need to worry about the people inside a business. People usually are irrelevant to the productivity management process and can be largely ignored or dispensed with altogether, because technology alone will produce abundant innovations. Save for executive development, technical training, and an overreliance on the latest "gee-whiz" high-tech training tools, people development programs remain outside the box.

Dangerous Company gives case study after case study in which this productivity solution fell flat. Instead of profit improvement, productivity declined. This book tells a story that senior management is just beginning reluctantly to grasp: developing human capital—better-educated, motivated people—through performance improvement is as much of a key component in business prosperity as implementing the latest technologies or management systems (Figure 5-3).

This situation was brought home to me as a keynote speaker at a Softbank Technology Performance Conference in Nashville. Here was a "techie" audience looking to me for solutions because of the inability of more and more of the workforce to use the latest business

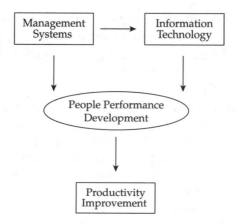

Figure 5-3 Productivity Management Process™

software. An example of this breakdown in the fundamental management process occurred when Westinghouse Electric executives made the commitment to purchase the installation of the R/3 operations network from the German software giant SAP. At the beginning of this process in 1994, the projected total costs were $65 million. But parts of the organization resisted change, the project slowed to a crawl, and costs soared with some Westinghouse divisions not installing many SAP modules. People performance development was not a management goal. "Implementing this type of software is not a technology exercise, it's an organizational revolution," says Harvard professor Michael Hammer.

Managing this process requires a new balanced approach. Above are the key elements of the Productivity Management Process that can be used to transform your organization.

The Human Capital Scoreboard

The knowledge company is what everyone wants to be. The problem is there's no established road map showing you how to get there until now. We've drawn the map. It is called the Human Capital Scoreboard™. Investing in human capital means all organizations must learn how to manage, measure, and balance the 3Ps: Productivity—Performance—Profit (Figure 5-4).

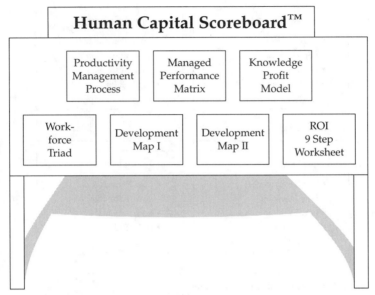

Figure 5-4 Human Capital Scoreboard™

As a first step, we need to analyze how the realignment of management systems and IT with people performance development can maximize productivity improvement. People need to learn how to better apply technology and how to better manage the results. Skeptics will point out that the workplace is already littered with failed quality, team, and leadership training that often produced only marginal operating improvements. To help avoid these mistakes, what business requires is a measurement system that benchmarks the organization's current and future human capital requirements—in other words, what brain power needs to be revved up.

Managed Performance Matrix

Who are the top performers in your business? What are their personal characteristics? The Managed Performance Matrix™ begins to benchmark, by quadrants, an organization's current human capital capabilities (Figure 5-5). By plotting the current position of their business on this matrix and comparing the results to those for their chief competitors, managers can more easily make decisions regarding how to invest

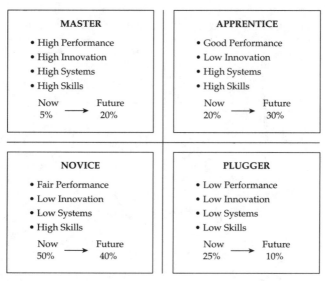

Figure 5-5 Managed Performance Matrix

in their human capital. The four performance profile quadrants are Master, Apprentice, Novice, and Plugger. The job description for a Master Knowledge Worker includes the following:

High Performance

- Meets or exceeds personal work goals and objectives, while leading others to high personal work standards
- Is not afraid to learn something new and try it out

High Innovator

- Good at solving problems, prioritizing solutions, and abstract reasoning/combinational logic; generates new ideas for services or product and getting the job done right

High Systems

- Understands how to motivate, coach, and lead people
- Understands the uses and integration of information and other appropriate technologies

High Skills

- Communication skills; oral, written and text comprehension exceed the 13th grade level

- Mathematical skills; computation and conceptual application exceed 13th grade level

The matrix gives organizations a tool that any manager can understand and use. It will help a business benchmark its human capital against the best and help predict a company's profitability five years out. How? By shifting the management focus from short-term, short-lived behavior training to the improvement over time of thinking skills that are the core requirement to increase employee productivity.

The Managed Performance Matrix builds an information bank on your human capital that can be used in preparing a reliable business plan and business strategy. Current estimates are that most businesses now have small numbers of Masters (5 percent) and far larger numbers of low-performing Pluggers (25 percent). To use this matrix successfully, a business will measure all people on four core competency areas: performance, innovation, systems, and skills.

For example, over a period of six months we assisted a Midwest light-industrial manufacturer with 500-plus employees in completing a workforce productivity audit. From the company president and professionals to the most recent hire, all managers' and hourly workers' four core competency areas were assessed. Test data were kept confidential, with individuals given coaching sessions to determine personal productivity goals. By using this data in the aggregate, management could benchmark against their leading-edge competitors. They then set targets on how high to raise the organization's productivity development bar to achieve individual employee performance goals and fulfill their business plan over the next five years. Individual employees were motivated by receiving coaching that showed them how they fit into the organization's strategy and how they could go about improving their core competencies.

In general only about 25 percent of all American adults in the workplace qualify for the Master and Apprentice quadrants of the matrix. (This is based on the results of the first national literacy audit done by the U.S. Department of Education in the early 1990s.) Most businesses will need to raise these numbers to about 50 percent of their workforce over the next decade. Why? Because technology and reengineered participatory management methods demand higher levels of performance, innovation, systems, and skills as described in our job description of a Master Knowledge Worker. To manage this performance matrix, your task will be to determine how many people need to drive their personal development profile from one quadrant to another—Plugger, to Novice, to Apprentice, to Master—thereby helping to meet targeted organizational productivity goals. This sounds fine in the abstract, but a business still needs a road map to begin this productivity journey.

On the Road to Human Capital Development

How can you draw a map of the lifetime learning needs for your employees? The Human Capital Development Map I (Figure 5-6) gives

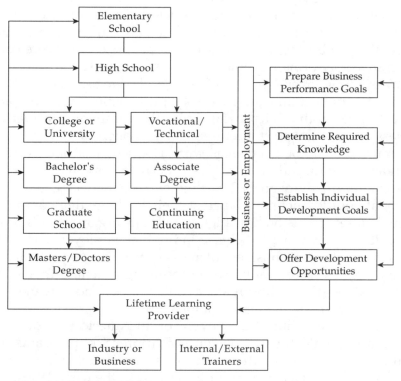

Figure 5-6 Human Capital Development Map I: Lifetime Learning Alternatives

an accurate picture of how this process can work for any business. It shows how components of lifetime learning are based on both school/business experiences that work in tandem. Business performance goals and people development goals are changing so rapidly that only by balancing these internal/external learning opportunities will people succeed in constantly updating the personal knowledge required to meet changing job requirements over their lifetime. How this map operates will vary by the community(ies) in which you have business operations. How well do you utilize and support these local education resources? Also, how well does your business culture support the concept of lifelong learning?

For the individual business, the Human Capital Development Map II (Figure 5-7) offers a specific method of assessing how well personal employee development is aligned with business objectives. Using this model, your organization can map the Managed Performance Matrix Applications/Benefits to the value they deliver to your business. The usefulness of this map is not only that it identifies the benefit in the form of a business objective; it also pinpoints the specific development application(s) needed to achieve the desired business objectives. Each division of an organization can use this Human Capital Development Map as a method to relate different business plans/strategies to the specific applications and benefits required of its training programs.

Knowledge Profit Model

Without support from the top, this people-performance-development process will slow to a crawl. Senior management needs policy, practice, and profit standards that will drive people through the quadrants of the Managed Performance Matrix. The Knowledge Profit Model™ (Figure 5-8) offers a useful management tool: Policy—a Workforce Education Triad™ of Skills, Training, and Education; Practice—a community of learning from many sources; and Profit—the measurement of business results by using a credible Human Capital Return-on-Investment Worksheet™.

Policy: Workforce Education Triad

Any person who needs skills, training, and/or education to help achieve the business plan will receive the requisite Workforce Educa-

Applications/Benefits

Business Objectives/Outcomes

	Performance Objectives	New Learning	Problems	Reasons Abstractly	Generates New Services and Product Ideas	Does Job Right 1st Time	Motivates Coaches Leads	Uses IT and other Technologies	Communication Skills 13th Grade
	Exceeds	Embraces	Solves						
Strengthen Customer Relationships									
Differentiate or Create New Products or Services									
Enhance Supplier Relationships									
Improve Cost Position									

Figure 5-7 Human Capital Development Map II: Applications/Benefits

112

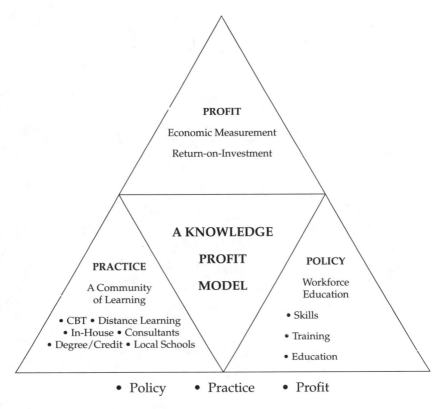

Figure 5-8 Twenty-First-Century Knowledge Profit Model

tion component(s) (Figure 5-9). Technology and globalization ensure that employees will need ever-higher skill levels that increase their overall personal comprehension and application abilities. Writing, math, reading, foreign languages, and English as a second language are important examples of what these skills can encompass.

An additional requisite component—training—underpins the newly flattened organization of the high-performance workplace. How can an employee be part of a participatory team environment without basic supervisory and management training? How can teams propose solutions to operational problems unless they understand how the entire business functions and makes a profit (service and production training)?

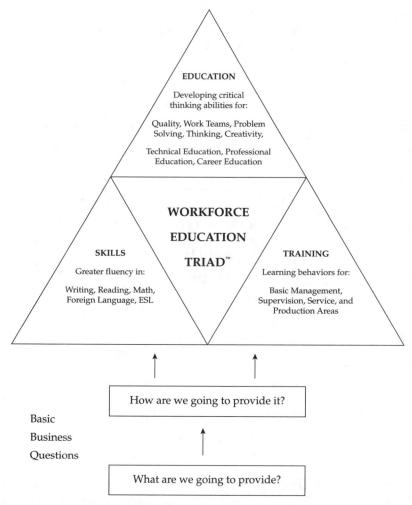

Figure 5-9 Workforce Education Triad™

Education is the third component of the Triad. It addresses knowledge related to business reengineering and deploying information technology. It includes background knowledge for problem solving and innovation, advanced technical/executive education, and career/school-to-work to prepare the next generation of workers.

The reasons for the Workforce Education Triad as a policy solution was best summed up at an Executive Council Meeting of the American

Management Association (AMA): "When the workers get the picture, they are better prepared to solve the problem. And without teaching them the fundamentals of business management and decision making, don't expect them to understand what you're doing." (*Management Review*, Autumn 1993)

Practice: A Community of Learning

No one single performance–development system will provide all elements of the learning needed to attain the business plan. Only each individual employee's careful selection of options from a community of available learning practices will maximize employee performance. These include (but are not limited to) computer-based training; distance learning; simulation-based multimedia; in-house classroom and small group individualized instruction; the use of outside professional consultants; external seminars; and credit/noncredit programs through local educational institutions. In most applications a combination of several practices will produce the maximum return for any performance development program.

Profit: Economic Measurement

The determining factor that will drive practice and policy is their accurate economic measurement. In Chapter 4 we discussed the nine-step Human Capital Return-on-Investment (ROI) Worksheet developed by an interdisciplinary business team that can help any organization more accurately calculate the ROI of specific employee–development–program alternatives. The Human Capital ROI Worksheet uses features found in a common business computer spreadsheet to help "run the numbers" to select from potential employee-performance-development-program alternatives.

"Doing" versus "Thinking"

Joseph Boyett and Henry Conn estimated in *Workplace 2000* that 80 percent of all workplace training done in the name of performance improvement is never used back on the job.[6] By any performance matrix, this seems like a lousy way for American business to annually invest $56 billion (American Society for Training and Development estimate, 1997).

The trouble stems from the many professional management fads, such as "action learning" or "accelerated learning," that promise to give people the ability to use "sound reasoning" to bring forth a gusher of brainwaves, but instead only deliver a behavior "how-to" shopping list of skills. This may work for the "doing" part of a manager's job: hard data, numbers, the right "words." But it falls far sort of the "thinking" manager embodied in personal hunches, ideas, and other so-called executive "wisdom."

Team building, interpersonal communication, and leadership development programs—the building blocks needed in this high-performance workplace—often fail to give people the critical competencies to apply these skills in the right combination and at the right time to meet performance expectations. More information alone seldom produces these greater insights—only greater confusion.

The failure of most information-age training is that it seems to place no value on learning these critical competencies that mentally process all this data and give it personal meaning. Can we match the rate of workers' increase in information—how "to do"—by also increasing their rate of acquiring critical competencies—how "to think"?

Building business leadership—the ability to use "sound wisdom"—often is seen as the exact opposite of "creativity." Most managers view creative types as mavericks. James Krohe, Jr., of the Conference Board thinks that many firms manage creativity as sanitariums used to manage lepers—you set them apart on their own, isolated from the healthy. Many managers disdain having "creatives" on the premises at all, let alone offering training that improves the thinking skills that are at the core of the creative process.

Yet many of these same managers have embraced the competitive concepts of the high-performance workplace, the continuous improvement process, and empowered work teams. Any comparison of quality gurus, Crosby, Deming, and Juran training systems finds a common call for people to master a range of complex thinking tasks that are integrated into their daily work activities. This requires that everybody make decisions, analyze systems, investigate, use combinational logic to invent new processes, classify, compare, and generally manipulate information in an insightful way—in other words, be creative on-the-job.

On the factory floor itself everyone is increasingly expected to be innovative and alert. Gone are the days of Frederick W. Taylor's decree:

"You are not supposed to think. There are other people paid for thinking around here." Today almost everyone gets paid for thinking.[7]

Even if this is beginning to sound like some of your organization's people development goals, the big question remains: how do you do it?

Rote Learning Is for Dogs

How we learn is still a matter of great debate. But over the past 20 years great strides have been made in successful business learning applications for performance development. At the forefront of this debate are two different approaches:

- Training rote behavior—"to do."

- Learning—"to think."

Good old Dr. Pavlov proved you could control a response to a situation by repeatedly reinforcing specific behavior to get more of it, or by punishing the wrong behavior to get less of it. Pavlov observed that showing food to a dog elicited salivation. Pavlov attempted to train the animal to salivate by ringing a bell before feeding the dog. With repeated training, the animal gradually responded by salivating when the bell rang even if he did not feed the dog. Pavlov believed that you could condition people in the same way by controlling specific environmental stimuli.

The U.S. Army conditions its recruits during basic training. The final objective is for the soldiers to learn a behavior checklist that reduces battlefield casulties. One key lesson is to always crawl close to the ground to offer the smallest battlefield target. This response is driven home in a field exercise during which live ammunition is whizzing overhead. The exercise is meant to condition the soldiers to always use crawling tactics in the presence of the enemy, whether or not they are under fire.

In the 1950s B.F. Skinner further advanced conditioning people's behavior by arranging environmental factors to bring behavior under specific stimulus control. For example, in some sales development programs, trainees consistently are videotaped in role-playing exercises until they can repeat specific selling steps. The idea is that the videotaping will keep reinforcing the desired behavior until they are able to automatically repeat the training program's "12 steps for consulting selling," the "8 steps for real-estate closing," etc., without having to "think about it." The problem is that the effects of this behavior checklist training often disappear soon after the videotape reinforcement is ended. Salespeople will revert to their old selling styles, having adopted few changes from the training program because it did not change the way they think about selling—only their short-term performance on videotape.

In contrast, a more "critical competencies" approach can help you deliver what managers want most—problem solvers and innovative thinkers who can apply what they have learned back on the job in new ways. This thinking approach to performance development stresses how we gain knowledge; organize it to make sense; process information, personal interpretations, and beliefs; and retrieve all this from our memory. We believe that employees are better able to process new information when it is made more meaningful to them and connects new ideas to their current knowledge of ways of doing business.

How does this happen? The latest research from the University of Chicago (1998), reported in the *Journal of Comparative Neurology*, confirms that various parts of the brain are physically "wired" at different times by the learning of different skills. This wiring of the brain creates a synapse as an electrical connection between two brain cells. Synapses are like telephone lines that allow the brain to communicate. Throughout childhood, adolescence, and adulthood, the brain constructs new synapses in response to learning.

"If a kid lacks advantages early on, does that mean he's doomed for the rest of his life? No. The new findings tell us that we shouldn't give up on people who haven't had all the right advantages," says Bruce McEwen, a Rockefeller University neuroscientist.

The good news for business is that the more complex "executive" functions such as reasoning, motivation, and judgment, the essential skills for success in a high-performance work environment, appear to develop gradually well into adulthood. These critical competency skills may take longer to acquire, but they are greatly influenced by environmental inputs such as education and training. So the bottom line is, we actually have a pretty good chance to develop an employee's thinking skills if we use the correct training procedures. As more informational connections are created, an adult's brain has a richer storehouse of knowledge to use.[8]

Two prominent business trends in the high-performance workplace—total quality management (TQM) and teams—emphasize a long-term, ongoing analysis of individual and organizational learning needs. This requires not behavioral training but rather training for the thinking that involves a gradual expansion of complex information over time. That is why the context for performance development has shifted to so-called lifelong learning. In sharp contrast is "managing behavior," which had its place in the assembly-line/mass-production industrial model that dominated twentieth-century American business culture, and its view that training was a one-time "event" of short duration.

The important management message: All training is not the same. Some training can permanently increase inner thinking abilities, rather than just rearranging surface performance behaviors.

Discovery Learning—Cook County Style

So how do you teach people to "think more clearly" and remember more? We now know how to present new information, as well as teach people ways to connect it to their existing knowledge.

Remembering new names at a business meeting is difficult for most people. An imagery memory exercise helps relate a new name to some other familiar idea, for later recall. A good example, is a personal story about the legendary Mayor Richard J. Daley of Chicago (1956–1978), related by a manager to this author.

In 1948, while serving as an election judge, she first met Daley, who was then Cook County Clerk. She complained to him when he visited her polling place that suburban election judges were compensated at a lower daily rate than City of Chicago election personnel. Daley noted her complaint and said he would look into the matter.

Fast-forward 20 years—it is now 1968. This same election judge was attending a political dinner with more than 1,000 other people in the Grand Ballroom of the Conrad Hilton Hotel. At the end of the dinner, the now-famous Mayor Daley worked the crowd, shaking hands as he walked toward the exit. As Daley approached the election judge, he recognized her and said, "Suburban election judge, you wanted more pay. You got it. Right?" She was struck speechless at Daley's amazing memory. One attribute of Mayor Daley's so-called political genius was his stunning, inexhaustible ability to recall a person by relating their individual needs to a face or a name. Certainly this amazing personal recall ability contributed to Daley's legendary success as a political leader.

Building the "Computer of the Mind"

Other thinking techniques can be used that help people discover how to recall memories or ideas and then relate them to new information as it is presented. This can be done through the use of thought-provoking, real-world problems; case studies; or action planning.

A concrete way to visualize this process of learning is comparing it to building the "computer of the mind." Knowledge is the content stored in this "computer." Like a computer's hard drive, memory is the "storehouse" where new and old knowledge is divided into different rooms (Figure 5-10). The "input" of new information first makes contact with the short-term memory. The adult draws on specific prior knowledge from the long-term memory selected by what personal meaning or perception is given to the new information. The working memory then combines all this when it interprets the new information to solve a problem. The "output" step is then performed.

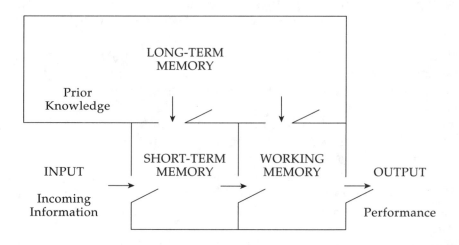

Figure 5-10 Memory as the "Storehouse of the Mind"

To make this computer work optimally, we have found how thinking skills can be trained for almost any work-related function. For example, adults learn team skills better if the skills' elements are introduced gradually, if they are taught through realistic role-play exercises that are self-critiqued, and if they are then practiced repeatedly back on the job. Spacing out these team-training exercises over time has been repeatedly proven to offer greater job productivity increases because they cause permanent improvements in employee thinking skills. This process is in sharp contrast to compacting team training to days or weeks, which usually produces only short-term behavior changes that will quickly fade and are often forgotten.

This long-term thinking skills training approach works better because it isolates the sequence of steps an employee must take while solving a work problem. It gives time for the adult's short-term, long-term, and working memory to absorb the new information and begin to use it generally across many new or old job tasks. It increases productivity.

This was the lesson that Mark Schmink learned in 1995 as manager of Dana's Stockton, California, plant. They make truck chassis for a single customer: Toyota Motor Corp. To win this business, Dana promised a 2 percent price cut over two years. In order to achieve this, Schmink created a "culture of inventiveness," with no change too small. He started by having everyone learn every job in the plant, so that each employee understood the big picture. And he insisted that no one receive a permanent assignment, thus not allowing a personal job bias to inhibit a steady supply of fresh perspectives.

To help encourage a culture of change and human creativity, Schmink opened a plant library and added tuition reimbursement for production workers. This signaled that mental work is as valuable as manual work—you go to school, and I'll pay for it!

Worker teams began questioning every routine of the plant, right down to the sequencing of individual welds. Schmink demanded that every worker suggest two ideas in writing each month. An amazing 81 percent offered enough productivity improvements to implement. Even those ideas that didn't work out offered the opportunity to learn from failure as part of what some experts called "incidental learning." Adult learners are interested in real-world applications and are capable of self-criticism. They learn from their mistakes.

Matt Johnson, a maintenance apprentice, came up with 180 ideas in a year, thanks partly to his having worked so many different jobs. "After moving all over I could see problems up and down the line," Johnson says.

Because the creativity process was continually encouraged, ideas begat ideas. Even the product design was open to criticism, and workers suggested changes. Continuous feedback was provided people by displaying minute-to-minute productivity numbers on electronic signs that looked like sports scoreboards.

Schmink celebrated the conquest of every goal with a motivational event: a family barbecue, a rib-eye lunch, free sodas for a day. He did everything to sustain the thinking skills of his workforce and show them that even small improvements were important.[9]

Critical competencies training develops the individual employee's memory. Training for these skills can be done within the boundaries of any specialized work area. Team skills for a cellular phone manufacturer, bank, hospital, or insurance business mean enhancing employee thinking skills by using the specific content and procedural skills that apply to each specific work environment. Significant performance improvement only happens when something is understood because it has been meaningfully rooted into the employee's existing knowledge. We believe that people must be actively involved in the training task in order to successfully learn and remember new information back on-the-job.

U.S. Gypsum used such mind-activating activities for sales training. This training was totally driven by the employee and featured a balance of coaching one-on-one, audio, video, self-study, and classroom training. A self-development guide was given to each sales representative at the beginning of his or her job (Figure 5-11). Each employee then initiated individual training activities to develop the skills required in a fully skilled sales rep. Employees used the guide and were responsible for scheduling their own training, following an outline for each training area, including meeting with the sales manager, writing reports, and attending a training class. As the sales reps completed these activities, they recorded each training component (Figure 5-12). This critical competencies approach has the following objectives: making the sales reps accountable for their time, promoting independent thinking, building self-discipline, and making good decisions.

**Sales Training Program
Independent Episodic Learning I
Self-Development Guide**

A. YOUR CORPORATE RESPONSIBILITIES	*B. YOUR TERRITORY AND ACCOUNT MANAGEMENT RESPONSIBILITIES*
1. Know Your Position Responsibilities	1. Cover Your Territory
2. Know Your Benefits	2. Know Your Competition
3. Know Your Company	3. Work with Trade Factors
4. Work with Key Company People and Departments	4. Work with Local Regulatory and Code Bodies
5. Know Plant Facilities	5. Lead and/or Cooperate in Team-Selling
6. Work with Your Manager	6. Participate in Special Marketing Efforts
7. Maintain Records and Files, and Submit Reports	7. Identify Large Jobs
8. Maintain Corporate Assets	8. Know, Sell, and Service Your Assigned Accounts
9. Control Your Budget	9. Identify, Approach, and Qualify Prospective Accounts
10. Represent the Company to Trade Factors, Business Groups, and the General Public	10. Plan and Initiate Account Calls
11. Inform and Advise Management	11. Determine and Meet Account Needs
12. Handle Special Assignments	12. Handle Pricing and Price Adjustments
13. Know the Legal Aspects of Your Position	13. Handle Objections and Concerns
	14. Ask for Orders and Close Sales
	15. Follow Through on Sales
	16. Handle Complaints
	17. Expedite Credit, Collections, and Claims

(continues)

Figure 5-11 Sales Training Program

These are the skills any company needs to have developed for a highly efficient sales force. This approach includes training critical competencies, important thinking skills, and/or data-driven skills for behavior management. By making learning independent and

C. YOUR PRODUCT KNOWLEDGE RESPONSIBILITIES

1. Know Sufficient General Concepts to Deal Efficiently with Other Professionals
   a. Blueprint Reading
   b. Physics of Construction
   c. Chemistry of Gypsum Products
   d. Construction Process (Building Stages)
   e. Building Codes and Code Bodies
   f. Fire Safety
   g. Sound Control
   h. Use of Literature

2. Know Features, Applications, and Benefits of Each Product Line and System You Sell
   a. Board Products
   b. Joint Treatment/Textures
   c. Construction Steel
   d. Plaster
   e. Systems

3. Become Familiar with Other U.S.G. Products

D. YOUR SELF-MANAGEMENT RESPONSIBILITIES

1. Know, Control, and Motivate Yourself
2. Plan and Schedule Your Activities
3. Talk and Listen Effectively
4. Communicate Interpersonally
5. Read Quickly and Accurately
6. Write Letters, Memos, and Reports
7. Gather and Organize Information
8. Identify and Solve Problems and Make Decisions
9. Develop and Make Persuasive Presentations
10. Conduct and Participate in Meetings
11. Establish and Maintain Productive Interpersonal Relationships.
12. Practice Safety in Driving, Visiting Construction Sites
13. Project a Professional Image
14. Negotiate Agreements, Resolve Conflicts
15. Keep Current with Industry, Company and Professional Selling Developments

Figure 5-11 (Continued)

episodic over a period of time, this training enabled the sales force to learn and retain more information, skills, and useful self-knowledge.

Your organization can learn much more about how to design and build management critical competencies through performance

Independent Episodic Learning II:
Training Progress Record
Sales Training Program

Sales Representative _____

Territory Number _____ Start Date _____

Position Responsibility Quarter 1		*Delivery System*	*Date Completed*	
			Target	*Actual*
A-1	Know Your Position Responsibilities	SDG		
A-2	Know Your Benefits	SDG		
A-3	Know Your Company	SDG		
A-4	Work with Key Company People and Departments	SDG		
A-5	Know Plant Facilities	SDG		
A-6	Work with Your Manager	SDG		
A-7	Maintain Records and Files, and Submit Reports	SDG		
A-8	Maintain Corporate Assets	SDG		
A-9	Control Your Budget	SDG		
A-11	Inform and Advise Management	SDG		
A-13	Know the Legal Aspects of Your Position	SDG		
C-1c	Products and Processes	SDG/LC		
C-2a	Gypsum Board Products	SDG/LC		
C-2b	Joint Treatment, Textures	SDG/LC		
C-2d	Plaster	SDG/LC		
C-2e	Acoustical Ceiling	SDG/LC		

NOTE: Quarter 1 Learning Center courses are contained in the product training binders

SDG = **Self-Development Guide**
LC = **Learning Center Courses**
DC = **Seminar: Division Conference**
CC = **Seminar: Corporate Conference**

Figure 5-12 Independent Episodic Learning II

improvement programs by consulting *FutureWork, The Revolution Re-shaping American Business* (1994) and *Enhancing Learning in Training and Adult Education* (1998), both co-authored by this writer.[10]

Increasing employee communication, problem-solving and analytical abilities will improve performance and productivity. However, executives also are increasingly faced with the sobering reality that the high-performance workplace requires the overall education bar to be raised far higher than the available number of "master" workers within most organizations. In the next chapter we will review how U.S. business is waging a war on manager and worker skill deficits as an essential part of a new strategic performance paradigm.

6

The Skill Wars

It's really pretty simple here. You just look at the paperwork, load the machine, and make sure your set-up is right. Then run it.

1970s MACHINE OPERATOR

Basically, the work here is the same as always. But it's changed too. There's a lot of paperwork now and participation. They will listen now and you can have ideas. Instead of being told they're dumb they say, "Let's try it." It's like "put up or shut up." Now you're expected to participate so you can see your ideas make a difference.

1990s OFFICE WORKER

The Quality Journey—What Does It Mean?

Calhoun Wire and Cable, an operating division of Techno Industries, is a corporation that develops new technologies from R&D, then invents new products addressing customer needs. The corporation holds more than 600 U.S. patents for tens of thousands of products. It employs about 10,000 people.[1]

Calhoun Wire and Cable emphasizes the production of high-quality wire and cable products that meet many exacting specifications for the information-technology industry. During a typical year the production floor manufactures more than 5,000 products, with specifications for thousands more available to customers. The operators on the production floor are classified in one of four levels, depending on machine experience and competence.

Over a five-year project Calhoun reengineered its organization in response to increased competition in the specialized wire and cable market. As part of the program it participated in the "Educational Requirements for New Technology and Work Organization Project" conducted by Stanford University. The researchers tried to determine what "new skills workers need for a high-performance workplace to succeed in the global skills wars."

Profile: Skilled Workers

Marta, a senior Calhoun machine operator, is a good example of how these new skills are meant to be used on-the-job. As she begins a new order, Marta holds up a transparent plastic envelope containing cable documents: a material list, production order, packing information form, material issue forms, and various printed labels. Marta will also complete several blank forms while she processes the order: the packing cost center report, wire spooling length distribution sheet, and packing quality checklist, as well as other paperwork.

Marta, like every other operator, has developed her own order completion routine to simultaneously spool wire and manage her extensive paperwork. She alternates between spooling wire, performing calculations, and entering information. With an increase in paperwork, operators also must be able to "catch" errors such as the juxtaposition of one pair of digits in a lengthy code. Marta is verifying that this paperwork makes sense. The significance of these quality control skills cannot be underestimated. If Calhoun's overall production system is to function profitably, it requires operators like Marta to be familiar with the larger context of that system.

The successful operator at Calhoun requires an impressive set of skills. Paperwork has proliferated. Decision-making activities have significantly increased. Operators must develop a good memory, methodically handle documents, constantly pay attention, follow instructions, and always use legible handwriting. The very abundance of information tends to be overwhelming. The important of oral and written communication has been greatly heightened as new management systems and IT are now appearing across the entire U.S. business landscape.

From Past to Present

In the past Calhoun Wire and Cable enjoyed decades of success due to its ability to produce specialized wire and cable applications that met highly specific and exacting specifications. Their patented products became world standards. Because of the absence of significant competitive pressures, Calhoun's customers had few alternatives but to accept product delivery on the company's terms. Orders were sometimes overdue. There also were variations in product quality. Management offered few incentives to control production costs such as reducing scrap wire and cable.

The big change came in the 1980s. First, patents began expiring. Then, foreign competition led by Japan invaded the specialty wire and cable market. Calhoun's management reacted aggressively by implementing strategies that raised the skills bar on the production floor.

An order entry system controlled by the operators attempted to reduce costs by recording data on the time, materials, and processing used to finish the product. Quality checklists were developed to speed up operator order handling.

PROD CON replaced Calhoun's existing pencil-and-paper production system. A computerized scheduling and production-control system, PROD CON sprouted in every department, generating extensive paperwork for each order. Calhoun took on the competition by successfully marketing its ability to satisfy customer requests for unique products. In theory this meant that operators needed to be skilled in the product specifications and process settings for approximately 24,000 different products!

To meet this goal, production management and engineering began training operators in statistical process control and other skills. They used these efforts to stabilize the processes for making so many products and reduce the variances endemic on the production floor.

Management's use of new systems and information technology had a major impact on operator skill requirements. Each operator needed to be able to process and comprehend a thick packet of order documents. Correctly handling this paperwork now required operators to possess considerable technical knowledge, differentiate what was important on the documents, perform required measurements and specific calculations, and enter data correctly throughout the forms.

Bottom-line results for upgrading the operators' skills were even more significant. Management now wanted the operators to see their role on the production floor as part of a unified technology system that was constantly changing. The operators needed to see themselves as involved in the company's long-term fortunes.

To complete successful projects, the operators' job descriptions included new tasks such as producing brief written reports, speaking at team meetings, participating in "brainstorming sessions," and determining cost/benefit alternative solutions. This shift in activities was very different for operators who had been originally hired for their ability to run machines. Now a whole new set of skills were required of the same operators. What dramatically changed is that this high-performance workplace now required everyone to possess information-processing skills and collaborative team-building skills. In the immediate future these skills will be entering a new, even more brutally demanding phase.

Welcome to the Future

Several years into its PROD CON system and IT reorganization, Calhoun Wire and Cable established NewSite as its "workplace of the future." NewSite was in reality Calhoun's first high-performance workplace where all the organizational and technological innovations would be fully used. Standardization of the production process was paramount. Each functional work area has a team of operators with the skills to assess ideas, resolve problems, or modify the machinery. NewSite's ultimate goal is to optimize productivity for the entire plant by improving worker performance.

The PROD CON computer terminals dominate NewSite. Now every operator must use a computer. They use their terminals to issue material orders, prepare minutes of team meetings, compose memos, and create charts and diagrams. Operator paperwork has been greatly condensed, with the computer creating new instant paper documentation. Cable and wire production equipment also incorporates computerized control panels that offer digital displays of run conditions.

Operator training has been greatly expanded as supervisors and engineers instruct operators in the analytical methods of the production process. This has included Total Quality Management, specifically conducting team meetings and group problem solving. Of equal importance was training in statistical process control, including flowcharting, histograms, Pareto diagrams, control charts, and other techniques. This has enabled operators to collect production data and interpret the results to establish process control.

The adoption of "just-in-time" (JIT) manufacturing has also increased the use of cross training to speed up the production process by enabling operators to move to several different work areas each day. This standardized peer training uses flowcharts and a formal checklist of tasks the operator must master in each work area before he or she can touch a machine.

NewSite's greater productivity has revealed how much time in the past was lost to correcting paperwork errors. Operators agree that both the accuracy and use of information has increased at NewSite. However, much of these improvements hinge on the individual operator's ability to collect, manipulate, and interpret reams of data. Thus, the operators' information-processing skills are now at the center of NewSite's performance and productivity process.

Calhoun now claims that NewSite has improved workplace productivity. Supervisors believe that they have provided workers with a more valuable bundle of skills that can be more easily transferred to future, better-paying jobs.

Skills and the New Workplace

The high-performance world of NewSite offers a good example of an increasingly complex workplace. Whether we focus on an industrial, manufacturing, service, or professional business environment, the new millennium's world of work has an important missing link between its description of a "knowledge worker" and job requirements that are solely translated into "bundles of skills."

In the past it was comforting to think solely in terms of "skilling workers." This simplified management's task when considering performance-improvement programs. For most people, learning to run a computer program, or to play golf or tennis, means acquiring a new set of skills. After you've learned them, it doesn't take a "conscious effort" to use them—just more and more practice. In fact, everyone will tell you that thinking just gets in the way of your best golf game.

However, you can sometimes learn the form and never master the content. The person who wrote the computer program must be somewhere in the loop. Also, somebody is needed who has the vision to figure out what the stuff means when it comes out at the other end.

A person may master all the skills and coordination of tennis and yet remain an average tennis player. If you are "blind-sighted," you will never acquire the vision to analyze an opponent's weaknesses and use this knowledge in formulating the strategies and tactics that will lead to victory.

In the past, by defining their production or service jobs solely as a list of skills, most managers felt absolved from the responsibility of helping employees learn the analytical abilities needed in the workplace. How can management develop strategies that teach these thinking abilities, so that more people can better process information in a high-performance business?

Setting Knowledge Targets for Business

In its 1995 U.S. economic survey, the Federal Reserve Bank of Chicago noted that American business is "becoming increasingly centered on the flow of information and knowledge creation. Surveys of new jobs being created by business suggest that new skill demands are higher than those of previous and existing jobs." The Federal Reserve's survey of firms included businesses located in Atlanta, Detroit, Los Angeles, and Boston. Thirty-two percent of these companies reported their skill needs have risen for all employment categories, even blue-collar jobs previously considered "low" skill. The report findings underscored the fact that "knowledgeable people," who can combine good technical skills with the ability to communicate and be team players, are in demand by all business sectors. The survey ranked by importance the specific knowledge/education abilities needed for these new jobs as follows:

Ability Needed	%
1. Customer Contact Skills	73
2. Reading	68
3. Paragraph Writing Skills	68
4. Arithmetic	68
5. Computer	56

(*Chicago Tribune*, December 19, 1996)

There is broad consensus on exactly what skills are needed by each business sector. In 1994, a national system of voluntary industry-led skill standards was established. More and more industry trade groups are formulating skill standards to restructure their response to education, work, and the market. A 28-member National Skills Standards Board representing business, labor, and government will provide the stimulus and leadership for this process. The National Alliance of Business hopes that by working collaboratively industry-wide, not business by business, powerful skill standards can be given the states to mandate career education programs, such as those established by the states of Oregon and Kentucky.[2]

A valuable comparison of several different "skill standards" provides the big picture on what knowledge people need in today's workplace. A research report by Eunice Askov at Penn State University, funded by the National Institute for Literacy, uncovered the following basic educational needs: Reading Comprehension, Writing, Oral Communication, Quantitative, Problem Solving, Critical Thinking, Knowing How to Learn, and Cross-Functional Skills (see Figure 6-1).[3]

Skill	Description
Reading Comprehension	Decodes, interprets, and comprehends information drawn from written documents, etc.
Writing	Communicates thoughts, ideas, information, and messages in writing; planning, generating, and revising text.
Oral Communication	Communicates thoughts, ideas, and information orally, attending to the comprehension of listeners and the demands of the setting.
Quantitative	Understands basic mathematical computations and problem solving procedures and how these procedures might be used to address various problems.
Problem Solving	Understands basic problem solving procedures and how these procedures might be used to address various problems.
Critical Thinking	Recognizes and can analyze the strengths and weaknesses of arguments and propositions using logic to establish the validity of these propositions.
Knowing How to Learn	Identifies and uses various alternative strategies for working on learning tasks, looking for examples, taking notes, and identifying alternative strategies for working with this material.
Cross-Functional Skills	Works with technology, people, resources, and systems to perform activities that occur across jobs.

Figure 6-1 Basic Educational Skills
Source: Eunice Askov, Penn State University, 1997.

In addition to these general skill foundations, the U.S. Department of Labor SCANS Report (1991) suggested the need for five employee-applied business competencies: resources, interpersonal, information, systems, technology (see Box 6-1).

SCANS FIVE COMPETENCIES

Resources: Identifies, organizes, plans, and allocates resources

A. *Time*—Selects goal-relevant activities, ranks them, allocates times, and prepares and follows schedules.
B. *Money*—Uses or prepares budgets, makes forecasts, keeps records, and makes adjustments to meet objectives.
C. *Material and Facilities*—Acquires, stores, allocates, and uses materials or space efficiently.
D. *Human Resources*—Assesses skills and distributes work accordingly, evaluates performance and provides feedback.

Interpersonal: Works with others.

A. *Participates as Member of a Team*—contributes to group effort.
B. *Teaches Others New Skills*
C. *Serves Clients/Customers*—works to satisfy customers' expectations.
D. *Exercises Leadership*—communicates ideas to justify position, persuades and convinces others, responsibly challenges existing procedures and policies.
E. *Negotiates*—works toward agreements involving exchange of resources, resolves divergent interests.
F. *Works with Diversity*—works well with men and women from diverse backgrounds.

Information: Acquires and uses information

A. *Acquires and Evaluates Information*
B. *Organizes and Maintains Information*
C. *Interprets and Communicates Information*
D. *Uses Computers to Process Information*

Systems: Understands complex inter-relationships

A. *Understands Systems*—knows how social, organizational, and technological systems work and operates effectively with them.
B. *Monitors and Corrects Performance*—distinguishes trends, predicts impacts on system operations, diagnoses deviations in systems' performance and corrects malfunctions.
C. *Improves or Designs Systems*—suggests modifications to existing systems and develops new or alternative systems to improve performance.

Technology: Works with a variety of technologies

A. *Selects Technology*—chooses procedures, tools or equipment including computers and related technologies.
B. *Applies Technology to Task*—understands overall intent and proper procedures for setup and operation of equipment.
C. *Maintains and Troubleshoots Equipment*—Prevents, identifies, or solves problems with equipment, including computers and other technologies.

Box 6-1 SCANS Five Competencies
Source: Adapted from U.S. Department of Labor.

The Maintenance/Repair Technician Industry Skill Standards written by a group of Indiana businesses adapted these employability skills into general employee behavior qualities. These behavior competencies included dependability, initiative, persistence, willingness to accept responsibility, attention to detail, stress tolerance, workplace ethics, and flexibility and adaptability to change (see Box 6-2).[4]

---

1. *Dependability*—Characteristic of someone who is reliable and can be depended on.

2. *Initiative*—Characteristic of someone who approaches work with a constructive, resourceful attitude and is a self-starter.

3. *Persistence*—Characteristic of someone who perseveres on his or her job despite the length of the task, discouragement, obstacles, or setbacks.

4. *Willingness to Accept Responsibility*—Characteristics of someone who is willing to be held accountable for something.

5. *Attention to Detail*—Characteristic of someone who is aware of and carefully attends to details.

6. *Stress Tolerance*—Characteristic of someone who is able to perform under conditions of pressure, strain, and tension.

7. *Workplace Ethics*—Demonstrates high ethics in the workplace and understands how they apply to the particular job, organization, and industry.

8. *Flexibility and Adaptability to Change*—Ability to adjust to new circumstances.

9. *Serves Customers (includes in-house)*—Works and communicates with customers to satisfy their expectations. Demonstrates politeness, understanding, and empathy. Exercises good judgement regarding when to listen and when to respond or initiate.

10. *Teamwork*—Works cooperatively with others for their mutual benefit. Negotiates and participates in give and take with the others.

11. *Ability to Work with Diversity*—Works well with people of both genders and a variety of ethnic, social, educational, and other backgrounds.

Box 6-2 Employee Behavior Skills—Maintenance/Repair Technician Profile
Source: Adapted from Industry Skills Standards Project, St. Joseph County, Indiana, 1996.

Murane and Levy's *Teaching the New Basic Skills* summarizes what all this means in the real world of business. They studied the skill requirements at Diamond Star Motors, comprising Mitsubishi and Chrysler. Diamond Star looks for workers who can keep improving their performance. They require five skills from employees: the ability to do math, reading, and mechanical functions; the ability to detect errors; the ability to communicate orally; the ability to work in teams; and perhaps most importantly, the ability to solve semistructured problems and originate improvements. All this seems very basic—yet countless business and governmental studies continue to show that these educational content areas are sadly lacking across much of the U.S. workforce.

The New Techno-Peasants

The late, famed *Chicago Tribune* pundit Mike Royko once asked a Chicago information operator for the number of *Chicago Magazine*.

"How do you spell that word?" she asked.

"Chicago?"

"No, that other word."

"Magazine?"

"Yeah."

"You don't know how to spell magazine?"

"Yeah."

On another occasion Royko was out of his office and called long-distance to get the phone number for the *Chicago Tribune's* Washington bureau.

"In D.C.," I told the operator who answered, "what's the number of the Chicago Tribune?"

"How do you spell that?"

"Spell what?"

"Are you talking about Chicago?"

"Uh-huh."

As gently as I could, I said:

"Are you telling me that you don't know how to spell the name of the third largest city in the United States?"

She responded by mumbling.

So I said:

"What would happen if I asked for something with Philadelphia in its name?"

Another mumble. Then there was a click. She cut me off.

You have to ask: How did that person get a job with the phone company?[5]

So she can't spell. Big deal for a low-end job. Tom Burke has seen far worse—executive blunders on their own résumés. Here's a composite letter constructed out of verbatim real examples he received over an 18-month period (published by *The Wall Street Journal*). He stopped after scanning the first 80 people in his flub file:

Dear Mr. Burk:

Thank you for accepting me recent phone call.

I hope you won't think me presumptions . . . my position has been recently has been eliminated . . . I am an executive for one of the neation's largest coporations . . . a Fortune 500 compan . . .

Regarding the current search you area conducting . . . as a follow-up our discussion . . . this is a close fit with by experience . . . attached is a one-page summery . . . I am a front-line professional with 14 years experience . . . as your outlined in your notice . . . my background give me a broad perspective . . . I am seeking a position on the Eat Coast . . .

In the years I have lead the organization . . . my strenghts are in understanding the industry . . . As for my company, it's losses now total $248 million . . .

I have worked in setting strategy that support objectives . . . managed a information development team . . . translated technical jargon into readable english . . . provided nuts and blolts information . . . am experienced in crisis advise and comminations to employees . . .

In Research and Planning I eloped the first issues-planning function . . . have been responsible for facility-citing issues . . . was chosen by the company as their keynote speaker . . . know what makes value-added services for client's or customers . . .

I have dealt with public saftey issues . . . was an assistant in the Lieutenant Governor's office from 1979–78 . . . represented our company at the Federal level in private and public meetings . . .

I'd like to discuss how I might compliment the right organization . . . Could I meet with while you're in San Diego . . .

[Signature missing]

P.S.–Please do not hesitate me for references.[6]

From coast to coast, the general lack of appropriate educational skills screams out for attention, as does this public notice in the *Los Angeles Times* (3/18/98):

South Pasadena   **LOS ANGELES TIMES**

Literacy Program

South Pasadena Rotary Club 3rd Annual Wine Tasting Extraveganza in Sapport of the South Pasadena Literacy Program at Grante Stat Bank, 901 Fair Oaks Ave. South Pasadena, CA 91030

It should be no surprise for most managers that a 1993 W.E. Upjohn Institute survey of employers discovered that:

- 30 percent of secretaries have difficulty reading at the level required by the job.
- 50 percent reported that managers and supervisors are unable to write paragraphs free of grammatical errors.
- 50 percent reported that skilled and semi-skilled employees, including bookkeepers, are unable to use decimals and fractions in solving math problems.

In just one industry, banking, losses of over $400 million per year can be attributed to these skill deficiencies with such consequences as low productivity, wasted or ineffective training, lost customers, and cash-drawer losses (American Banker's Association, 1991). Multiply this across all U.S. business sectors, and we begin to approach one Commerce Department estimate of $300 billion as a potential indication of annual lost productivity.

Ask Motorola. Ask the residents of Harvard, Illinois, who had been anxiously waiting for the opening of Motorola's new $100 million, state-of-the art cellular-telephone manufacturing plant and the arrival of its much-publicized 3,000 new jobs. Begun in June 1994, and completed by the spring of 1996, in 1998 the factory is still standing idle. Why? Motorola cannot find enough skilled workers to open the plant.

This shocking development shouldn't surprise U.S. executives. A National Literacy Audit conducted by the Department of Education (1993) found that nearly half of the 191 million adults living in the United States were functionally illiterate. This included approximately 20 percent of all managers and supervisors.

An American Management Association (AMA) Research Report (1998) had similar findings. Four out of ten companies now conduct tests on potential new hires for reading, writing, and math. Of 166,506 job applicants tested, 37,965 or 23 percent revealed deficiencies that disqualified them from the position they sought.

A separate United Way Business Survey (1994) pointed toward the same results (see Table 6-1). One basic reason to focus on 12th-to-13th-grade-level reading comprehension as a basic indicator of a "knowledge worker" is that most business software manuals now are written at this level of reading fluency.

Worse yet, the American Society for Training and Development (ASTD) contends that nine-tenths of all new jobs will require postsecondary skill levels in reading, writing, and math. It seems no exaggeration to state that too many Americans are rapidly becoming the new techno-peasants of the information age.

What has caused this workforce literacy gap? Until the most recent decade, the nation's schools were expected to produce mostly a grunt labor force of minimally educated adults for work on the mass-production assembly line. Large number of students were never expected to achieve better than fourth- to sixth-grade reading, writing, and math abilities. The unwritten definition of "factory worker" included a lack of education. The entire educational system was organized around this model. High schools were two-tracked. Basic education and vocational training was given to the majority, who

Table 6-1 Workforce Reading Fluency

Reading Levels	Manufacturing Workers	Service Workers	White Collar Workers	Total
1. Non-Fluent (Grade 0–4)	32.3%	25.7%	2.0%	11.1%
2. Functionally Fluent (Grade 5–8)	29.0%	31.4%	11.7%	17.6%
3. Marginally Fluent (Grade 9–12)	25.0%	20.0%	32.8%	29.6%
4. Fully Fluent (Above 12th Grade)	13.7%	22.9%	53.6%	41.7%

Source: United Way 1994.

would enter the working world. College-prep classes were for those few who entered management and the professions.

Today technology and globalization have rewritten the rules. By the year 2000, 80 percent of all jobs will require at least 12th- to 13th-grade-level reading, writing, and math comprehension abilities (U.S. Labor Department). In turn, the government has estimated that more than 90 million current managers, professionals, supervisors, and support and production workers fail to meet these standards. *The Wall Street Journal* (1994) recognized this dilemma facing American business when it noted:

> *It's bizarre that certain pundits and prognosticators want to focus on high-tech network access subsidies for the masses barely three months after the Department of Education published a survey claiming to show that fully half of American adults are close to functionally illiterate.*

The National Center for Educational Statistics (1992) also revealed that only about 3 percent of potential jurors can fully comprehend a written account of how the jury-selection process works. On graduation as many as 15 percent of college graduates have only marginal educational skills. Most importantly, only 17 percent of *all* working American adults are sufficiently well educated to function effectively as "master knowledge workers" in our complex techno-logical world.

At a time when U.S. corporations have an unprecedented need for these knowledge workers, they are simply unavailable. With unemployment levels in the late 1990s reaching a 25-year low, a survey by the American Business Conference of midsize growth companies found that 41 percent believed that employee competency had declined, and at the same time, 71 percent had become more dependent on modernization. Motorola discovered (1992) that about half of their 25,000 manufacturing and support people in the United States failed to meet the seventh-grade yardstick in reading and math. And they can't find more knowledge workers on the current job market.[7]

These results were further corroborated in a 1997 study, by Grant Thorton, of 4,500 National Association of Manufacturing (NAM) members. More than one-quarter of these companies regularly rejected 75 percent of all job applicants because they lacked relevant technical skills and work experience. More than 50 percent found their current workers had serious math, writing, and reading skill shortcomings.

Seventy-three percent said they either cannot improve productivity or cannot upgrade technology because of skill deficiencies. "The shortage of skilled employees is not a distant threat anymore," says Ernest Deavenport, chairman and CEO of Eastman Kodak Co. and chairman of NAM. "The skill gap is now catching up to us and could threaten the amazing growth and productivity gains of the past decade." The shortage of well-educated people has a broad bottom-line impact for companies in manufacturing, and it is just as pressing for many service, technology, and professional businesses. "This labor shortage isn't just simply an inconvenience for businesses anymore," commented Carol Ann Meares a policy analyst at the Labor Department. "It's starting to affect competitiveness" (*Wall Street Journal*, December 1, 1997).

In mid-1997 the Information Technology Association of America documented 190,000 unfilled information technology jobs in the United States. They projected that this number would grow to 1.5 million by 2005.

The high-performance workplace will deeply depend on a broadly educated and skilled workforce capable of operating advanced technologies, of making decisions, and of directing their own education and training. To be employable in the first decade of the twenty-first century, most workers will have to be both technically and socially competent. That means that engineers must be able to write and speak so others will understand them. It also means that liberal arts graduates need to be skilled with the personal computer and understand science and technology. But most importantly, it means that anyone who graduates from high school, but not college, must also possess these same educational abilities. Without them most people will not find any jobs—anywhere.

Searching for a Solution

Management desperately needs new practical strategies to fill the "skills gap," which is far broader than American business first projected. This skills gap now includes many professionals, managers, technical workers, support staff, and production workers. Included in this gap are the following: reading, math, grammar training, management writing skills, office practice, computer skills, software knowledge, English as a second language, foreign language skills for business, problem-solving abilities, conducting meetings, meeting participation, report/form writing, and blueprint reading. These are the workforce education areas that TQM, ISO 9000, and other advanced managerial quality-control systems take as the minimal abilities of all production or service employees. The question remains: "How do we train the majority of our adult workers and our students in school to meet the educational requirements for knowledge workers in twenty-first-century business?"

Since the 1970s American business has sought solutions that will improve employee productivity. In the first phase of their drive for competitiveness, high-tech equipment and computers were introduced into almost every office and plant. This led to the dramatic downsizing of management and production forces that still continues. In many instances high technology did fulfill its prophecy of accomplishing more work with fewer workers. Thus, significant productivity gains were realized by American business in 1992, reversing the erosion of American productivity from the 1980s.

However, senior management is just beginning to realize that high-tech, computer-driven equipment requires a greater number of better-educated employees than are generally available anywhere in the

United States. Of far greater concern is the sobering fact that many managers, technical workers, professional office support staff, and production workers require extensive workplace educational programs to realize additional real productivity gains.

In the "reengineered," "down-sized," "right-sized" workplace, the employees who remain must daily be able to perform complex tactical and strategic tasks. This means that many more people than ever before in the typical workplace must assimilate increasing amounts of new knowledge, possess personal thinking/application/problem-solving abilities, and handle high work loads with extremely variable content.

Creating more of these "knowledge workers" will take time and money, two commodities in short supply in today's short-term, profit-driven environment. So a long-term training solution is not even an option being considered by most organizations.

Also common business wisdom dictates that you can't retrain an older workforce. In a Wyatt Worldwide survey (1998), 773 chief executives in 23 countries thought that productivity peaks around age 43. Though few employers are reluctant to make this overt link for fear of being accused of age discrimination, there are some strong indicators that this survey is on target.

James Lardner in "Too Old to Write Code?" (*U.S. News and World Report*, March 16, 1998) points out that a chronic shortage of computer programmers and other information technology jobs could be filled in part by "retraining" the large number of unemployed IT workers over the age of 50. However, "retraining," according to one headhunter, is widely associated with hand-holding and unacceptable delay.

Instead, U.S. business increasingly is pursuing the strategy of recruiting from overseas. This is not the first time. Following the Second World War the United States lowered its immigration barriers for a time, to allow displaced skilled European workers (tool and die makers, machinists, etc.) an opportunity to come to America.

Since 1992 the number of foreign-born IT workers admitted to the United States has almost tripled to 15,000 from 5,700 according to the Institute of Electrical and Electronics Engineers (*Wall Street Journal*, January 8, 1998). New legislation was proposed in the U.S. Congress (March 1998) to allow 90,000 special visas for IT workers, up from 65,000 a year. Earlier in the debate, however, Tom Waldorp at Intel pointed out it may not be in the United States' best interests to have people come here, get additional experience and education, and then go back to other countries to compete against us—in other words, a "brain drain" in reverse. Also this writer and others repeatedly have observed that by failing to develop our own U.S. knowledge infrastructure, and in the short run relying too heavily on foreigners to make up for the "brain shortage," we may deny future American generations access to these high-pay, high-skill jobs.

Another operating strategy is to continue to dumb down the entire business process, thereby blunting the need to constantly update worker skills. This has been a popular solution as computer chip power has increased and the use of PCs has spread throughout every workplace. Unfortunately, it often fails to work because, as Les Black at BGF Industries sees it, "Even if you can dumb down the job by using computers, we still need educated people who can think systems."

The final solution being pursued to fill the skills gap is to move industry offshore. Shopping the world for skilled knowledge workers enables U.S. multinational companies to circumvent this issue at home. By 1997, one ominous estimate was that 11 percent of overseas production by American companies was being imported into the United States rather than being sold in foreign markets. If this management practice continues to grow, it will tend to undercut the development of America's future industrial infrastructure and limit the availability of more remunerative jobs for many Americans.

The Workforce Education Solution

Today U.S. business needs significantly larger numbers of better-educated people than in past generations. Typifying this solely as a need for "better skills" is both inadequate and misleading for developing any meaningful discussion within the business community on how to build a globally competitive workforce across the service, manufacturing, industrial, and professional business sectors.

Workforce education is a new strategic business paradigm that encompasses twenty-first-century educational, training, and skills standards. Conceptually there is much more to workforce education than merely acquiring better reading, math, writing, or thinking abilities.

This is a macroeconomic issue, not a technological program to be solved, or just another business cost. To succeed in the twenty-first-century workplace, senior management must acknowledge workforce education as the driving activity that supports people performance and organizational productivity. Workforce education is the strategic linchpin of future technology, business innovation, and renewed employee commitment.

Many people need to improve their personal skill competencies in reading, writing, math, foreign languages, or English as a second language (ESL), but in a work-applied manner that will solve day-to-day and future workplace problems. Workers cannot be efficient team members if they are inarticulate. "Better communication abilities" means developing personal verbal and listening skills. Improving individual self-esteem and motivation are critical for better management that empowers workers to think for themselves with less supervision. How well can we educate every adult worker to become more adaptable? Can we enhance personal creative-thinking and problem-solving skills? These abilities are the foundation of the interpersonal and team skills needed for group effectiveness. All of these workforce education changes are being driven by competitive necessity.

Workforce education has long been the "poor man" of corporate training and the "bastard" of the American educational system. Born in adversity and mired in political controversy, until now it has remained isolated from the mainstream of business training and development.

Past/Present Training Program Failures

Before 1980 this was not a training issue. Most businesses vehemently denied that managers or workers experienced this problem. They would never consider an in-house education solution. By the late 1990s some businesses began using computer-based training and classroom instruction to raise educational levels. Unfortunately, the majority of these programs typically experienced dropout rates of at least 50 percent. What was the problem? Employees perceived little correspondence between the training activities and their day-to-day job needs. Instructional materials were often inappropriate for the workplace, and instruction was "lock-step" rather than individualized to meet the adult's personal learning problems.

Current research suggests that management strategy seems fixated on using multimedia technology (CD-ROMs, distance learning, etc.) for employee training while outsourcing nonessential business core areas. A survey by *Training Magazine* of the Fortune 1000 focused on the strengths and weaknesses of using multimedia training (see Figure 6-2).

On the plus side, this type of training delivery is good for self-paced learners, and it can be delivered almost anywhere and at any time. Management has a great deal of control over its content. This medium is particularly useful for the best-educated employees who are highly motivated and ready to learn more on their own.

Unfortunately, multimedia training as a stand-alone system lacks the important social component to learning. Interacting with a machine cannot substitute for interacting with capable instructors and interested peers who are part of a classroom learning experience. Even the most advanced "intelligent tutoring systems" continue to have difficulty overcoming this need.

Based on prior experience and years of research on how people learn, this author contends that, for most of your employees, multimedia is a tool, a means to an end, not an end in itself. As a stand-alone,

When asked about the strengths and weaknesses of using multimedia training, here is how the Fortune 1000 responded.

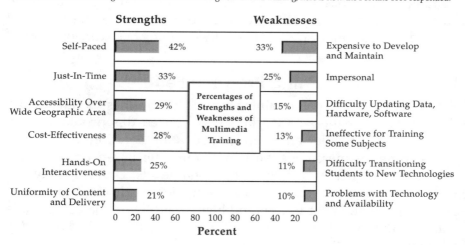

Figure 6-2 Strengths and Weaknesses of Multimedia Training
Source: Adapted from *Training Magazine,* "Multimedia Training in the Fortune 1000."
September 1996.

multimedia will not produce a total employee learning system. Business has gone down this path before and failed.

As a consultant in the late 1970s, I saw billions of dollars squandered on workplace learning centers filled with early computer "page-turning" software. It simply failed to teach most people. Let's hope we don't have to repeat this wasteful lesson all over again. Granted that today's multimedia training is far more attractive and stimulating, and much of it has better written content. However, such training is delivered by impersonal machines that cannot think. For the most part people learn best through thoughtfully directed interaction with other thinking people. A well-educated employee can profitably use CD-ROMs to rapidly update facts. But that is not new learning—it is personal data acquisition. For most mortals, learning to sell, improve interpersonal skills, solve customer service problems, or increase the clarity of written communication requires teaching—time—and trying it out, first in a class, then back on the job. Learning is a continuous process, not a half-day training event, or taking a disk on team problem-solving home to use after putting the kids to bed.

Training Media's Review Bill Ellet believes in classroom training because:

- It's the ultimate interactive system.
- It has the social context that brings about changed behavior.
- It can be customized at a fraction of the cost of media-based programs.
- It has a better cost to earnings ratio.

Ellet says, "Line training is capable of infinite interactivity. A seasoned teacher can respond meaningfully and in real time to an endless number of ideas, problems, and questions. The point isn't to write-off multimedia as a training tool—it's that Multimedia and live training work far better as allies than as adversaries in making training more effective. That means they take better care of the bottom line than single-minded solutions."[8]

New approaches to training and learning are needed because complex tactical and strategic tasks demand expanded personal thinking abilities for on-the-job applications. Twentieth-century command and control/assembly-line business structures relied heavily on employee behavior training or psychomotor technical-skill training. Now management's new performance and productivity expectations require workforce education that improves employee thinking and problem-solving abilities. Brains have become more valuable than brawn.

Workforce Education Triad

A comparison of the most commonly used quality programs—Crosby's 14 steps, Deming's 14 points, and Juran's 7 points—finds a common call to expand training that promotes employee problem solving on the job. All three call for empowered work teams that will integrate a wide range of complex thinking processes into their daily work activities. This quality-driven, "continuous improvement process" requires that people make decisions, analyze systems, investigate, invent new processes, classify, compare, and generally manipulate information. Increased personal creativity has become the name of the game for American business.

To succeed in this new knowledge-manipulation environment, business needs to encourage employee education throughout the ranks. The $60+ billion annual corporate training budget sounds impressive. Yet it is only a fraction of America's $400 billion annual business capital hardware bill.

As part of any company's strategic business plan, managers need to reevaluate their training programs by assessing total local workforce skills. What are your employees' educational skills in comparison to those of domestic and foreign competition? If an educational skill gap exists, is it increasing or decreasing compared to key competitors? Motorola is not a national industrial leader by accident. Continuous employee education is at the heart of their short-term/long-term strategic planning. They documented the savings earned by training people in problem-solving methods and statistical process control. Motorola's rate of return was about 30 times the training dollars invested!

Training is useless unless change results, and unless it is part of a process that awakens people to their own intellectual strengths and weaknesses. In the past, behavior-based training often taught adults what to think. In the move toward a more cognitive-based training paradigm, learning the "how to" of thinking moves to center stage in meeting quality program-implementation requirements.

In the past 15 years these new adult learning strategies have been employed to stimulate critical thinking and intelligence. Frederick Goodwin, Director of the National Institute of Mental Health, believes that though training programs cannot make a 70 IQ person into a 120 IQ person, we can change their IQ in different ways, perhaps as much as 20 points upward based on more effective cognitive training. We now know how to raise adult intelligence, personal critical thinking, and abstract reasoning abilities, along with improving personal attitudes, planning capabilities, flexibility, and persistence. Is there a new fundamental conceptual framework that will help us organize this human development revolution reshaping American business?

I propose a Workforce Education Triad™ as a graphic representation of the process (see Figure 6-3). Business will continue to offer basic "training," such as supervision, management, service and assembly behaviors—the fundamentals of how any business operates and makes a profit. However, this "training" will be offered to most employees rather than restricted to current managers. Why? How can any employee be expected to analyze and solve work problems unless he/she really understands how the company operates and how their individual work influences final service or product results?

Most businesses will add the second triad component, "skills," to address the need for improving overall comprehension through better writing, math, reading, foreign language, or English as a second language (ESL). Continued growth in complex technologies and unabated foreign competition will continue to increase the need for higher skills in both salaried and hourly employees.

Only after addressing these two employee developmental components will a business be able to successfully address the "education" issues at the top of the triad that build critical thinking skills for: TQM, ISO 9000, work teams, empowerment, problem solving, personal creativity, and career education programs. I see the winning of the "skill wars" as based on this Workforce Education Triad of training, skills, and education. Both the lessons learned from current behavior-based training and newer concepts of thinking-skill education will provide the "best practices" to maximize the talents of all people.

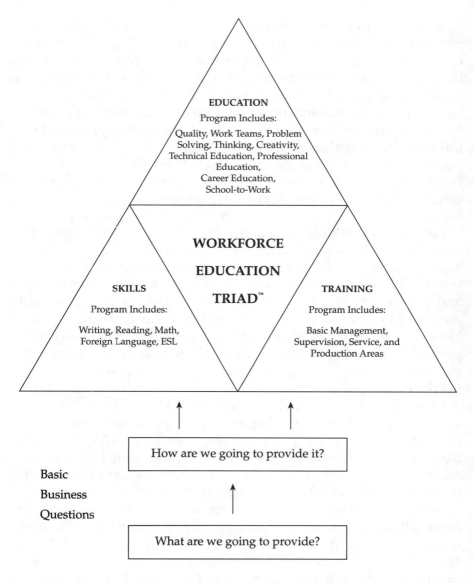

Figure 6-3 Workforce Education Triad™
© 1999 Edward E. Gordon. All rights reserved.

Report from the Trenches

Metra: Working Today to Prepare for the Future

The Northeast Illinois Metropolitan Transit Railroad Authority (Metra), the commuter rail division of the Regional Transportation Authority (RTA), provides all the commuter rail services for the six-county Chicago metropolitan area. Begun in 1982, Metra is the second largest commuter rail system in the United States. It generates more than 270,000 trips on an average weekday using rail lines radiating north, south, and west of downtown. Metra has one of the best railroad safety records in the country. It intends to maintain its excellent safety/customer service record, and it wants to utilize the latest technological innovations in passenger railway service.

America's railroads dramatically changed during the 1980s and 1990s. Now, profits are up, employment numbers down, and high-tech railroad applications mushrooming throughout day-to-day operations. Computers now drive a new generation of diesel locomotives, eliminating the "little red caboose" on most trains; fewer but better-trained "maintenance of way" (rail-track) workers are required to maintain steel rails for greater safety and operating speed. A key ingredient to implementing all these high-tech rail applications is a new management commitment to employee training.

Railroad employees live in an increasingly high-tech world. The application of their educational skills to computerized technology has already started and will continue to accelerate. Nationally, the number of railroad employees has declined because of the increasing use of these technologies. Railroads need workers to be better trained and educated than in earlier years because of the increasing complexity of these jobs (Gordon, Morgan, and Ponticell, 1994).

Microprocessors are now in every locomotive, and computers operate advanced signaling devices. High-speed/high-tech trains are now operating daily in Europe and Japan at speeds of 125 to 185 mph. Ever-greater suburban sprawl could make this an attractive future technology for a railroad that wants to increase its ridership by shortening travel times over expressway alternatives. Metra's vision of the future prompted much research and the decision, in 1992, to begin training their employees in order to fulfill their long-term goals.

Metra's workforce education program is designed to train current workers who have educational skills below the 10th-grade level. This "people program" gives an older, well-established workforce the opportunity to improve their reading, math, and communication skills (such as English as a second language). Employees participating in the program are specifically interested in improving current job skills or gaining promotion to a new job at Metra.

Classrooms are located in the Metra railroad marshaling yards scattered throughout the Chicago metropolitan area. This places the training program near the individual employee's daily work activities. In the briefing sessions held for all employees before the program began, workers were told, "This program is like a floating crap game. It can go wherever you want it to go." From the beginning a key concept was building the entire training effort around what Metra's training manager described as "on-the-job trust."

In the two years prior to the program, Metra stressed its commitment from the top down. The executive director made a major commitment to the concepts behind this workforce education effort. Fifteen unions were briefed and lent their support to beginning the program. Question-and-answer presentations on workforce education were made during general management and small committee meetings.

An information campaign was then begun for all 2,100 Metra employees. Flyers were distributed to all employees, and information was published in the Metra newsletter (see Figure 6-4). Even more important, face-to-face briefing sessions were held in Metra rail yards for all employees, who attended on a voluntary basis. Metra's workforce education program is offered to all employees who wish to volunteer for the training classes. All program test scores are kept confidential. Progress reports on each worker are given to Metra's human resource department rather than to the employee's immediate supervisor.

At its inception approximately 200 Metra employees volunteered for the program. Maintenance-of-way personnel, coach cleaners, engine machinists, and workers in many other job classifications were tutored in groups of five, using a rapid-learning-program curriculum. Every effort has been made to use realistic, on-the-job training materials and other instructional materials applicable to personal interests or daily life.

The Workforce Education Program became a viable source of "job readiness" for employees seeking to improve reading comprehension,

Workforce Education Program
Training Bulletin

For more information, contact Training and Development at 8913, 8932, or 8922; We're at your service.

Workforce Education Program

A new educational opportunity will soon be coming our way—Metra's *Workforce Education Program*. This training program, open to all employees, will provide customized instruction in math, reading, and language skills. This is an opportunity to brush up on some old skills or even learn a some new ones.

Metra has been awarded a grant from the Illinois Secretary of State to implement this "pilot program." The grant provides matched funding for 30 Metra employees who will receive 40 hours of customized instruction in the educational skills they want to improve.

The classes will be small—five to a class. What's also interesting is the approach. Metra's Training division will be working with an outside expert in the field of adult education—Dr. Ed Gordon. "This is a people program," said Dr. Gordon (he prefers "Ed") at a presentation to the members of our Labor/Management Technical Skills task group. Dr. Gordon stresses the fact that each class will incorporate "real world" examples from the job or other areas of personal interest to participants. "For example, we might use a racing form to work with fractions," said Gordon, "anything to make it more enjoyable."

This program has received the glowing endorsement of many of our Labor officers. One highly supportive General Chairman (Mark Wimmer, General Chairman B.M.W.E.) wrote to the Director of Training, John Wagner, commenting on the *Workforce Education Program*, "Metra appears to be very committed to enhancing basic education as well as work skills . . . most importantly n a confidential and non-threatening environment." Participation is voluntary and costs the employee nothing, the classes will be provided after hours utilizing Merta facilities easily accessible to the employee.

Field presentations to explain the *Workforce Education Program* will take place in mid-November. Following these presentations, interested employees can arrange for an orientation session with Dr. Gordon's staff to discuss their particular interests.

Programs using the same approach are being provided by Federal Signal, First Bank of Chicago, Nabisco, and by many other Illinois employers. It is worth noting that among the 57 grants awarded by the state, Metra's *Workforce Education Program* was the only transportation entity and the only public sector employer to be successful. For additional information on the program, you can call the Training Division (x8932)

Figure 6-4 Metra Newsletter Announcement

math skills, and language skills, including ESL. More than 180 employees participated in this voluntary education program with minimum commitments of 10 weeks (40 instructional hours) and the majority participating in 20 or more weeks of instruction geared to meet specific individual needs. This program annually provided over 800 classroom hours of instruction at several Metra work sites.

An Apprentice Prep Program became a subset of Metra's overall workforce education effort. This optional program was offered to internal candidates for the Mechanical Department Apprentice Program as a means of improving individual math and/or language skills. There were several "success stories" involving 10 of the 28 apprentices, who, through enrollment in workforce education classes, subsequently met the verbal and math requirements after 10 to 20 weeks of classes.

Between 1992 and 1998 hundreds of Metra employees have successfully participated in the Workforce Education Program. They have increased their overall productivity on-the-job, and some employees have passed job-proficiency examinations that qualified them for promotions.

In addition to increased productivity and promotion gains, Metra employees recognized what the company is doing personally for them. One illustration of that benefit is a letter one trainee voluntarily addressed to Metra's executive director during a writing assignment.

11-93

Dear Sir:

I just want to take the time to acknowledge your commitment and support to the educational workforce project. I am a current class member in my second term class.

The workforce project has instilled into me educational values, self assurance and confidence. I am preparing myself for the GED test and after that more higher learning for job advancement.

I am proud to be a Metra employee for the first time in fourteen years. I have the self assurance to forge ahead for advancement within the Metra family. I think I can speak for all the workforce project members when I say thank you Phil Pagano.

Sincerely,

[Employee's name is withheld for reasons of confidentiality.]

The following reply was sent to the employee:

12-93

Dear Sir:

I am in receipt of your recent correspondence in which you conveyed your appreciation for Metra's Workforce Education Program. I am pleased to hear that you have found this program to be of great value.

Testimonials such as yours and the feedback I've received from others solidify Metra's continued commitment to the program for the future. It is my belief that Workforce Education is perhaps the most successful program ever undertaken here at Metra. I am encouraged by your success and have high hopes for your continued educational advancement.

Thank you for taking the time to write me about Workforce Education. It is always a pleasure to receive letters as yours containing such positive feedback.

Best of luck to you in preparing for your G.E.D.!

Philip A. Pagano

Executive Director—Metra

The student's letter is of interest because he wrote three drafts and then voluntarily sent it to Metra's executive director. It was his honest, unsolicited personal thinking about how his workforce education skills training had changed his educational perspective, self-confidence, and personal commitment. Here is a typical technical worker expressing his strong personal loyalty (and that of his fellow workers in the training program) to top management. Why?

What happened to this railroad worker is that Metra's training made him aware of the connection between personal educational advancement and his future work-life advancement. What may surprise some readers is that many American workers still don't make this basic future work/life connection.

As a result of the Workforce education Program, other Metra employees have:

1. Passed the GED high-school equivalency examination
2. Enrolled in community college courses

3. Gained promotions to conductor, supervisory, and other new jobs

4. Volunteered to become team leaders

5. Voluntarily encouraged other workers to enroll in the classes

A major goal of the program was to also prepare Metra employees to enter union apprenticeship training. Over the next decade American business faces the fact that many skilled technical workers will be retiring from the workplace. The Metra workforce education program

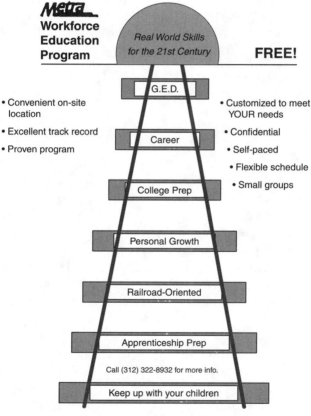

Figure 6-5 Metra Flyer for Employees

is part of the organization's strategy to prepare other employees for successful entry into a wide array of advanced technical apprentice-ships (see Figure 6-5).

Metra has made a long-term budgetary commitment to do what-ever it takes to meet all the educational requirements of its high-tech workplace for all employees. The Metra workforce education pro-gram is a serious, long-term commitment to broaden the availability of training and development services for all workers. It is breaking out of the box with "new" management wisdom that has helped re-define performance-improvement strategy.

"New" Management Wisdom

Many upper-level U.S. executives don't know about workforce edu-cation as a performance improvement strategy, or they don't believe in it. For many managers their workers are "too old" or "too dumb," or effective education "just doesn't exist." They are being blinded by their own, at times disagreeable education experiences. This leads most executives to ignore the startling performance improvements of employees over the past 20 years in the use of applied on-the-job edu-cation programs. Thomas Sticht (1998) points out that the U.S. mili-tary has used this strategy since World War II. Troops in job-related skills programs feel they are getting job training, rather than "reme-dial" or "basic skills" training. In the same amount of time they made four to five times the amount of skill improvements over other per-sonnel enrolled in generic skills training.

For many of these adult learners, small-group training and other new training methods help overcome lifetimes of being considered "slow learners." Many adults in the workplace (including man-agers) suffer from a learning disability (often called dyslexia). Peo-ple with these perceptual disorders experience such difficulties as seeing letters reversed. Although their intelligence may actually be above average, learning to read is difficult for them. When asked how they survived all these years not reading, some say their bosses did all the reading for them, or they used elaborate strategies to keep their poor skills a secret. What is of equal interest are the in-creasing skill problems among professionals and managers in this new workplace environment.

Management Communication Skills

Do today's managers need improved communication skills for more effective leadership? A national survey conducted by the U.S. Labor Department concluded that 20 percent of all U.S. managers lack effective communication skills. What has brought about this leadership communication-skills gap?

Managers are victims of a high-tech work environment. They were educated as accountants, managers, marketers, financial analysts, or engineers, or in other professional collegiate programs. A highly skilled secretary was once always available to correct writing, grammar, or spelling errors. Those days have ended. Now managers must compose their own letters, memos, reports, or proposals on a PC. Even if secretarial help is available, managers cannot always rely on the current generation of secretaries for rewriting or corrections. In a heightened competitive environment, engineers, accountants, and attorneys also are finding that they must learn how to take highly technical information and write clear, concise reports that are understandable and salable to clients. Another aspect of the technology revolution is that managers receive more messages, not fewer, in a variety of formats that must be read and understood, and then communicated throughout their organization.

As American business looks to overseas markets for expansion, it has become necessary for managers to possess some degree of fluency in a foreign language and local business customs to achieve successful business penetration. Global leadership development is often held back by major roadblocks in corporate communication. Prior to the 1980s, typical U.S. executives had not given serious consideration to a foreign language as part of their personal education for the business world. A recent study of 320 high-level U.S. executives now working in the Pacific Rim and Western Europe indicated that 82 percent received no training in foreign business practices. Only 15 percent were given any language training. The Columbia University Graduate School of Business indicates that, by the year 2000, there will be a significant shortage of U.S. managers equipped to run global businesses.

At present many business schools at universities across America are offering specialization for international business. This writer was discussing the leadership issues with a current business graduate student. She informed me that she was conversant in four languages: Spanish,

French, Italian, and Greek! Even though this is an encouraging development, it will take at least a decade before there are adequate numbers of university-trained, entry-level international business executives. Until then American business must marshal its own internal training resources to master the global leadership competitive challenge. Increasingly, organizations are using individual coaching in skill/educational programs for professionals and managers.

The Medium Must Have a Message

As accounting firms have begun to competitively market their services, the writing skills of CPAs have come under increased client scrutiny. The jargon and acronyms of the accounting profession often create an unintelligible audit report, document, or "annual accounting letter" for the client's board of directors. Besides their technical inscrutability, these documents are often boring, with little variation in basic analysis from year to year. Until recently, few college schools of accounting offered students a serious business writing program. CPAs, until the current era, had little opportunity or inclination to practice improving their writing skills. More than one CPA has admitted to this writer that being able to avoid writing projects in college (i.e., term papers) was one reason why they chose accounting as a profession.

Such communication practices have caused some accounting firms to lose clients to competitors. Accountants must now be able to produce financial reports that are individually written, clear, concise, and punctuated with careful recommendations to improve corporate financial management.

Price Waterhouse, in Chicago, has worked with this writer in offering their CPAs an advanced written communication leadership program. Individual CPAs were trained by a writing specialist with a background in financial reports. The one-on-one skills training was conducted on site, with two 60-minute classes held each week for 10 weeks.

Each CPA's written reports were studied by the trainer prior to the program. The accounting firm selected specific examples of "model letters" as course goals. These documents paralleled the firm's management perspective, tone, and accounting philosophy. These training modules were designed to diagnose specific writing weaknesses and undertake individual skill improvements to attain the firm's writing standards. Personal allowances were made for the individual writing style of the CPA. This advanced written communication program was used as individual needs were identified by Price Waterhouse for continuing professional education.

Many other organizations also adopted this leadership communication skills format. An executive in U.S. Gypsum's data support area was given training to improve her writing skills. A staff trainer at the Hartmarx Corporation was given a specialized tutorial to write inhouse training programs. This program included proofreading and self-editing techniques. Other executives at Santa Fe Railroad and Carson Pirie Scott & Company (retailer) were tutored one-on-one in communication programs that assessed their specific writing needs and incorporated practice with appropriate company job-related writing assignments.

The engineers of a large container corporation and Metra, Chicagoland's commuter railroad, participated in a technical writing program. These communication programs resolved the growing problem of helping these technical professionals improve their communications with other non-engineering staff.

A technical writing professional offered these communication skills on a 1:5 basis to sharpen these engineers' writing skills for clarity, vocabulary usage (nontechnical), conciseness, and organization. The principles of effective technical writing were practiced with typical business memos, reports, and letters for internal use or client correspondence.

We have repeatedly trained managers and professionals who had already attended group writing-skill seminars. Even though some of these seminars were conducted over several sessions, there was little time to practice writing, critique the result, and try again. In addition to addressing writing standards, the goal of a successful business communication program is the acquisition, review, and application of problem-solving and thinking skills to written communication.

Internal Communication—At Home

Since the 1980s large numbers of foreign students have attended U.S. universities for their professional and technical education. Many have stayed to work for American companies as mid- and upper-level management employees. On the whole, they have exceptional business/technical abilities and read English well. But their ability to speak, understand, and write in contemporary American English is often inadequate. Organizations such as W.W. Granger, Morton International, Tellabs, Inc., and Continental Can have helped engineers or executives improve their interpersonal and group communication skills on the job. Specialized industry vocabulary and specific common written documents were included in the customized one-on-one tutorials.

Both American and Japanese companies are relocating Japanese and other foreign nationals for "tours of duty" within the United States. Though the average overseas executive's prior foreign language training is considerably more advanced than his American counterpart, these managers often arrive at an American company at an unacceptable English-fluency level. Motorola, Panasonic, and Honda offered one-on-one tutorials for these managers, and in some instances their entire families. ESL training increased proficiency in spoken English, identified pronunciation problems, and dealt with related idiomatic business expressions.

Internal Communication—Overseas

In the 1990s globalization became a driving force for U.S. business. Any company that needs to export its products or services had better get busy improving its communication skills in order to remain healthy and profitable.

As the world marketplace continues to merge overseas corporations with their American operations, it is now necessary for American executives to function effectively in languages other than English. Few corporate training programs are geared to teach foreign languages applied to a specific industry's vocabulary and terminology.

Indramat, headquartered in Frankfurt, Germany, is an automotive engineering and manufacturing company with U.S. operations in Chicago's northwest suburbs. Engineers in the American office needed German for their telephone conversations, written correspondence, or face-to-face business negotiations with their Frankfurt counterparts. The training was given through small tutorial groups of five engineers led by a German-language trainer using appropriate materials. Grammar, vocabulary, and usage were specifically linked to content areas of automotive engineering and manufacturing. Twenty class modules were used, built one on another, until the individual engineer reached the proficiency level required by his/her job assignment. This leadership communication program was conducted over a two-year period with more than 40 participating engineers.

Another international business application is the preparation of corporate marketing or management staff for overseas operations. Motorola conducted French language training for overseas marketing assignments. This small-group tutorial emphasized those language skills needed to conduct negotiations in the electronic industry.

A sales manager at NutraSweet (Deerfield, Illinois) worked in South America and spoke excellent Spanish. However, he needed to rapidly acquire advanced Portuguese language abilities. Because of tight scheduling and travel, classes were conducted on a one-on-one basis and made extremely flexible. The curriculum also made use of specialized Portuguese training tapes to be used while traveling.

In similar circumstances other NutraSweet marketers learned Spanish for their South American operations. One manager was even trained in Chilean-dialect Spanish. All of these foreign-language leadership communication programs necessitated precise individualization for the company's products and a shortened time frame to achieve the fluency required by the job.

A vice-president of international sales at Newly Weds Foods (Chicago) received one-on-one French language training to assist in business negotiations. Although this executive also used a French interpreter, he had felt out of touch when French was being spoken.

Europeans in business can generally speak some English. However, many will naturally begin a business discussion in their own language. Any visiting American business representative should at least make an attempt at using the local language and following accepted local business customs. Americans traveling abroad have often told us that if they make a sincere effort to speak their hosts' language, even imperfectly, their hosts will use enough English to conclude the negotiations successfully. Greater personal foreign-language fluency brings enhanced long-term business results and success in the global marketplace.

Closing the leadership communication gap will improve personal performance for many more managers. Technology does not replace the need for human interaction. The bottom-line productivity message: there can be no substitute for developing better interpersonal communication skills—whether written or oral—to win the competitive battles of global business in this century or the next.[9]

Workforce Education Diversity

Some employees who have been enrolled in workforce education programs are using a Rapid Learning Program® that maximizes performance improvement. This audience has included attorneys, accountants, engineers, executives, managers, supervisors, legal secretaries, administrative assistants, office support staff, and production and service workers, as well as technical trainees. The skill content areas for these programs include reading, math, writing, English as a second language, foreign languages, and office practice skills (see Figure 6-6).

For more details on these programs, consult the Workforce Education series co-authored by this writer, which includes *Enhancing Learning in Training and Adult Education* (1998), *FutureWork, The Revolution Reshaping American Business* (1994), and *Closing the Literacy Gap in American Business* (1991).

The past 20 years has seen an increase in the diversity of businesses across America that have established workforce education as part of their management strategy for increased productivity and profit. They are winning the skill wars by investing in their human capital. Here are some brief program snapshots from a cross-section of small to large businesses across North America:

Allied Signal—Aerospace manufacturing (Arizona, California, Connecticut, Maryland, New Jersey). Worker retraining program to upgrade the skills of defense workers for a high-performance workplace, including quality, customer relations, technical, and occupational training.

Dudels Manufacturing—Metal fabricating (Chicago, Illinois). Workforce education in ESL, shop math, measurements, and recordkeeping for SPC.

Elco Industries, Inc.—Fastener manufacturer (Rockford, Illinois). The Elco "Learning Resources Catalog" offers more than 60 courses ranging from reading and ESL to computer training,

COMPANY	POPULATION TUTORED					
	Professionals	Managers	Office Support	Production	Service	Technical
Angus Chemical Co.			X			
Christ Hospital			X			
Clorox				X		
Continental Can	X^a					X^b
Courtyards by Mariott					X	
First National Bank of Chicago	X					
FMC Corporation			X			
Fox Secretarial College			X			
Homequity			X			
Indramat	X					X
KDK Job Training Service			X^a	X^c	X^c	
Mariott Residence Inn					X	
Metra Railroad	X^a				X^c	X
Morton International		X^a	X^b			
Motorola	X^a	X^c	X^c			X
Newly Weds Foods		X				
Northern Trust	X					
Nutrasweet		X				
Premark International			X			
Price Waterhouse	X					
Sante Fe Railroad		X				
Schless Construction		X	X			
Tellabs		X				
U.S. Gypsum		X				
W. W. Grainger		X				

Figure 6-6 IIP Workplace Programs Overview
Source: Imperial Consulting Corporation, Oak Lawn, Illinois.
Notations a,b,c pairs "Population Tutored" to "Tutoring Content" for end program.

COMPANY	TUTORING CONTENT					
	Reading	Math	Writing	ESL	Foreign Language	Office Practice
Angus Chemical Co.			X			X
Christ Hospital						X
Clorox	X	X				
Continental Can			X[c]	X[a]		
Courtyards by Mariott	X	X		X		
First National Bank of Chicago			X	X		
FMC Corporation			X			
Fox Secretarial College	X	X	X			
Homequity			X			
Indramat					X	
KDK Job Training	X[c]	X[c]		X[c]		
Mariott Residence Inn	X	X		X		
Metra Railroad	X[c]	X[c]	X[a]	X[c]		
Morton International			X[c]	X[a]		
Motorola	X[c]		X[c]	X[a]	X[b]	
Newly Weds Foods					X	
Northern Trust	X					
Nutrasweet					X	
Premark International			X			
Price Waterhouse			X	X		
Sante Fe Railroad			X			
Schless Construction			X			
Tellabs				X		
U.S. Gypsum			X			
W. W. Grainger				X		

Figure 6-6 Continued

from specific machine skills to leadership and managing change. Some courses are provided one-to-one, others are in class groups. Self-study and computer-based training are also used. Elco spends about 1 percent of payroll on 12,000–15,000 hours of training annually (12 hours/person). It is working to reach a future goal of 20 hours of instruction per employee.

Hampden Papers—Paper products (Holyoke, Massachusetts). Skills training program in English as a second language, GED classes, and tuition assistance for technical schools and college courses related to the workplace. One and a half percent of its payroll is budgeted annually to send its workers to school.

Hardy Industries—Automobile accessories (Portland, Oregon). Teamwork and educational skills training in reading, writing, math, algebra, participatory skills, quality, problem-solving, and company-paid tuition courses.

Institute for Career Development—Steel industry (Indiana). More than $24 million invested by 14 steel companies in worker basic-skill enhancements, technical-skills training, personal development, and tuition assistance.

Lumonics, Inc.—Laser, laser-based systems (Kanates, Ontario, Canada). In 1990 began English as a second language program. Workplace Language Program addresses oral communication, team participation, problem-solving, reading, and writing. ISO 9001 and TQM leadership training are also offered.

MacLean-Fogg Company—Car parts supplier (Mundelein, Illinois). BASE Program enrolls about 8 percent of employees in reading, writing, math, and ESL classes. Every employee also receives 20 hours of job training per year (approximately 400,000 hours of training). Tuition reimbursement is given for college courses.

Methodist Medical Center—Health care (Peoria, Illinois). Education programs have been a long-standing tradition at this hospital. Programs include ESL, math, reading, and GED.

Motorola University—Employees, suppliers, and customers take quality-related courses that cover such topics as statistical process control (SPC), customer satisfaction, problem solving, and benchmarking. More than $120 million annually is invested to train Motorola's 120,000+ employees.

Navistar International—Truck components (Waukesha, Wisconsin). Education Center since 1988 offers instruction in educational skills: writing, reading, ESL, math, computers; site-specific training: blueprint reading, SPC, founding applications, QS 9000; personal enrichment; career education: GED, college prep.

Warner Lambert Company—Confectionery manufacturing facility (Rockford, Illinois). One-to-one skills tutoring programs for workers. Established in 1989, it has been expanded each year.

Will-Burt Co.—Auto parts, metal fabricating (Ohio). Since 1985 a company-wide workplace education program offering courses in blueprint reading, geometry, SPC, leadership, creativity, self-esteem, logic, a mini MBA program, and many other quality-training areas.[10]

Smith & Wesson—Firearms manufacturer (Springfield, Massachusetts). All 676 front-line workers were assessed in math and reading. For more than three years, classes were held on company time to improve attendance. Each class of up to 15 employees met four times a week for an hour each day. ESL classes were also provided. The results? Smith & Wesson sees a continuing need to ensure that new workers are ready and able to use state-of-the-art manufacturing techniques (see Figure 6-7).[11]

The Age of the "Knowledge-Based Business"

Sir Graham Day, former chairman of Rover, in an address to the Canada–United Kingdom Chamber of Commerce, typified the entire English-speaking world as "an educational achievement problem." Rover initiated its own workforce education program, called Rover Learning Business, after Day discovered that his best assembly-line workers were unable to learn statistical process control. Rover's program offers everything from remedial English and math to job-skills enhancement and college-tuition reimbursements.

Smith & Wesson Workforce Education Program Results

In support of the claim that basic skills classes have helped them do their job better, students wrote the following comments in response to the question, "What is the most important thing you do better at work because of this class?"

- I can read charts on the boards that I couldn't understand before.
- I read the ISO book better.
- The most important thing I do better is read the bulletin board more often.
- I feel more confident about writing notes for second shift.
- I can write work orders and better communicate with people.
- I can use fractions and decimals better.
- Helps me feel more comfortable speaking at the meeting I have every morning.
- It's easier to talk to my team.
- Better communication with my supervisor.
- I communicate with my supervisor.
- I use the computer a little better.
- I've learned how to write about machine problems.
- I'm not afraid to write a note because my spelling got better.
- I can chart statistical process control better.
- Better problem solving with math.

Figure 6-7 Smith & Wesson Workforce Education Program Results
Source: Adapted from *ASTD Technical Training*

"It is important for you to know, " Day told his audience, "that the commitment to education and training by Rover had nothing whatsoever to do with altruism or social responsibility. It had everything to do with Rover's survival and the enhancement of its future prospects."[12]

Education is a big deal at Driv-Lok, a 138-worker small manufacturing company 60 miles west of Chicago. About 3 percent of its $4.5 million payroll is spent on a workforce education program that contains everything from engineering, to computer design, to critical thinking, to basic math. At any time about 15 employees are being reimbursed for their college courses.

It was pointed out to Driv-Lok President W.E. "Bud" Duffey that sending his workers to class costs money. "So?" Duffey replied, with an intimidating pause. "It costs money to ship rejects back, too." But if his workers became more highly trained, he'd have to pay them more. "That is the least of my worries," Duffey said. "Pay them more, they'll produce more."[13]

Duffey's thinking has been confirmed by two employment studies. The University of Washington in its survey of 544 employers in Washington State found that an increase in the complexity of many jobs will require more training for workers to obtain greater skills in the low-wage labor market.[14] The American Society for Training and Development (ASTD) in a study of employers training (1997) also addressed the issue that such training is often not provided because of the fear of high turnover of low-wage workers. ASTD discovered just the opposite effect was true. The more training offered to these employees, the greater was the likelihood of their staying with the same employer. Why is this happening? The high-performance workplace is now yielding to the coming of the knowledge-based business: people know they need to learn more and remain employable as jobs rapidly change.

Stan Davis and Jim Botkin in the *Harvard Business Review* (September/October, 1994) prophesied that the next wave of economic growth is coming from businesses in which increasing employee knowledge drives performance, productivity, and profit:

> *Knowledge is doubling about every seven years, and in technical fields in particular, half of what students learn in their first year of college is obsolete by the time they graduate. In the labor force, the need to keep pace with technological change is felt even more acutely. For companies to remain competitive, and for workers to stay employable, they must continue to learn. . . . Business more than government, is instituting the changes in education that are required for the emerging knowledge-based economy. . . . Over the next few decades, the private sector will eclipse the public sector as our predominate educational institution.*[15]

Only at great peril can management continue to ignore the workplace as an arena that broadens and deepens the need for learning. An impetus for change is building that challenges many current management practices. This review of workforce education shows how innovative businesses have already established programs that develop the knowledge and skills of people at all levels in their organizations. These employees aren't just learning more—they're working smarter to improve how they work, and thinking more about innovations that can be applied to their work and in their lives.

CHAPTER

7

A Message from the Competition

The demands created by advancing technology require increased levels of knowledge, skills and understanding to achieve a basic education. Workforce education is a means of acquiring the understanding and ability necessary to improve living and working conditions.

INTERNATIONAL COUNCIL FOR ADULT EDUCATION

World Workforce Skills Challenge

American business managers grumble, "Why are only U.S. workers falling victim to the 'skills gap' opened by advancing high-tech?" The answer may surprise you. America is not alone. In 1980 the European Parliament reported that the functional illiteracy rate among the member nations of the European Community (EC) (including Great Britain, France, Germany, Belgium, Denmark, Ireland, and the Netherlands) stood at 4 to 6 percent. This means that 10 to 15 million European adults possess an educational-ability level lower than that of a 13-year-old student. The same report placed the functional education rate of southern Europe even lower, at an astounding 24 percent.[1]

Since then this skills gap has only widened. A 1997 report sponsored by the Organization for Economic Cooperation and Development (OECD) from the International Adult Literacy Survey (IALS) covered Europe, Canada, New Zealand, and the United States. It showed big skill gaps in every country. On a 1- to 5-point scale, at least one-quarter of the adult population fails to reach a minimal skills levels for high-performance-workplace employment. Level 3 is regarded by many experts as the basic level of competence needed to cope adequately with the complex demands of everyday life and work.

The United States has a large number of adults at levels 1 and 2 on all scales (i.e., those who do not meet even minimal skill standards). Fortunately, there are also many Americans at level 4/5. What this means is that a tremendous skills gap exists in American society between the best educated and over 40 percent of the population that are in danger of becoming the new techno-peasants of the information age. Among the world's industrialized nations the United States has a greatest concentration of adults who are at the lowest levels of literacy.[2]

As the statistics show, American business is not alone in its dilemma over the low educational levels of its workforce. There is not a single Western industrialized nation that sees its education and worker-training programs as up to the demands of twenty-first-century productivity. William E. Nothdurft, in a Brookings Institution study in 1989, found that the industrialized economies of Western Europe are struggling with the same workforce education issues. However, there is considerable evidence that several are succeeding in educating for higher worker productivity, making economies grow faster, and lowering poverty rates and unemployment. Is there any common principle behind these results? In these nations, business, labor, and government have reached a consensus that investment in their population's human development is a fundamental economic necessity. This has not always been the case in Europe's history.

In 1851 a London industrial exhibition caused grave concern in the elegant boardrooms of some major English manufacturers. American products were stealing the show. They were mass-produced at high levels of quality with interchangeable parts and sold at a competitive price. These American products upset the British industrialists' belief that their world economic dominance was unassailable. The English conducted a personal fact-finding tour and learned that the American secret was not better machinery or process innovations, but a higher level of basic worker education. The New England industrial heartland of the day boasted a 95 percent literacy rate, compared with only 66 percent in Great Britain. Over the next 150 years, England never closed this worker talent gap. This was a decisive contributing factor to Britain's long decline as the world's foremost industrial power.

The fundamental issue of global competitiveness has led to a contemporary European consensus on developing strong training/

education systems, including specific preparation for work. Unlike Europe, America lacks a nationwide consensus on these issues of workforce competencies and business-sponsored programs to ensure that school graduates are ready, willing, and able to enter and remain in the world of work successfully. Even though the diversity of the workforce in the United States dwarfs the problems faced by our European competitors, we share with Europe many common economic, political, and cultural values. We can learn much by listening to this message from the competition.

A Sleeping Giant Awakes

We now interrupt "the American century" with this news bulletin from The Netherlands Foreign Investment Agency:

> *Holland's workforce is one of its strongest business assets, embodying an extraordinary combination of language and technical skills, know-how, discipline, work ethic, and "can do" attitude. We have about the highest productivity as measured by relative unit labor costs in manufacturing in the European Union. English is virtually a second language. Government policy and spending forge strong links between education and industry. Thirteen universities and more than 100 technical institutes train the management and staff you need in Computer Implemented Manufacturing, telecom, biotech, med-tech, information processing, office automation, software, and microelectronics.*

This compelling portrayal of its workforce by a small member of the European Union must be recognized as a direct, legitimate challenge to the future profitability of American business. What's more, this competitive message is being trumpeted again and again by other nations in Europe and Asia. These trends will only accelerate. American business must meet the international workforce education challenge or face a grim future of declining market share, lower profits, and a substantial lowering of our overall standard of living.

All industrialized nations in the world face the challenge of producing quality products and services—at a competitive price. Until the 1970s, American industry was successfully meeting this challenge in nearly all sectors. The United States emerged from World War II with the world's premier industrial base. It did not have to worry much about human resources with an enormous population and a steady influx of immigrants. Meanwhile, Europe and Japan took advantage of the need to rebuild a destroyed industry with state-of-the-art machinery. Of course, this would not have been possible without the help of American human capital, especially the Marshall Plan. However, unnoticed even by the experts, Europe and Japan at the same time were developing their *human capital*.

The Japanese and Europeans invested heavily in systematic industrial education and training programs. Modern and well-equipped schools and training centers arose everywhere. In the United States, however, vocational high schools were dismantled and degraded under the guise of providing every student an "equal opportunity" to obtain a college education. Americans have forgotten the basic economic premise that capital and manpower cannot exist separately, but belong inextricably together. Now, America is paying for this neglect and awakening to the need for investment in a systematic approach to manpower development from elementary school onward.

At present all over Europe and Asia, new tech programs and initiatives are arising and growing. The same trend is emerging in the United States. However, many American initiatives are sporadic and lack a consensus on theoretical foundations and practical methods. As well as wasting precious time, America is wasting the talents of the majority of its children who will not ever complete college. Much energy and money could be saved if Americans would study and adapt the experiences of other nations.

Many of our foreign competitors developed a system of industrial education that is not limited to classic production industries, but also includes modern service businesses. It integrates centuries of experience and new scientific insights in teaching methods and logistic processes. These insights are already fruitful in pre-vocational programs during the elementary years (e.g., basic skill development through arts and crafts for all children). They are consistently applied in all apprenticeship and training programs throughout the European Union.

Here, too, the assumption of educators is that skills and positive work characteristics cannot be separated. This principle has served as a base for highly effective training programs. Quality products require not only skills, but also positive behavior patterns (they used to be called "virtues"), such as reliability, punctuality, and accuracy. We know that neither skills nor personal characteristics can be simply acquired, but must be absorbed over time. It is easier to develop both skills and behavior patterns in younger individuals, but it is still possible with older trainees. There will be no lasting effect, however, when these two are separated.

It will be a long way back, but the United States is again on the right track toward regaining its previously vaunted "American work ethic." We now realize that even the smallest training program must consider the inseparable components of financial capital and human capital, and of skills and work characteristics.[3]

Europe Is Back

Since the end of the Cold War with the fall of the Soviet Union in 1992, Americans have begun thinking of themselves as "the last remaining superpower." We are Numero Uno, "top banana," Mr. Big. Yet just when we weren't looking, there has been a fundamental shift in the world arena: Europe is back.

After fighting two devastating world wars, the microeconomies of Europe (an exception being Germany's huge $1.45 trillion GDP) are embarking through the European Union (EU) on creating a new Europe. In two bold moves toward a truly continental economy, 11 of the EU's 15 member states have launched a common currency with a fire sale on their old bank notes. And in a second step, overcoming centuries of distrust, the western EU members have begun the process of bringing a handful of former East Bloc nations into the EU fold.

Across Europe millions of people and thousands of businesses are benefiting from the huge new European single market. The removal of frontiers inside the European Union in 1993 is now a fact of life. Companies have entered new markets, have struck up transnational partnerships, and have restructured production to exploit the opportunities of a unified European home market of 370 million people. Most European borders now resemble state lines in America. Even national flags have been replaced by a circle of 15 stars on a blue field, the European Community (EC) symbol, with the welcoming nation's name inside.[4]

The United States experienced a similar economic integration in the 1880s and 1890s driven by two major factors. After the Civil War the federal government began issuing a national currency to replace the confusing array of individual state bank notes valued at different levels. This unified single national currency gave a boost to interstate commerce.

The railroads completed the process. By 1869 a golden spike created the first transcontinental railroad and signaled a railway boom from 35,000 miles in 1865 to more than five times as much in 1890, more than in all of Europe. By the 1870s a refrigerated carload of California fruits and vegetables could be shipped to the Eastern markets. These spectacular achievements helped create unparalleled productivity and competitiveness. By 1900 the United States was a major world economic and exporting powerhouse.

The EU and its unified markets are now recreating these same favorable economic conditions. In terms of international weight the new European "Euro" will be second only to the U.S. dollar. The gross domestic product (GDP) of the Euro-11 countries will be roughly the same as America's. But their share of international trade will be larger (see Figure 7-1). In the future we also can expect EU international companies to establish more and more overseas production platforms in the United States and around the globe.[5]

Europe's single market has several major flaws. One is that European labor mobility is thwarted by linguistic and cultural differences; in contrast, Americans generally perceive no barriers in moving from

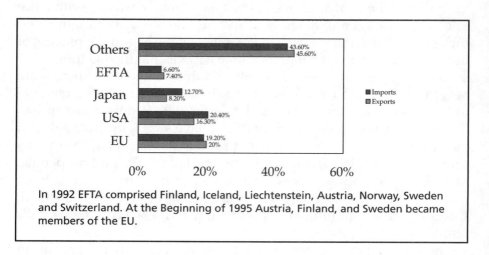

In 1992 EFTA comprised Finland, Iceland, Liechtenstein, Austria, Norway, Sweden and Switzerland. At the Beginning of 1995 Austria, Finland, and Sweden became members of the EU.

Figure 7-1 Share of World Trade—1993

Source: Adapted from Organization for Economic Cooperation and Development (OECD) 1996

state to state in search of a new job or a better life. The second issue is the still-strong instinct of national self-interest. In almost every industry each national government still seeks to protect its own commerce with layers of red tape.

The 1992 Maastricht Treaty that created the European Union (EU) addressed both of these issues by establishing European transnational general education and career–vocational educational programs. The EU recognizes the primary responsibility of each member state for the organization of its educational system. However, the EU's task is to promote cooperation among its member states through Europe-wide programs that supplement individual national measures.

The decline of the "rust-belt" industries has brought economic and social havoc to many parts of Europe. New technology along with the globalization of markets has had an even bigger impact on Europe's less diversified microeconomies than it has in the United States. Areas that were at the forefront of the nineteenth-century Industrial Revolution, such as Newcastle in the United Kingdom or the Ruhr Valley in Germany, have suffered unemployment in the 1980s and 1990s that ranged from 12 to 20 percent of the workforce.

To help revive the general European economy and reduce unemployment, the EU launched a number of cross-border programs centered on training, education, and youth. Collaborative projects have been launched through student exchange programs and networks drawing participants from many sectors such as employers, unions, government, universities, youth organizations, and other educational agencies. These include such programs as Erasmus, Lingua, Petra, Comett, Force, and Adapt (see Figure 7-2 for more details).

These EU programs recognize the importance of high-quality initial education and post-school learning opportunities. Successful career education should help young people move from school to work, and help them retain what they have learned through work opportunities that use their knowledge and develop appropriate skills. This transformation process becomes the linchpin of a lifelong learning process, rather than just "getting through" a schooling process associated with youth.

This strategy for lifelong learning requires active collaboration among a wide range of players. The Organization for Economic Cooperation and Development (OECD) has outlined the strategies

Program/Initiative	*Target Audience*
ERASMUS	Promote student exchange among higher education institutions (180,000 students by 1994).
LINGUA	Improve knowledge of foreign languages in vocational education, and business personnel.
PETRA	Two-year vocational program after "high school" featuring cross border joint training projects.
COMETT	Cooperative programs between business and higher education.
FORCE	Preparing training staff and training employees in quality and other performance issues.
ADAPT	Retraining for 600,000 unemployed.

Figure 7-2 European Union Training/Education Programs
Source: Education and Training, Commission of the EU, Brussels, 1991.

needed to help make this process work (see Figure 7-3). The European Union and its 15 member states have long experimented to secure a better relationship between education/training and the labor market.

A 1995 European Business Survey by Grant Thornton International reported that 16 percent of employees received training from their business (see Figure 7-4). There was great variation between nations, the Scandinavian countries reporting the highest level, 35 percent, and Italy the lowest, at less than 10 percent.

As a whole, service-sector companies invested more in training for a higher proportion of their staff than manufacturing or construction businesses. Technical and operations training were reported by 59 percent of all organizations. Forty-nine percent of all training was in sales and marketing. Sixty-four percent of smaller companies trained their employees, compared to 81 percent of all mid-sized and larger businesses.

Individual countries reported that same ranking of training subjects (see Figure 7-5) though the UK and Finland conduct more general management training. France, Italy, Switzerland. and Luxembourg offer less training in sales and marketing. The training of secre-

Assessment	
Goal:	A smooth transition to work.
Means:	Apprenticeship-Type System Develop an education and training partnership between the schools, the government at all levels, and the occupational society. Make certifications portable between different working and learning environments. Provide workplace-based vocational programs as a major part of the upper secondary education system. Align on a nationwide level curricula, assessments, and certifications with the occupationally-based structure of the labor market that young people enter. Have the occupational society not only support but take an active hand in designing, implementing, and managing the system. Provide workers with the capacity to learn continuously throughout their lives.
Cost	$4,700–7,300 per student per year (1993 dollars)
Allocation	• Partnership between Government, Education, and Employers • Portable Graduate Certification • Workplace-based Vocational Programs • Nationwide Alignment of Standards and Curricula with Entry-Level Jobs • Continuing Education Programs
Implementation:	Public/Private The occupational society, jointly with all levels of government and the education system, develop and implement a nationwide structure with regional variations.
Assessment:	The Organization for Economic Cooperation and Development's assessment demonstrates lower ratios of youth to adult unemployment in nations with strong apprenticeship work-based vocational education systems —Denmark, Germany, Austria, and the Netherlands.

Figure 7-3 Economy and Jobs/Preparation for Life and Work
Source: Adapted from Organization for Economic Cooperation and Development (OECD).

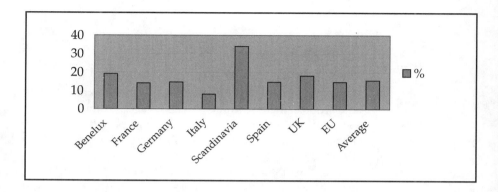

Figure 7-4 Proportion of Staff for Whom Training is Paid
Source: Adapted from "European Business Survey," Grant Thornton,
International Business Strategies, Ltd., Spring 1995.

tarial and clerical workers is more prevalent in France, the Nether-lands, Belgium, and Spain.

Companies reported that 72 percent had supported some form of business education (see Figure 7-6). This ranged from secondary school to postsecondary undergraduate, graduate, and postgraduate education.[6]

Let us look at some of these messages from the competition and what ideas the United States might apply.

The German Model: Will It Pay in America?

In a Hamburg classroom a group of 18-year-olds sit reviewing the con-cepts of double-entry bookkeeping. In the next room their classmates monitor bubbling chemistry experiments in a well-equipped science lab. These are scenes from a secondary school in Western Europe. However, these students are not in a school building, but in class-rooms at a company, Beiersdorf (producer of Nivea face cream). Their instructors are Beiersdorf employees. When the classes change, the ac-counting students will attend chemistry class (among other subjects) at Beiersdorf and the chemistry students will study accounting.[7]

In the German Dual System, schools and industry are cooperating with the government to prepare about 70 percent of high-school-age youth for the world of work. There are more than 370 specific careers

Country	% Who Train	General Management	Sales & Marketing	Technical Operations	Clerical/Secretarial	Other
Belgium	76	28	47	66	44	11
Denmark	60	23	49	46	31	22
France	82	13	36	61	46	14
Germany	71	30	55	59	30	13
Greece	78	36	50	53	26	10
Ireland	73	40	62	61	38	7
Italy	33	28	37	54	23	12
Luxembourg	75	14	33	72	35	14
Netherlands	54	28	51	63	46	13
Portugal	59	33	57	55	9	20
Spain	53	16	53	49	45	20
UK	76	45	53	68	39	13
EU Average	64	27	49	59	36	14
Austria	74	36	58	61	36	16
Finland	51	53	70	64	42	23
Malta	65	20	53	48	20	6
Sweden	83	30	48	47	43	19
Switzerland	61	23	35	67	38	12
Survey Average	65	28	49	59	36	14

Figure 7-5 Training over the Past Year and Subjects Covered (%)
Source: Adapted from Grant Thornton, 1995.

Country	With Business Education	Pre-University	Graduate	Post-Graduate
Belgium	72	37	50	25
Denmark	93	35	40	9
France	56	36	53	11
Germany	85	10	69	23
Greece	85	10	69	23
Ireland	67	54	39	25
Italy	77	54	39	8
Luxembourg	71	37	56	15
Netherlands	71	34	58	8
Portugal	63	60	34	8
Spain	75	35	48	25
UK	56	49	38	23
EU Average	72	44	47	15
Austria	79	67	41	5
Finland	87	20	71	14
Malta	65	53	41	7
Sweden	75	43	42	16
Switzerland	76	69	25	12
Survey Average	72	44	46	15

Figure 7-6 Level of Formal Business Education (%)
Source: Adapted from Grant Thornton, 1995.

with accredited training programs and internationally recognized diplomas (the so-called "Journeyman's Certificate"). The government provides a portion of the funding, industry takes care of the practical training, and the schools are in charge of the theoretical and educational aspects. All three agencies are involved in the accreditation process, with the major responsibility staying with the specific trade associations.

Roland Wacker is an 18-year-old German enrolled at the Mercedes technical training center in Sindelfingen. He is in a high-quality apprenticeship program in which he is paid about $600 per month during his training. This program is a fast track to a high-tech adult job. Roland's academic studies are demanding, and they dovetail with the high-tech job training of the Mercedes-Benz apprenticeship. Because Mercedes takes the viewpoint that its training center is an investment in its next generation of employees, it has the most advanced technology in order to maximize what Roland can be taught.

The company's estimate of the full cost for Roland's apprenticeship is over $60,000. Can Mercedes believe it is getting its money's worth from this investment in human capital? "If you accept that this is an investment into possibly a lifetime's work, then it's an excellent investment. When they are through with their apprenticeship, you have really first-class specialist," asserts Helmut Werner, Mercedes' chairman.[8]

The German educational system encourages businesses to take a long-term view of training. Employers share with the government the cost of worker training. The business pays apprentices a small stipend and the government funds classroom instruction. In the 1990s German industry and government was investing about $15 billion annually in its apprenticeship training. To match this effort, the United States would need to expend roughly $60 billion.

Training youth is accepted as the price of operating in Germany. Motorola has its most productive/profitable and expensive manufacturing operations in Germany. In 1997 Motorola announced a $1 billion expansion of these facilities. Why? Because of high consistent employee performance. The German economy today is productive largely because of one outstanding factor: a highly skilled labor force. In the case of Motorola and much of German industry, the strength of this asset more than offsets some major disadvantages, such as some of the world's highest labor costs and income-tax rates that per hour are 60 percent higher than in the United States.[9]

For decades Germany's best companies have remained profitable by keeping operations simple, avoiding diversification, and focusing on the core skills that make employees productive. The rest of the world is now only beginning to learn these lessons as Germany exports its operating wisdom around the world.

Herman Simon in *Hidden Champions* (1996) uncovered how Trumpf, the world's seventh-largest machine-tool maker in terms of sales, is number one in Germany with only 3,100 workers: concentrating on the continuous skill-education of its people. Berthold Leibringer, CEO of Trumpf, describes this operating wisdom:

Our numerically controlled machines are serviced solely through employees of Trumpf Japan. The importance of training our Japanese employees cannot be overemphasized. Continuous contacts between the parent company and Trumpf Japan guarantee that each service technician in Japan is always up to date and has access to the most recent information. Our own manufacturing operation in Japan allows us to make spare parts available within forty-eight hours. This wouldn't be possible if they had to be shipped from Germany.

Thinking Early about Careers

The German primary school curriculum gives all children the opportunity to develop their technical aptitudes through hands-on tasks on units. They and their parents also receive information on 343 defined occupational tracks. General aptitude and skills testing is also given each child to guide them in their potential career interests. At about the age of 10, the German family must choose one of three school tracks for their child (see Figure 7-7):

1. Grammar School (Gymnasium)

2. Intermediate Comprehensive School (Realschule)

3. General School (Hauptschule)

If the children choose the Gymnasium, this means they will attend a university. The other two schools lead to an earlier career. However, reforms in this German system now allow children to switch from one track to another by taking additional courses.

During the 1980s and most of the 1990s about 25 percent of children went to the university and 70 percent pursued education for a career-entry certificate. This certificate is only issued after the comple-

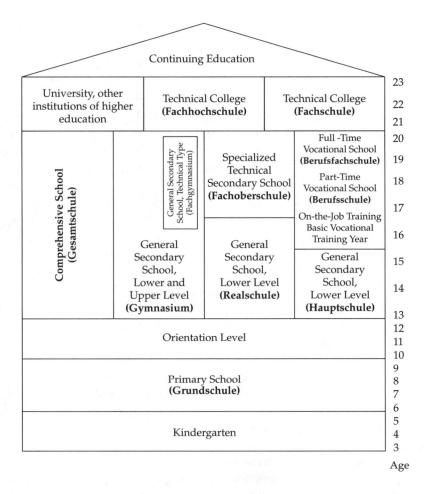

Figure 7-7 Structure of the German Educational System
Source: Courtesy of Federal Republic of Germany

tion of a comprehensive apprenticeship program that is built around a "dual system": classroom instruction and on-the-job training. Students must attend school full-time for nine years. They then sign a "contract" to complete a three-and-a-half-year training program.

The real backbone of the dual system is a business culture that supports a major commitment by industry. The student is expected to find an employer who will support his or her apprenticeship. The student then signs a contract that entitles him to a small monthly stipend, classroom training, and technical on-the-job educational experiences.

Each of the 16 German states implements the dual system in different ways. Helmut Schaible is the director of the Robert-Bosch-Schule Technical Training Center in Ulm, located in the state of Baden-Württemberg in southwestern Germany (see Figure 7-8). He heads this huge 3,000-student technical training center in a city that was the home of Albert Einstein, Count von Zeppelin (inventor of the lighter than-air-rigid airships), and World War II's famous commander Field Marshal Erwin Rommel.

Helmut told me that school class time varies in the 16 German states from 8 to 13 hours per week. Baden-Württemberg is the only 13-hour state. He maintains that the school needs more time because theory is becoming more complicated. This represents about 45 percent of the educational program; the rest is practice, with equipment located right in the classroom. The Ulm technical training center is one of three such schools in this state. Baden-Württenberg has a multitude of smaller high-tech businesses. As a result much of the student's technical training is done at the Ulm center rather than on-site at the business.

Many different career occupational opportunities are offered by these businesses to students. This diversification is not necessarily the situation in other German states. In Hamburg much of the heavy industry has disappeared and has not yet been replaced by other businesses. As a result a high proportion of students choose to enter the university and avoid the dual system entirely.

There are other issues. Helmut spoke of the tensions between tradition and reality. The increasing cost of training has reduced some of the support by German industry. Workers and employers want broader career training for better job flexibility and mobility.

Major industrial associations are working with the state's 130 technical schools to update the integration of on-the-job training, company education, and traditional classes. Helmut points to the progress made over the past 10 years in combining technical areas (reducing them from 550+ to 343), thereby broadening career employment opportunities.

Whatever the shortcomings of the "dual system," Germany has been very successful in inculcating the values of teamwork and cooperation in most of their children. The popular culture of Germany has

Figure 7-8 Germany's 16 States
Source: Courtesy of Federal Republic of Germany.

forged strong links among parents, schools, and businesses. The bottom line is that the Germans have done a superior job in providing strong academic skills for more of their children. They have also made the content of elementary and secondary education relevant to the changing career needs of society.[10]

As a nation, Germany fits Michael Porter's description of leveraging an important competitive advantage:

> *There is little doubt that education and training are decisive in national competitive advantage. . . . Education and training constitute perhaps the single greatest long-term leverage point available to setting policies that link the educational system to industry and encourage industry's own efforts at training.*
>
> THE COMPETITIVE ADVANTAGE OF NATIONS (1990)

There is much for the United States to learn and adapt from this message from Germany. Stihl Co. (home office in Stuttgart), manufacturer of chainsaws, lawn blowers, and trimmers, established a plant in Virginia Beach, VA, in 1974. Originally, parts were shipped from abroad and assembled in the new plant. There was no problem in finding about 40 unskilled workers for the assembly line. However, a need soon arose for skilled craftsmen to update and replace the machinery that makes the precision parts for the chainsaws.

In Germany, Stihl uses only custom-made machinery. Designed and built in-house, not only are these machines more efficient, but the people who designed and built them are available immediately whenever problems arise. Thus, the running time of the machinery is close to 98 percent, with only short interruptions for maintenance.

Because of this success, Stihl decided to set up its own machine shop in Virginia. Unfortunately, the company was unable to find any local tool-and-die makers or other highly skilled craftsmen. Instead of importing labor from Germany, which would have been difficult and only a stopgap measure, the management decided to start a half-million-dollar training program in Virginia modeled on Germany's dual system of industrial training.

The curriculum goes beyond mere production skills. All related competencies are included. For example, the tool-and-die makers must take blueprint reading, electronics (CAD), welding, cost calculations, etc. On each level, the apprentices get the blueprints and the appropriate materials for each task. Once they have learned to use tools and machines, they can use any tool and machine in the shop for their projects, which are meticulously evaluated in terms of accuracy and quality. With Stihl products, for instance, a tolerance of 1/100 of a millimeter (ca. 4/10,00 of an inch) is the norm.

In Virginia Beach, the Stihl training program started with 35 apprentices. Four did not complete the program; five left for employment with other companies. However, incentives and fringe benefits usually keep the top people once they have completed their training. The case of a maintenance worker at the Stihl Virginia Beach plant is a good illustration. During his four-year apprenticeship, he accepted a pay cut, making only about $8.00 an hour. Two nights each week, he and his fellow apprentices attended the local community college. Stihl persuaded the college to adapt the curriculum to their needs, including using German standards for some of the apprentices' technical courses.

This program proved beneficial for all the parties involved: the community college, the students, and the employer. For instance, the former unskilled maintenance worker now makes about $50,000 a year crafting and maintaining machinery. Stihl also confirmed the experience of other German companies in the United States that such training programs are a good investment. It costs Stihl about $50,000 annually, for up to four years, to train an apprentice to build and maintain a machine. With 35 apprentices, this is still below the cost difference between a custom-built machine with maintenance, and one built and maintained by in-house personnel.

Within five years, Stihl became the biggest manufacturer in Virginia Beach, with close to 500 workers (there were 40 in 1974!). In spite of a depressed market (in 1981, the sales of chainsaws in America dropped 50 percent), no workers were laid off. In 1993, its revenue doubled to $200 million, and the production rate (power tools produced per worker) increased from 800 to 2,100.

Many of our competitors in western Europe are committed to the norm of lifelong learning for all employees. They don't see training as narrow skill applications or just on-the-job experiences. Instead, they invest 4 to 5 percent of their budgets on employee learning, supporting world-class quality standards such as ISO 9000 or the "6th sigma" approach of a 99.99 percent defect-free production rate. Unless America raises its training standards for more workers to these levels, how can we expect to compete successfully against the increasing pace of technological change in the world workplace?[11]

The British Lion Wakes Up

Britain's former Prime Minister John Major and the late Princess Diana have something in common: they, like 67 percent of all British youth, left school at age 16. Few school-leavers rise as high as Major or Diana. As a group, they are a key reason why the United Kingdom (UK) is losing its economic competitiveness to better-schooled nations.

"We are far behind other countries in training students for the job market," remarks Hilary Steedman, a researcher at Britain's National Institute of Economic and Social Research. "It's our most serious problem." According to a 1991 study by Steedman, productivity per worker is 22 percent higher in France and 45 percent higher in Germany and the Netherlands. Is it any wonder that UK auto, steel, and shipbuilding industries that were once world leaders went into a tailspin beginning in the 1950s?

Noble Effort

Not that Britain hasn't been trying to address this problem. In 1981, Margaret Thatcher's government embarked on the Youth Training Scheme (YTS). This initiative sought to create opportunities for employed and unemployed adults to expand, update, or strengthen their skills by providing trainees with a certified standard of skills, as well as encouraging young students to pursue formal education or training until at least age 18. The YTS program provided an average of 25 weeks of off-the-job training over a two-year period. This component was combined with on-the-job training and planned work experience. It was the intent of YTS to lead toward recognized vocational qualifications. Trainees received small training stipends and direct contact with the realities of the workplace. In 1989, 450,000 students were enrolled in YTS.

A Better Idea

In addition to this program, the Thatcher government launched the Technical and Vocational Education Initiative (TVEI) with the aim of increasing the creativity and problem-solving skills of students age 14 to 18. This program empowers managers and executives to act as curriculum advisors, tutors, and student mentors at local schools. An actual work experience is a central component to all TVEI programs.

Special vocational/technical courses also have been introduced in craft and design technology: art, design and graphic communications, business studies and information technologies, and technology sciences.

By 1987, TVEI programs were under way at nearly all "local education authorities" (i.e., school districts) in England, Scotland, and Wales. This program was considered so successful that, by 1992, it was mandated to be universally available in all secondary schools and for all students.

On the other hand, it was clear in 1994 that the YTS had never lived up to its billing. About half who enrolled in the program dropped out after the first six weeks! Consequently, this approach was scrapped in favor of a "modern apprenticeship" program that eventually will link up 150,000 school dropouts and private-sector employers. Employers get tax credits for joining the program. Apprentices get paid jobs.

Older workers, too, are being retrained in new technologies. One training organization, Mari, which specializes in retraining both unemployed adults and school dropouts, has established 28 offices across Britain offering training for information-technology occupations. As many as 2,000 trainees are now enrolled with Mari, with up to 20 percent in a work placement. Two-thirds of these trainees have never used computers!

In 1986, when Mari first offered adult retraining, ex-shipyard workers, crane operators, and welders were being trained in PC use and computer maintenance. "They surprised us with their ability to gain skills as PC users and in some cases, programmers," say Ann Cooper, a Mari group managing director (*London Times*, 1994).[12]

There were an estimated 15,500 apprenticeships throughout the United Kingdom in December 1995. These ranged from engineering (38 percent), to business services (17 percent), to retail and hospitality (13 percent). Most of these apprentices (58 percent) were recruited to small businesses of less than 25 employees. Both younger and older workers participated in the apprenticeship programs.

By 1998 the government also had established 82 Training and Enterprise Councils (TECs) in England and Wales and 22 Local Enterprise Companies (LECs) in Scotland to develop training solutions based on local labor-market needs. The TECs are local, nongovernmental organizations directed by leading business and education leaders from within the community. They design collaborative training initiatives using local business and education resources and have helped overseas-based corporations develop the requisite local workforce.

"Investors in People" is the TEC's national program that encourages business to invest in "Better People—Better Business." This program carries out training needs assessments and lays out relevant training and employee development plans. The "Investors in People" provides a framework for improving business performance and competitiveness.[13]

In Northeast England, the Tyneside TEC played an important role in attracting Siemens to the region. Olivia Grant, chief executive of Tyneside TEC explains, "We were able to reassure Siemens that we had the right people to put together a recruitment and training package to meet their needs. Proof of this has been in the breadth of training we have been able to offer. TEC has sponsored about 50 training programs on Siemens' behalf."[14]

When Siemens announced its planned microelectronics facility in Tyneside, the local university was asked to provide over 200 engineers with training in the German language that exactly matched Siemens' needs. The need to develop good foreign language skills for business is a major objective of the UK educational programs. Greater language fluency reduces miscommunication and increases quality. Problems arising from the limited understanding of another language are common throughout Europe. In some cases the results can be funny, as illustrated by these unique signs in English collected over the years by employees of Air France:

Leipzig, Germany, elevator: "Do no enter the lift backwards, and only when lit up."

Paris hotel elevator: "Please leave your values at the front desk. If you lose them in your room, we are not responsible."

Rome laundry: "Ladies, please leave your clothes here and spend the afternoon have a good time."

German camping site: "It is strictly forbidden on our Black Forest Camping site that people of different sex, for instance men and women, live together in one tent unless they are married with each other for that purpose."

Copenhagen airline: "We take your bags and send them in all directions."

Invest in Scotland

In the northern British Isles, Scotland began shifting to high-tech in the 1960s to compensate for a steep decline in its heavy industry: shipbuilding, steel, coal mining, and textile manufacturing. Its chief assets were a hard-working, well-educated technical labor force and a strong university system.

To heighten these advantages, local Scottish governments added tax abatements, subsidies, and, most importantly, employee training grants. By 1995, a 70-mile swath between Glasgow and Edinburgh attracted more than 300 high-tech companies employing 45,000 workers who make $9.5 billion worth of products. This includes many American companies such as Motorola and Hewlett-Packard. Fifty-seven percent of Europe's workstations are built here, as are 25 percent of Europe's PCs and 10 percent of Europe's semiconductors.

Another key competitive educational advantage is Scotland's development of research consortia between universities and companies. One example is a consortium working in optoelectronics. With 350 researchers, the four universities involved have a research budget of $20 million per year. This helps support 20 Scottish companies that yearly produce optoelectronic products valued at $167 million (*Electronic Business Buyer*, 1995).

Something fundamental must be working here, and it is not necessarily cheap wages. Scotland's employee wage base may be lower than other parts of Europe, but it is comparable to most of the United States.

An "Invest in Scotland" ad in *The Wall Street Journal* that touts Scotland's high priority on education stated, "Instead of learning how to memorize, they [Scottish students] learn how to think." If this business–education collaboration works so well in Scotland, why not in America?

A school–business connection is essential to improve the relevance of education and technical training. It assures students that an actual job exists for them in the working world when they complete their education. The ideological differences between the Conservative and Labour political parties in Britain were overtaken by the convergence of local job/education concerns that bridged the ideological/political chasm. In Britain's version of workforce education, local school officials, parents, business people, unions, and others succeeded in implementing school reforms that achieved the different aims of these diverse partners while benefiting the community as a whole.

This policy approach gives each community the power to interpret workforce education in a realistic manner for the local job market that profits everyone: students, employees, and business.

More than 3,500 companies have now established themselves somewhere in England, Wales, or Scotland. Over 40 percent of all U.S. investment in Europe is now in the UK, making the United States by far the largest investor in this nation. This includes IBM, AT&T, NCR, Hewlett-Packard, DEC, Hughes Microelectronics, Honeywell, Tandy, and Sun Microsystems, to mention a few.

Take, for instance, the Motorola experience. Between 1990 and 1995 Motorola invested more than $1.5 million a week in the UK. This company is now Scotland's largest employer with more than 5,300 people. In 1969 Motorola opened its first Scottish plant. Today their East Kilbride fabrication assembly and test facility is by far the largest in Britain and the largest manufacturing operation in Scotland. This does not include other operating facilities at other sites in Scotland. According to Chris Galvin, Motorola's president, it was the technology base and the expertise of the workforce that convinced them that Scotland was the right place to expand. In Livington, New Town, Motorola also established a European research and development center with about 30 engineers designing manufacturing systems and controls for all its European plants.

Edinburgh University is a leading university in semiconductor production R&D. It worked with Motorola in developing graduate and postgraduate training programs in electronics, particularly in semiconductor technology. These two centers collaboratively developed training materials and delivery systems for Motorola subsidiaries worldwide. They also conduct training in Scotland and assist Scotland's technical secondary schools in preparing the next generation of workers.[15]

Faced with industrial oblivion, the UK has taken the difficult steps necessary for fostering locally driven business–education–governmental partnerships. This has not been done easily or without great investment by many. But it has begun to pay off for all concerned. Perhaps America can take a page from British workforce education reform? Can we establish a new corporate culture that values developing the "wisdom" of many? Throughout the United States we need to empower local communities to interpret workforce education into realistic local programs that will profit all the key players: business, unions, education, and all students.

Turning Europe's Forgotten Half into an Asset

Here is a quick investigation of Ireland, Denmark, Switzerland, and the Austrian business communities' rationale for providing more learning opportunities for young people: greater profits and growing economies.

Ireland's Saints and Scholars

Once Britain's poor colonial stepchild, Ireland now boasts Europe's fastest-growing economy. With growth rates over 6 percent throughout the 1990s, Ireland is surging while the rest of the European Union (EU) has been struggling. Dell Computer, Intel, Motorola, Gateway 2000, and Fruit of the Loom, Inc., are among the many international pharmaceutical, computer technology, and food-production businesses setting up shop. Foreign investors have been attracted by access to EU markets and a well-educated, English-speaking workforce. The country received 40 percent of all U.S. investment in the European electronics industry from 1980 to 1998.

Throughout Ireland's history it has been known as the land of saints and scholars. Today Ireland remains very focused on education. Companies such as KAO Infosystems have found Ireland to be a cost-effective location for their call centers. KAO, which markets its own brand of diskettes and also handles telemarketing for software companies, set up a Dublin call center. The company boasts Russian and Lithuanian speakers among its 60 call-center employees.

Irish President Mary McAleese gave a passionate call to action at the International Federation of Training and Development Organizations (Dublin, 1998) for increased investment in training and development. She drove home training's return-on-investment in her case study of the upswing in Ireland's economy.

Ireland's Industrial Development Authority reports that 20,000 Irish university students are studying a foreign language as part of their coursework. This ensures meeting the rapid growth needs of the telecom boom. Ireland's language training agency in 1995 established a database of multilingual people interested in working in the telecommunications industry.

Ireland also offers training grants to industry for in-house programs introducing new technologies. This is meant to supplement integrated student programs that provide education and work experience leading to a specific career certificate.[16]

Denmark's "Sandwich System"

This Scandinavian country has committed itself to providing all of its young people with the knowledge and skills they need to enter the technological workforce. Nicknamed the "sandwich system," the Danish educational program features alternative periods of school/work apprenticeships. It bears a superficial resemblance to the German dual system. However, its salient feature is its flexibility. Its goals are to provide all students with the basic knowledge and skills for leading any life they want.

At age 16 students can go in three directions: the gymnasium (similar to the best American high schools); the technical college; and the business college (where the focus is on entering the workforce, more project-based and hands-on). Students in all these schools take the same examinations, and if personal aspirations change, the Danish system allows them the flexibility to take another path.

All three schools include heavy doses of academic coursework that sometimes rankles with students who are impatient with theory and want to work with their hands. What this means is that students do not learn only narrow skills. Danish firms tend to be small, so workers need to be crossed-trained to remain employed or employable.

The private sector is a major player in Denmark. Danish business leaders, to a person, have a remarkable moral commitment to providing learning opportunities for young people. They believe that they have turned Denmark's "forgotten half" (the students who do not go to a four-year college) into a real human capital asset for business. The Danes have met their challenge. American business might do well by learning from their experience.[17]

Switzerland/Austria Work Empowerment

In Baden, Switzerland, a high-school student studies at the giant Swiss–Swedish engineering firm of Asea Brown Boveri (ABB). His apprenticeship studies are in a state-approved, partially state-financed high school located on the factory's premises. When asked by American visitors what qualities are essential for success at work and in life, the student told us, self-discipline, independence, creativity (imagination and problem solving), team effort, personal competence, flexibility, focusing on customer needs, honesty, loyalty, and helping his fellow workers. Maybe he has read Tom Peters?

At the Union Bank of Switzerland in Zurich, students have been receiving training for over 125 years. As much as $23,000 per apprentice per year is invested by the bank, over and above what the state pays for secondary education. The bank's curriculum stresses a broad range of skills and values: self-initiative, effective team playing, decision-making ability, good concentration, communication skills, flexibility, attention to personal appearance, good grades in school, enjoying people, and persistence. The apprenticeship program enjoys high prestige among students, parents, and the general public. Often Swiss apprenticeship programs have requests for enrollment that are triple or more the number of available slots.

In 1990 Switzerland set up the Advanced Training Campaign to create more apprenticeships and revitalize advanced vocational education. By 1995, 610 new projects were underway involving employers, employees, and educational institutions. More than $150 million was provided by the government as seed money to help companies get started and then institutionalize the process permanently.

In nearby Bregenz, Austria, the Julius Blum precision cabinet-hardware manufacturer employs 22 full-time and 11 part-time trainers to serve the educational needs of their 130 student apprentices. Blum's training philosophy is summed up by its two mottoes:

Never underestimate the capabilities of our youth. Rather, find out what they are, and utilize them in helping to create a successful adult.

and

A positive role model is the best way to form a young mind.

The 19- or 20-year-old students completing their fourth year of combined schooling and on-the-job training are earning up to $1,700 a month. In Bregenz's public high schools, where these apprentices study, the students work on state-of-the-art technology. As Blum's apprenticeship director says, "We want our students to have the very best technology; if the equipment in the plant is better than in the schools, they will look down on the schools." Blum's leaders practice what they preach: "Smart workers are our best asset."

Blum's four-year apprenticeship program costs about $5 million a year. But CEO Gerhard E. Blum told *The Wall Street Journal* that it pays for itself in better products and market share. "The thorough education is one of the hidden strengths in the European economy."

In 1992 Blum learned how true those words were when he opened his first U.S. plant in Stanley, North Carolina. He found plenty of cheap labor, but nobody qualified to run the high-tech machines. Blum had to send 20 Austrians to the United States to do the crucial jobs. The firm has recently opened a high-school apprenticeship program based on its Austrian tech-prep curriculum near its Stanley plant. Will Blum be able to transplant the same high standards and performance to its New World outpost?

As an American observer in all these European countries, I try to gauge the extent to which the Europeans are encouraging individualism versus a mind-numbing, repetitious automation-like employment. In almost every case I see them as stressing what made America great: skilled, thinking people who are creative problem solvers in a stressful, fast-paced world. Two world wars, an American occupation, and the Marshall Plan, have proved to the European mind the cost of becoming the victims of ignorance. This is a lesson that should not be forgotten by Americans.[18]

Silicon Valley: East

The United States has done it again. The 1999 trade deficit hit another high. Why is this happening? One common answer is the huge competitive edge provided by cheap, unskilled labor in developing countries. Even with the current economic problems, the fact remains that almost anywhere you go in the Pacific Rim, local workers are very busy working at the same high-skill tasks you expect to find in the Silicon Valley or Chicago or New York. One of the new facets of the global economy is the increasing balance of skills in the world.

This trend has emerged with the worldwide shift to market economics. Since the Second World War, there has been a steady improvement in education, particularly in Asia. Link these factors to the decades of training done by multinational corporations, and what emerges is a highly competitive global workforce in fields ranging from finance and architecture to computer software and hardware.

As we have noted in earlier chapters, an acute shortage of technicians in the United States has already motivated many companies to relocate to Europe and now Asia. But now we can take the deterioration of our labor market a step further.

In a jarring keynote address to the annual convention of the Institute of Electrical and Electronic Engineers in September 1994, Edith Holleman, Counsel to the U.S. House of Representatives' Science, Space and Technology Committee, sounded the warning that the invention of new high-tech products in the United States "cannot be counted on to spin off into domestic manufacturing facilities providing employment for many engineers and skilled workers."

Motorola exemplifies this trend. Its Scriptor Pager was developed almost entirely by its Singaporean industrial designers using Singaporean software. This was done at Motorola's Singapore Innovation Center, a $35 million paging-device plant employing 75 local engineers.

Most of the Malaysian electronics industry has already made the transition from the labor-intensive operations of the 1970s, which originally attracted multinationals such as Motorola, Hewlett-Packard, and Phillips Electronics, to the capital- and technology-intensive industry of today. In-house training by these companies has helped to make up for any shortcomings of the local educational system. The Malaysian Penang Skills Development Center, a partnership between the public and private sectors, is an international model of successful career education that includes school-to-work training. This 360-student polytechnic institute for local high school and even university graduates is funded by 57 foreign companies, including Hewlett-Packard; Intel; Motorola; Taiwan's biggest computer firm, Acer; and France's telecom giant, Alcatel. Since 1989, about 10,000 people have been trained in computers, programmable automation, and other high-tech areas.

This learning doesn't come cheap. Intel donated a $140,000 microprocessor lab. A 20,000-square-foot "team-building park" was built by Seagate Technology for leadership training along with a clean room to teach vacuum technology for hard-disk manufacturing.

Motorola chipped in $320,000 for PC software training and a bachelor of science program.

India and China are also following on the successes of Malaysia and Singapore. Their potential is great given their schools' heavy emphasis on math and basic science. Intel's Chief Operating Officer, Craig R. Barrett, observed, "I see a ton of people [in these countries] who are as technically well-educated as people in the U.S." India has 100,000 English-speaking software engineers and technicians. Hundreds of Indian companies now supply software to Western customers. The number of these engineers could double by the year 2000.

According to John Naisbitt in *Megatrends Asia* (1996), Asia's answer to Silicon Valley is India, Inc. In 1986 the Indian government began offering economic incentives to high-tech businesses. There are now seven software development parks with five million employees exporting software worldwide. As a result, many Indians who went abroad for their education have returned home to start up their own versions of Microsoft. At these firms, professional employees expect a big investment in continuing education as part of their employment. Functional and managerial education is in constant demand. Retention of these professionals requires continuous first-rate education.

This demand for more education in the workplace is not limited only to India. Germany's Volkswagen, America's Procter & Gamble, and McDonald's all run their own training centers in Asia. Investing in these facilities helps these organizations establish themselves in a foreign market by promoting their own technologies.

In China, Northern Telecom Ltd. has opened a lab employing 250 engineers that is a part of Beijing University of Posts and Telecommunications. Northern Telecom will develop cellular phones, multimedia transmission devices, and software at this lab. Motorola and AT&T have also built plants or facilities in China. Europe's Airbus Industries and America's Boeing are both installing flight simulators in China to train pilots to fly their aircraft. Microsoft has set up four training centers in association with Chinese universities.

Initially all these activities will focus on the enormous needs of China. But ultimately it is only a matter of time before the Chinese start selling these products globally. Albert Sin, the Human Resources Director of AT&T China, said, "I've never found people more open to learning. They soak up everything."

Dedication to education is one of the critical factors for the rise of South Korea from one of the poorest countries in the world a generation ago to the 11th wealthiest before the 1997–98 Asian recession. It is a certainty that education will help bring about a faster turnaround for Korea's current economic malaise.[19]

South Korean students score at or near the top in most international education studies. South Korea ranks second only to China in the number of doctorates earned at U.S. universities, many paid for by Korean business.

The key to the Korean economy is how well it can develop its human capital. Before the 1997–98 recession, Korea outstripped its supply of technology managers, software designers, and systems engineers. To fill in these technology gaps, Samsung, Hyundai, Kia Motors, and Pohang Iron and Steel operate their own technical high schools. This strategic move helps guarantee that the skills of graduates match the needs of business.[20]

Though the strides Asian business has made to competitively educate its workforce are impressive, the 1997–98 Asian economic downturn shows that there is no easy path to solid economic growth. Also, the outflow of skilled work to less expensive Third-World havens is only a temporary phenomenon. As we have already noted, the wage gap closes as economies mature. Another critical economic factor is that these countries are still not producing enough skilled workers to guarantee their nation's advancement up the economic ladder. But then, there still remains Japan, Inc.

Japan first expanded its economy through the wholesale copying of foreign ideas. A high regard for education in school and significant expenditures for worker training in industry also helped explain the meteoric rise of Japanese industry. As recently as 1996, the government subsidized 50 percent of the wages and expenses for employee training programs that enhanced production technology or introduced workers to new high-tech business skills.

Another indication of its support for the practical is the fact that Japan is a world leader in the proportion of qualified scientists and engineers (about 60,000 per million people). About 800,000 Japanese work in research and development—more than in Germany, the United Kingdom, and France combined.[21]

This infatuation with all things educational begins with the fact that Japanese parents take a deep personal interest in their children's education. A close connection has been forged between home and school. This parent–teacher partnership is a critical foundation for later high performance throughout adult life.

However, in another aspect of educational preparation the United States and Japan are remarkably alike. Like America, Japan at the high-school level does not support apprenticeship education equivalent to the German dual system. Japanese companies prefer to do specific job training, and they do a lot of it continuously. High schools are left to concentrate on a rigorous academic program, and they do an excellent job. Japan has one of the highest literacy rates in the industrialized world.

Like the Germans, however, the Japanese have developed a support system that helps students secure a track into an adult career. They have consciously forged close ties between local schools and business. Recruiters from industry visit high schools during senior year to select students for their technical, clerical, or blue-collar jobs. How well students perform during high school significantly influences their future career paths. It helps determine how good a university a student will attend or what kind of occupation and business will employ the student.

As a result, Japanese high schools are a serious place for academics. From the seventh grade through high school, all students are required to take two years of science, six years of math, and six years of literature. Every student takes calculus. This subject is very important to Japanese industry. It is telling to note that high-school students are hired by business to do their statistical process control (SPC) calculations. This is a critical high-performance task that even most American college graduates are incapable of performing.

By the time Japanese students have graduated from high school, they have completed four more years of education than a comparable American student. This is because of a 240-day school year, compared to 180 days in the United States It is not surprising that many of these young people are doing comparative college-level work.

Most Japanese companies require students to take rigorous employment qualifications tests. Business is looking for dedicated knowledge workers, and even more importantly they want entry-level workers who can show them they know how to learn.[22]

Bottom Line Management

What ideas can U.S. business adapt and transfer from these people-performance-improvement programs from Europe and Asia? Here are some policy guidelines:

1. Skill Standards

Unlike other countries, the United States will probably not mandate career-education laws and regulations on a national basis. However, many U.S. trade associations are in the process of determining core skill standards by specific industry. A federal National Skills Standards Board (NSSB) also has been established. Over the next several years these groups will issue suggested guidelines on the education appropriate for entering specific career areas.

But the real action will be in the 50 individual state legislatures. The education laws of each state must be changed. The state legislatures constitute a key arena for the lobbying efforts of the business community.

By 1998 only two U.S. states, Oregon and Kentucky, had mandated by law specific high-school career education credit requirements for graduation and made these credits transferable either into postsecondary career-education certificate programs or toward a two- or four-year college degree. In order to institutionalize career education, your state needs to start here and mandate these career credits, guided in part by what skills the local business community thinks are needed for success on-the-job.

This starts with you! I have interviewed too many local business people, association executives, and school officials who have already established quality local career-education programs, only to see them disappear because key supports retired or relocated, or because a single business partner's priorities changed. Today many feel frustrated because their state governments have not changed the law to institutionalize their efforts and safeguard them for the future. Local business–community–trade associations, such as the Chamber of Commerce, Rotary, Lions Club, and Kiwanis, might serve as an organizing group to give you a voice in lobbying for the specific career-education program your state needs. We are talking about the future livelihood of your children or grandchildren—not somebody else's.

2. What Careers?

Career concentrations must be defined by state law. Each state will do this differently with some general similarities emerging over time. Existing businesses will play a large part in determining what career programs are established in each state.

However, most states will not want to limit potential economic growth by ignoring new industries or those that are now underrepresented in their region. There are 16 major career occupational areas for national employment. Such resources as national trade associations can be utilized in any state that needs to develop new career-skills programs rapidly for businesses moving from overseas or from another region of the United States.

3. Student Choice

Career-education activities need to begin in elementary school. Children need to learn about many different career possibilities, not just what is popular. Schools need a plan to uncover and develop the different aptitudes and interests of all their students, not just the top performers.

Businesses can help by such means as supplying teachers with current career information, providing company tours to school groups, or encouraging employees to speak to elementary school groups about their jobs and the education needed for such careers.

Students need continuous exposure to accurate career information throughout their school years. This needs to begin in the primary grades. If career information is delayed until high school, it is often too late to overcome faulty career choices based on information supplied by peers, parents, or the media—information that is often inaccurate.

4. Flexible Career Prep

Students should be able to move easily from one career-education study program to another. This should be based on their personal interests, their aptitudes, and their understanding of local/regional/national/international-labor-market job needs. A child should be educated for a broad career, not a specific job. In fact, the typical twenty-first-century child will change jobs, if not careers, at least five or six times over a lifetime of employment.

5. Shared Economic Investment

States must provide business with the economic support to make universal career education possible. This is a shared economic investment that needs to be divided between government and industry. It will not be cheap.

Each individual state must decide how to best fund these career programs. This means that tax-paying parents must agree that these changes are needed for their children's future livelihood as well as their own. The business community must decide that workforce education has become an integral part of competitive business management, and not a "do-gooder" side-show fit only for "corporate charity types."

6. Who Will Teach?

In each state, business and higher education need to collaborate in the education of future teachers. They need to know how to teach their future students how to apply math, science, and the humanities for different career opportunities.

States need to fund and require current classroom teachers to enroll in continuing professional education that provides current information on the education necessary for specific careers.

7. Program Management

The local-community level is the best place to manage career programs. The local chambers of commerce, broadened to include union, education, and governmental representation, might provide the forum for collaboration on career education at the grass-roots level. They could also act as conduits for disseminating local labor market and economic job-development information to the public, and serve as neutral players for mobilizing civic leadership.

These local career boards could then organize their programs around local businesses in the service, manufacturing, industrial, or professional business sectors. Individual businesses in each sector could voluntarily collaborate on a joint career program, whether the company is small, mid-sized, or a multinational. In this way career internships or apprenticeships could be planned by an entire business sector, rather than relying on the sole support of an individual company.

8. Parental Involvement

Local career councils need to educate not only children about potential careers, but more importantly, parents. As parents, you need to be given the opportunity to receive an accurate, up-to-date picture of future career opportunities for your children. Even if you don't have any children, it is in your best interests as a manager to win the skill wars for your local community businesses.

Multiple Answers

9. As we have seen from our foreign competitors, there is no "one size fits all" career-education system. Local leadership is needed with the wisdom to determine how to best invest in our human capital at a local community level. That means you!

10. More and more each day, managers are crying out, "Give me skilled workers!" Business now understands how hard and costly it is to reskill its current workforce. In the short term, workforce education may now appear too expensive for most businesses. However, in the long term, globalization and technology will make winning the skills wars an economic business necessity for survival in the battle for productivity and profit.

In an earlier chapter, I pointed out that about 100 years ago America experienced its first education revolution by establishing successful work-based learning at the local level. This was not an easy task. There was great opposition from many parts of society. Child labor was cheap for business. Many parents needed their sons' and daughters' extra income. Whoever heard of sending girls to high school in 1900? Do you want to pay more taxes to educate someone else's child—especially an immigrant child?

Yet, state by state, Americans overcame these reactionary arguments and went on to establish and build local community-supported elementary, secondary, and vocational high schools. The people of that era were proud of what they were doing for their children and the future of America. They were progressives, business and labor leaders, parents, educators, Democrats and Republicans. They understood that to compete in the early-twentieth-century world of mass production and urbanization, America needed literate youth and adults ready for work. One hundred years later, has anything really changed?

Now we again need to revamp work-related education experiences and classroom education to keep pace with our current challenges. Future careers are changing. This does not mean abandoning liberal arts high schools or colleges, but it does mean recognizing that adding new technology career education is just as important. How about a blend of the best of both worlds?

My own father was an intelligent, well-educated carpenter. He graduated from a Chicago vocational high school in the 1920s. At that time every Chicago high-school teacher had to have a master's degree in order to teach. My father learned basic carpentry and drafting in high school. He lived his life as a successful small-scale carpenter contractor who built a few homes, but remodeled thousands of residences over his 50 years as a skilled craftsman. The English, geometry, and math he used to design his projects, write his customer proposals, and negotiate with clients and suppliers earned him a good living and a sterling reputation as a master builder.

My father did not write books, but he did read the paper every day of his life. My father did not earn millions, but he supported the local educational programs that helped his children shape their future lives.

The truth is that our children in the next millennium will need even greater educational diversity and opportunity than that given to this current generation. We must educate the minds of all children to seek out the ideals and truths from the liberal arts, at the same time offering all students greater opportunities to develop their technical skills and aptitudes. If this means a longer schooling experience, who ever promised that living in the twenty-first century was going to be easier?

Twentieth-century technology has already freed many from the heavy physical labor of the past. I believe that the twenty-first century will focus on the development of people to think, to build, to be leaders in a global competitive society. Management investment in human capital will become a cornerstone for a "second American century."

This will not come about easily or cheaply. In many other nations, business and taxpayers alike are making a large investment in career education. Many of these nations have no natural resource to develop other than their people. After the Second World War, Germany and Japan were urban and industrial wastelands. With the help of the United States and their strong civic dedication to education, it is amazing what these two nations have achieved over the past 50 years.

I agree with Stephen Hamilton, Cornell University, that the most important lesson we can learn from the European and Asian career-education systems is that many of the problems we in the United States attribute to "youthfulness" are in fact traceable to the lack of the right societal institutions. The Germans and others make clear that young people are quite capable of assuming what Americans see as adult work roles, if they have adequate education and training and are given good job opportunities. Our current skepticism results from the wall we have intentionally built between education and the U.S. labor market.

Looking at our chief competitors with comparable economic systems shows that career education is more than a good idea. It is real. It exists. Our examination of the smooth transition from education to careers in Germany for most youth underscores this point.

Career education cannot be dismissed as an impractical, socialist idea that will never work. Profit-driven corporations pay $10,000 a year or more to educate each intern or apprentice because they believe it is a good investment in human capital. The issue before America is not whether local career education is feasible or effective, but how to adapt this basic idea across the United States to local values, traditions, and organizing institutions.

Germany proves that these programs can function on a mass scale in a world competitive economy. Career education has not been marginalized for young people who cannot succeed in "regular" school. Instead it is the largest form of upper secondary education in Germany. Its scale encompasses enough diversity and flexibility in each German state to make it work in technologically complex business environments.[23]

The most serious challenge the United States faces is the absence of appropriate local institutions that undergird a career-education system. No mass youth career education program can be sustained without some overarching coordinating institution with enforcement powers. Some countries have used the equivalent of our U.S. Chamber of Commerce to mandate by law the involvement of employers, schools, unions, and older workers in designing and overseeing these programs. With so many successful models to choose from, I can't believe that local community leaders across the United States will not confront this issue and solve it.

In many ways we find ourselves in a new watershed era, trapped between two worlds—one of twentieth-century mass production, the other of twenty-first-century limitless techno-cyberspace. Are we less enlightened than past generations? The future competitiveness of every business and the future livelihood of all our children is at stake. Some communities and businesses have already begun this "Second American Education Revolution." Can yours afford to be left behind?

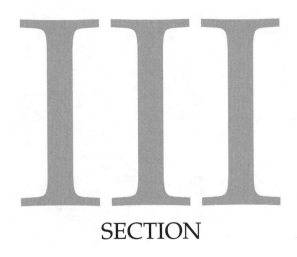

SECTION

Developing People

Help Wanted: Creating
the Next Workforce

Work—*Conscious effort, other than that whose primary purpose is either coping or relaxation, aimed at providing benefits for oneself or for others.*

Career—*The totality of work one does over a lifetime.*

Career Development—*The total combination of educational, economic, social and psychological factors that combine to shape the career of any given individual over a life span.*

KEN HOYT, KANSAS STATE UNIVERSITY

Sultan, Washington, is an old lumber-mill town just north of Seattle in the Pacific Northwest. In the late 1960s, Boeing constructed a huge 747 plant in nearby Everett. High-tech industries serving the plant developed along Interstate 405. All this development brought major population increases to the area. At the same time, lumber production, fishing, and farming began to decline, economically depressing smaller communities such as Sultan, Gold Bar, and Index. Local residents lacked the skills to work in the high-performance workplace and had little personal inclination or education opportunity to change.

I traveled to Sultan (named after a local Indian chief) and met with local parents, students, and educators. We discussed what is happening in the American workplace and how to prepare students adequately with education for the high-tech careers of today and tomorrow. There was a great sense of urgency in the air. Boeing had just announced that deliveries of a dozen 747 aircraft scheduled for September would be delayed because of a shortage of technical professionals. Boeing is trying to increase jetliner output to record levels to meet its record sales. But the company and its suppliers are having trouble keeping up. They cannot find enough new high-skill employees.

Washington State and its business community are trying to fill this "knowledge-worker" gap. According to Carver Gayton of the Employment Security Department, "Throughout the state, 60 high schools are using workplace standards developed in Washington to teach students in school-to-work programs the skills required for future careers." Before moving over to his job with the state, Gayton was the former school-relations manager at Boeing. He points with pride to the 500 Boeing school-to-work internships available to students leading to an average annual starting salary of $27,000.

Progress Report

Boeing's program is not an isolated example. Since the initiation in 1995 of a new national awareness campaign regarding the need for school-to-work, more than 100,000 students have received paid or unpaid internships, while 200,000 students have obtained job-shadowing or mentoring assistance, according to the Department of Labor's School-to-Work office. More than 900 community-based business–school partnerships now cover 41 states and at least 5,400 high schools. Highlights of these programs include:

- More than 3,000 high schools use some career-related curriculum. Integration of academic and career instruction occurs in classes at 2,700 institutions.

- 2,300 high schools have integrated academic and work-based learning classes.

- 12,000 students are now enrolled in multiyear apprenticeships.

- More than 200,000 businesses nationwide have initiated programs with almost 59,000 offering on-site, work-based learning experiences.

- 86 percent of participating companies were small businesses that offered students work-based learning.

Though these numbers sound impressive, only a small fraction of the U.S. business community has thus far chosen to participate in school-to-work programs. With more and more organizations facing severe shortages of properly skilled workers, education that prepares the huge numbers of Americans who never will complete college for the new careers of the twenty-first-century marketplace would seem to make a great deal of sense.

The "New" Silent Majority

According to the Department of Education, only about 25 percent of Americans will ever obtain a B.A., M.A., or Ph.D. degree. What makes this figure even more interesting, after considering the massive doses of current federal/state/private college tuition aid now available, is that about the same graduation rate has held steady since the 1920s. What happens to all the others?

As we previously reviewed in the U.S. Twentieth-Century Knowledge Economic Model, the average life span is divided into three parts: education, career prep, and work. The typical pattern in the education phase has been school attendance from age 6 to 18. But beginning in the 1960s, increasing numbers of teens began dropping out of high school, and the numbers have been rising ever since. High-school vocational education flourished before World War II only to go into general decline following the war and most schools' general push toward a college-prep curriculum.

In the last decades of the twentieth century, a social consensus has been building that college attendance is the standard path to career success for America's youth. Although an increasing number of students have been admitted to colleges and universities, many do not graduate. On the other hand, an ever-shrinking proportion of students have entered formal postsecondary technical schools or been admitted to union-controlled apprenticeship-education programs. As a result, according to a Commerce Department report of 1998, more than 190,000 professional technical jobs are now vacant, while employers search in vain for qualified applicants. This agency projects that by 2005, U.S. business will need more than one million new high-tech workers.

For most twentieth-century Americans, entering the world of work signals the end of their education. Their high-school graduation is remembered as the year they "got out" and went to work. The result is a very real wall between the world of work and the world of education career/prep. Traditionally, business and schools have very little contact. They talk in different languages and remain deeply suspicious of each other's goals. Business still expects that the people who come to them for a job are "job ready." Only managers and professionals are exempt from this rule. They still represent about 20 percent of the workforce that annually receives some form of continuing professional education or training. The rest usually receive only the most rudimentary on-the-job training (OJT). Except for the periods during the two world wars when training was greatly expanded across every industry to rev up production, most American workers receive little or none. The U.S. economy functioned very well with a minimalist public school system that educated many workers very poorly but gave them good-paying jobs in a mass-production economy. Only the top 20 percent of the population was needed for managerial/professional jobs in the economy. They got the best education.

By 1997 technology and the globalization of business had turned this world upside down. The new high-performance workplace needs a "good education" for about 50 percent of the entire U.S. population.[1]

The Neglected Majority

The good news is that many economists believe that 70 percent of the good jobs in the current and future American economy will not require a four-year college degree. As it is currently the case that about 75 percent of all U.S. teenagers will never actually finish a four-year college, this does not look like a problem. This percentage has held fairly constant, even though the number of students who have "access" to higher education (i.e., enter a college or university) over the past three decades has shot upward from 6 million to nearly 13 million. According to the international Organization for Economic Cooperation and Development (OECD), entry rates to U.S. colleges are still the world's highest.

But "access" to higher education doesn't seem to be the question. It's what happens—or doesn't happen—once a student gets there. For many the answer is "not much."

For the high-school class of 1982, this was their academic record by 1993:

9 percent	Less than 10 credits; left after one year
16 percent	More than 10 credits, but less than two years of credit
5 percent	More than 60 credits, but no degree
4 percent	Certificate earned
6 percent	Associate degree earned
27 percent	Bachelor's degree earned

(1997 National Center for Education Statistics)

The bad news we can deduce from these numbers is that only about 10 percent of the class of 1982 may be job-ready today for many of the good jobs that do not require a four-year degree. The OECD found that the United States has one of the highest university dropout rates in the industrialized world: 37 percent. Maybe too many students starting college just aren't ready, or aren't really that interested.[2]

According to the "career-education guru" Ken Hoyt at Kansas State University, the workplace can be divided between "secondary labor market" jobs—dead-end, low pay, short-term jobs with few benefits—and "primary labor market" jobs—professional or technical jobs with good wages and benefits. According to the U.S. Bureau of Labor Statistics (BLS), between 1992 and 2005 more than 26 million new jobs will be created throughout the United States. Ten million will require only a high-school diploma or less. The other 16.3 million new jobs will require some form of additional training and education.[3]

The BLS *Employment Outlook 1994–2005* projects that these jobs will grow faster than the overall rate of the job growth (see Figure 8-1). While jobs requiring additional education, such as an associate degree (A.A.) or technical training certificate, represented less than 30 percent of all jobs in 1994, by 2005 they will account for almost 45 percent of all new job growth. In fact, labor economist John H. Bishop believes that this figure may actually reach as high as 60 percent because of the dominance of new technologies in the U.S. marketplace.

Ken Hoyt believes that career education should begin in elementary school. By the time students graduate from high school, everyone needs the following career-related skills:

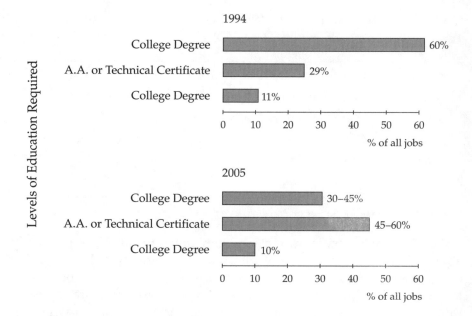

Figure 8-1 Jobs in the Future Will Require a Different Education

Source: Adapted from U.S. Bureau of Labor Statistics, *Employment Outlook 1994–2005* and John H. Bishop. "Is the Market for College Graduates Headed for a Bust? Demand and Supply Responses to Rising College Wage Premiums," *New England Economic Review*, May/June 1996.

1. The "basic" academic skills (i.e., reading and math comprehension/application skills at the 12th-grade level)

2. A set of productive work habits

3. A strong and personally meaningful system of work values

4. A set of job seeking/finding/getting/holding skills

5. Basic career decision-making skills

The bad news is that the non-college-bound student remains a low priority in most American high schools. Dale Parnell dubbed them "the neglected majority." This remains a group that many segments of society don't want to cope with.

Most business people see education as the exclusive job of the schools. They don't see career preparation as part of their mission or related to their responsibility of making a profit. Unions fear that high-school apprentices will displace their members or lower the wage scales. Teachers see career preparation as an intrusion into their classrooms, an assault on the "liberal arts," and even a plot to establish dumbed-down "factory schools" controlled by corporate America. Some conservatives are ideologically opposed to the use of public taxes for funding student career preparation.

But the biggest obstacle to change is the typical parents' mindset regarding their child's future lifetime career. Says Tom Kean, the former governor of New Jersey, "The American public doesn't really understand what's going on in schools. They don't recognize it's their child who isn't getting the kind of education which would enable him or her to earn the kind of living that they deserve. I don't think we've really energized ourselves to understand that this is a national priority. This is really a crisis."[4]

The resulting career market distortions are amazing. Nina Munk, a *Forbes* editor, tells how a senior manager in New York City called her in shock over the labor market (July 1997). He was looking for a new secretary. The dozens he interviewed demanded $50,000 as a base salary; one required a 20 percent signing bonus, another extra pay for work over 37.5 hours per week. His check of the *New York Times'* classified ads yielded an astonishing 470-odd postings for executive and administrative assistants. Though the supply of highly educated secretaries is dwindling, the Department of Labor forecasts 390,000 new jobs between 1994 and 2005, the tenth largest increase in new jobs in the United States. Lauren Sacks of Manhattan Impact Recruiting reports that secretarial salaries have jumped 20 to 30 percent.

Present wisdom has persuaded bright young women that secretarial work is demeaning. So women crowd into law schools only to graduate into an increasingly overcrowded profession. Yet some recent college graduates now see secretarial positions as a valid way to enter the world of business, says President Julia Slick of the famous Katherine Gibbs School. She reports that in the past five years student enrollment in their secretarial program at the main New York campus has more than doubled. And they aren't all females.[5]

The Career Game

A recent study of what careers young Americans think about suggests that teenagers have wildly high expectations about their future. Since

1992 researchers at the University of Chicago and the National Opinion Research Center have asked a national sample of some 1,000 students grades 6–12 what they want to be when they grow up. The answers are amazingly unrealistic.

Most young Americans expect to have high-status and high-paying jobs. Almost one in three expects to have a professional career. Ten percent expect to work in the sports or entertainment industry. Another ten percent think they will be doctors. Few imagine themselves working in service, craft, or technical industries. Yet government labor and economic indicators predict that most new jobs will be created by these business sectors over the next 10 to 15 years.

"Our kids' aspirations, overall, represent a considerably more potent, better-rewarded economically, higher-status set of occupations than probably these kids are going to enter," says Charles Bidwell, one of the principal investigators for this career study.

They found out that the vast majority of young people expect to graduate from a four-year college, and a large number expect to go as far as a Ph.D. Yet they have scant knowledge about what specific careers actually entail. When asked for precise information about the fields they hoped to enter, such as the average income, the educational requirements, or the prospects for job openings, few students could provide it.

The University of Chicago study argues that schools need to provide better career information to both students and parents about the knowledge and skills required for a broad range of occupations and work and to integrate that information throughout the elementary and high-school curriculum. Today's high-school counseling is focused primarily on college, not careers. The social status and economic prosperity of individual communities seems to be the main influences on whether students are channeled into four-year or two-year colleges or enter the job market right after high school.[6]

Unfortunately, this system is now breaking down because it was based on a commonly held myth.

Myth: A bachelor's degree is the best route to a good job and secure lifetime career.

Reality: For a few, the 15 to 25 percent who will earn any degree, a B.A. does provide access to the upper tier of American society. In fact, only about one in four U.S. workers holds this degree. The vast majority of future jobs with career-growth potential will require only a year or two of postsecondary education and continuing lifelong educational updates.

The new definition of "career" focuses less on a progression up a career ladder in a profession or corporation and more on recognizing opportunities and adapting. Rather than focusing on a one-career preparation path, current and future workers need a higher quality of education that integrates general knowledge in both the arts and sciences with emerging technology. The well-educated technician of "Star Trek" is a much more realistic twenty-first-century career model than the attorney of "L.A. Law" or corporate moguls on "Dallas."

By the end of the 1990s, it was once again apparent that most U.S. businesses are not emphasizing workforce education. This should not be too surprising, since the mass production system that spawned America's post–World War II economic expansion functioned by simplifying work and reducing the skills needed by most employees. Starting in the 1970s, some U.S. employers began moving away from this approach as more sophisticated technologies and work organizations took shape. "The Learning Organization" of the 1980s and early 1990s made some progress in the business community toward promoting lifelong learning. However, the current drumbeat toward short-term, maximized profits has driven most employers back to earlier management schemes in which learning and training are not significant employee activities.

Workforce projections indicate a growing demand for technicians in many fields. Since the Second World War, the U.S. military has trained large numbers of technicians who later adapted their skills to the civilian workforce. As the military services shrink, employers throughout the economy will find it increasingly difficult to hire the technicians they need.

Joseph Boyett and Henry Conn also predicted in *Workplace 2000* (1991) a growing shortage of appropriately educated people to support our high-performance economy. It now seems that most members of the U.S. business community are content to accept the larger implications of *Workplace 2000* predictions that are now unfolding across America. The U.S. economy will lose its capacity to sustain a high standard of living for more and more of its citizens. The business challenge of reorienting the nation's labor economy is enormous. However, the alternatives are so bleak that it makes more sense to shoulder this undertaking rather than to accept continued decline.[7]

Brave New World—Where Are the Job Seekers?

One of the chief problems business will face between now and 2020 is an undereducated population in the past. America's high-volume, low-cost, mass production economy demanded little from the majority of workers who entered the job market after high school. For many, a high-school diploma required achieving only seventh- or eighth-grade reading/math abilities, showing up most of the time, and not causing too much trouble. This is far removed from a "classical liberal arts education." One reason for this education disconnection has been our budgetary priorities. The U.S. public spends on average $19,940 (1990) on the education of youth between ages 16 and 24 if they go to college, but only $9,130 if they do not.[8] As complex new technologies continue to increase the demand for highly educated people, the general education curriculum at many American high schools leaves large numbers of students who not only will never graduate from college, but also lack the general or specialized education to be job-ready. This has become a major labor market block that is already beginning to slow down parts of the U.S. economy.

A 1997 survey of the 4,500-member National Association of Manufacturers conducted by Grant Thornton LLP discovered:

- More than 25 percent regularly reject 75 percent of all applicants as unqualified.
- More than six in ten companies believe their current workforce have serious performance problems such as a lack of timeliness and absenteeism.
- More than 50 percent find their workers lack appropriate math, reading, comprehension or written language abilities.
- About half believe their employees cannot read and translate drawings, diagrams, and flowcharts.
- Only 19 percent believed that the local community schools were doing a good job in preparing future workers.[9]

These dismal numbers underline the reality that for the great mass of today's students there is little or no connection between what they might want to do as adults and what school has to offer them. The United States needs to recreate an environment in which more students see a connection between learning and careers.

Jobs expert Marc Tucker sees the goal as "rebuilding a system in which all young people are motivated to work hard in school because they know that hard work in school will pay off by enabling them to learn what they will need as adults, in and out of the workplace."[10]

In *Teaching the New Basic Skills*, economists Frank Levy and Richard J. Murane contend that the skills needed in the workplace can best be determined by examining companies that make highly efficient use of their employee's education. They studied two high-performance companies: Diamond-Star Motors, the joint automaking venture between Chrysler Corp. and Mitsubishi, and Honda of America. What they found was the need for six essential skills:

1 and 2.   Math and reading comprehension abilities at the 9th- to 12th-grade levels

3.   The ability to solve problems where alternative solutions must be considered and tested back on-the-job

4.   The ability to work in groups or teams

5.   The ability to communicate effectively both orally and in writing

6.   The ability to use personal computers for everyday job tasks

"There are a lot of jobs that pay a middle-class wage that require a lot more than this," says Murane. "But we would argue that, outside of professional sports, there are virtually no jobs in this economy that pay middle-class wages without at least these new basic skills."[11]

Other hints abound. Business leaders told the U.S. Department of Education they particularly need graduates skilled in math and science. *The Formula for Success: A Business Leader's Guide to Supporting Math and Science Achievement* (Business Coalition for Education Reform, 1998) states that "entry-level workers at Intel must have one year each in chemistry, physics, and electronics along with solid basic science skills."

More than 80 percent of surveyed corporate human resource managers see knowledge of the basic sciences as a requirement for future entry-level jobs. Math education must support using science in many typical jobs. For example, auto technicians must be able to calculate the mean of various measurements to meet manufacturer rules. The chemical industry requires the use of differential calculus in many essential job tasks.

Some communities are responding to these new career education requirements. About 650 schools in 21 states are already using the Southern Regional Education Board initiative "High Schools That Work" program. It obliges career occupational students to enroll in at least three full-year math courses with two of those courses in college-preparatory math, four full-year college-prep English courses, and at least three full-year courses in science, with two credits in a lab course.[12]

For the past 50 years only around 30 percent of all jobs have required a four-year college degree. Only 20 percent of all these jobs have been in the professional ranks. These numbers are not going to change much in the next 20 years, except that some professions will actually shrink. Projections from the U.S. Department of Labor through 2005 paint the chilling scenario that at least one-third of all four-year college graduates will not find employment that matches their degrees. For those with graduate degrees in virtually all professional fields, graduates will exceed employment opportunities by at least 50 percent!

Contrary to the wisdom of students and parents, there is a worldwide surplus of accountants, chemists, engineers, language teachers, and marketing and financial specialists. Also, women have almost reached numerical parity in all professional employment areas except engineering.

In 1998 one in four new job opportunities are being created in technical areas. By 2010 some expect this to rise to 50 percent. Not only does America have an educational shortfall for a large part of its population, it also is schooling too many in its better-educated segment for the wrong occupations.[13]

In his book *Reinventing Education*, Lou Gerstner, IBM's CEO, commented on these enormous handicaps for U.S. industry. "Thirty percent of companies cannot reorganize work activities because employees can't learn new jobs and twenty-five percent can't upgrade their products because their employees can't learn the necessary skills."

One example of this problem is in the semiconductor industry. C. Douglas Marsk, Lithography's president of U.S. operations, says that there is a dangerous shortage of qualified workers to manage and operate the growing equipment base. This industry needs to bolster the ranks of virtually every occupational area: on-line operators, support technicians, process engineers, equipment service engineers, and applications specialists.[14]

In the automotive sector, dealers, manufacturers, and independent repair shops alike are all having trouble employing enough qualified mechanics. Across the United States the entire industry is suffering from a shortage of about 60,000 technicians.[15]

The Information Technology Association of America estimated (1998) 346,000 unfilled information-technology jobs. The Department of Labor projects that the number of unfilled IT jobs will swell to 1.1 million by 2006. According to Jim Papas, staffing manager of U.S. Cellular Corp., "The market is increasing 10 to 15 percent a year."

"I've never seen a situation like this in the 32 years I've been in the computer business," relates Mike Blair, president of the Chicago Software Association. With 20,000 tech jobs unfilled in Illinois alone, "A lot of us are saying that our growth next year is not going to be based on how much we can sell," Blair said, "it's going to be based on how many people we can get to implement and to consult."[16]

At the same time, traditional societal high-status jobs are in decline. The *American Bar Association Journal* reported that of the law school class of 1988, 84.5 percent had full-time legal jobs six months after graduation. By 1994 only 69.6 percent of the class did, and 15.3 percent had no jobs—part-time or otherwise.[17]

Part of the blame for these out-of-sync labor market numbers, says international jobs expert Hans Schieser, is that the U.S. education system is unrealistically based on the assumption that all our children are equally endowed with the same aptitudes, interests, and intellectual capacities. We have long known that about 50 percent of the population can be educated to develop abstract reasoning and problem-solving abilities, and about 50 percent has more practical intelligence that can successfully deal with the concrete realities of everyday life.[18]

One psychologist, Robert J. Sternberg, sees seven human abilities areas that education can tap for job/career development: linguistic, logical–mathematical, spatial, musical, bodily–kinesthetic, interpersonal, and intrapersonal intelligence (see Figure 8.2). Using such an approach as a model for an individual's potential career development, Iowa State University assessed 13-year-olds attending a summer academic program; included were each student's math, verbal, spatial, and mechanical abilities, and preferred career interests and

Type	*Skills*
1. Linguistic	Reading a book, writing a report, giving an extemporaneous talk.
2. Logical–Mathematical	Solving math problems, proving a logical theorem.
3. Spatial	Traveling through unfamiliar areas with ease; figuring out how to fit suitcases into the trunk of a car; playing right field well.
4. Musical	Remembering a tune; singing a song; composing or playing music.
5. Bodily–Fine-gross Motor	Used in playing golf, tennis, performing gymnastics or ballet.
6. Interpersonal	Used in figuring out what other people mean from what they say; understanding body language, facial expressions.
7. Intrapersonal	Understanding why someone is sometimes overconfident; takes rejection so poorly; or fails to achieve an important goal.

Figure 8-2 Human Ability Areas (Intelligence)
Source: 1996 Robert J. Sternberg

values. Students were then counseled regarding the career implications defined by their personal abilities (intelligence). Such a career assessment needs to be part of every student's local middle-school program.[19]

Perhaps the most attractive feature of using such a personal career management strategy is that it identifies the personal strengths and preferences of each individual and matches them to workplace opportunities of the twenty-first century. Such programs also help highlight that the mastery of reading, writing, and math, abstract reasoning; the ability to work with others; and even technical aptitudes can be encompassed within a liberal arts education.

These are also the same qualities identified with the modern twenty-first-century workplace. America needs to provide many more students with a world-class liberal arts education that also features individually appropriate career-education components.

As Harvard University's Howard Gardner puts it, "The single most important contribution education can make to a child's development is to help him toward a field where his talents best suit him, where he will be satisfied and competent. We've completely lost sight of that. Instead, we subject everyone to an education where, if you succeed, you will be best suited to be a college professor. And we evaluate everyone according to whether they meet that narrow standard of success."[20]

The Transition from Education to Employment

According to the American Society for Training and Development, the current U.S. system for making the transition from school to work is the worst in the industrialized world. As we have seen, many business representatives indicate that the growth of their firms is being restrained because trained or even trainable workers cannot be found to fill job openings.

The results of state and local career-education systems so far represent mere tokenism. Only two states, Oregon and Kentucky, have made school-to-work a main part of their overall school-reform agendas (Mathematical Policy Research, Inc., May 1997). In six other states—Florida, Maryland, Massachusetts, Michigan, Ohio, and Wisconsin—school-to-work competes with other reforms. Only Oregon has pulled together the key components in 1991 school-to-work legislation that directly links academic and workplace skills, which will be discussed later in this chapter.

Since 1994, more than $643 million has been funneled to 37 states through the federal School-to-Work Opportunities Act (*Vocational Training News*, May 1997). This seed money has been used to help states design work-based or school-based learning systems. Thus far, only 2 percent of students are engaged fully in these programs. However, many of these students are in work-based classes that are unrelated to their career goals.

Eighty percent of high-school seniors now complete career-interest inventories. More than half go on to visit a work site. Unfortunately, there is little evidence that these activities eventually lead to a specific career path. Students spend more time learning job skills when the school and a local business partner provide an internship. However, few states have changed the laws that mandate graduation requirements, leaving little time for students to participate in work-based learning.

In July 1997, Colorado became the first state to offer a 10 percent tax credit against the state income tax to employers investing in a local school-to-work initiative. This addressed another major reason why these programs lag behind their rhetoric—lukewarm support by the American business community. Even though many major U.S. corporations have established their own school-to-work programs (American Express, Citicorp, McDonald's, GM, Ford, Walgreens, Boeing, and the National Restaurant Association, to name a few), most small local businesses aren't interested.

One of the chief problems has been general confusion on the "how-to" of this process. Some favor a career-education-program system, other the newer school-to-work program, or a combination of both.[21]

One Best Solution?

Since about 1900 the United States has used several different work-based learning approaches. In 1906 one of the first vocational education programs began at the University of Cincinnati. By 1913, Dayton, Ohio, businesses helped launch the first vocational high school. Students spent half of their time in the schoolroom and the other half at the workplace in employer-supervised education.

Although vocational education enrollments have diminished since the 1970s, about 150,000 high-school students in the 1990s graduate annually with vocational credits. About 8 percent of all high-school students are enrolled in these programs. Around 50 percent of all high schools provide such opportunities[22]

After the Second World War, vocational education began its long decline. Beginning with the G.I. Bill, which paid for veterans to return to school, most Americans began to focus on earning a college degree as the surest guarantee of participating in "the American Dream." However, beginning in 1974 a new effort for career education was launched across the United States. Career education is a life-long process that places a "careers" emphasis in every subject and at every grade level. This begins in the primary grades and continues throughout the high-school years. Local or regional councils that include business, education, labor, government, the professions, and community-based organizations serve in an advisory role. Private sector participation is voluntary. Career awareness activities begin in the early elementary school grades. By middle school career exploration begins and continues through high school. An emphasis is placed on decision-making skills and on seeing the classroom as a "real" workplace.[23]

In 1994 a national school-to-work system was proposed that expanded current vocational education through federal/state/local school/business partnerships. It encouraged the adoption of a system of voluntary occupational skill standards developed by a National Skill Standards Board. School-to-work seeks to integrate school-based and work-based learning in high school and beyond. It seeks to prepare young people for specific careers at an entry level.[24]

According to Donald Clark, president of the National Association of Industry–Education Cooperation, "The main cause for optimism in the United States is that efforts to combine academic and occupational curriculum with work-based learning appear likely to provide the best preparation for young people entering an economy where learning and work are intertwined. The fact that most other industrialized countries either have been moving in this direction for some time or are now beginning to do so corroborates the logic of these initiatives."[25]

In the late 1990s there certainly exist strong economic, social, and educational arguments for better unifying academic and career preparation into a more coherent system. From a business standpoint, the argument is that a high-skill economy requires all its workers to have higher levels of general education. Such an economy calls for new types of knowledge that overcome the current boundary separating school from career (see Figure 8-3).

Areas of Competency	Outcomes								
Life Skills	Set Goals	Make decisions	Apply problem solving skills	Accept responsibility for actions	Resolve conflict	Maintain personal health	Access human service	Manage personal finances	Demonstrate civic/social responsibility
	Demonstrate family responsibility	Balance work and family							
Communication	Demonstrate active listening skills	Synthesize information	Follow oral directions	Take accurate messages	Use appropriate language for situation	Demonstrate phone skills	Interpret body language		
Problem Solving	Recognize the problem	Define the problem	Use a problem solving system	Evaluate solutions					
Employability Skills	A: Demonstrate time management skills	Demonstrate computer literacy	Dress appropriately	Work cooperatively with others	Perform job tasks with minimal supervision	Exhibit professional behavior	Demonstrate work etiquette	Manage job stress	
	B: Write a resume	Fill out application correctly	Write a cover letter	Demonstrate interview skills	Execute a job search				
Reading	Use word identification strategies	Demonstrate comprehension skills	Follow written directions	Comprehend popular publications	Recognize figurative language	Access information			
Writing	Use legible penmanship	Write a complete sentence	Write a complete paragraph	Utilize writing process	Write an essay	Follow accepted rules of punctuation	Use accepted rules of grammar	Format writing	
Mathematics	Add whole numbers	Subtract whole numbers	Multiply whole numbers	Divide whole numbers	Use a calculator	Compute fractions	Compute fractions to decimals	Convert fractions to decimals	Compute using ratios/proportions
	Compute percentages	Convert fractions to percents	Convert percents to fractions	Use measuring equipment	Convert units of measurement	Compute units of measurement	Solve work problems		

Figure 8-3 Higher General Educational Goals: All students completing high school will be able to read, write, solve mathematical problems, and think critically in order to achieve personal goals and be prepared for a life-time of career changes

The business and the education community must plan for more flexible, diverse elementary/high-school learning. The world of work is moving away from a twentieth-century era of preparing for one specialized job or career, to the twenty-first-century reality of multiple careers over a lifetime. The difference between jobs will be greater, thus demanding a greater variety and depth of personal knowledge.

Kenneth Hoyt at Kansas State University thinks that efforts currently being called "school-to-work" can be viewed "as vehicles for use in helping persons make some but not all of these changes. They are necessary but not sufficient. A broader perspective is needed."[26]

A practical drawback for a more narrow school-to-work education is job obsolescence. It may give a business a skilled entry-level worker immediately, but it does not adequately prepare employees for ongoing technological job changes. A limited school-to-work education in one type of technology will not enable a person to comprehend complex manuals or computer software resulting from ongoing advances in the same or another area of high-tech.

In the late 1980s, E.D. Hirsch used some of the same arguments in the much-discussed book *Cultural Literacy, What Every American Needs to Know*. Hirsch pointed out that rapidly advancing technology demanded fast and complex communications. He argued that society and business demand more broadly educated, highly literate people. "We must understand more than the surface meanings of words, we have to understand the context as well. The need for background information applies all the more to reading and writing. To grasp the words on a page we have to know a lot of information that isn't set down on the page."

He makes the point that "many young people under 30 years of age, lack the information that writers of American books and newspapers have traditionally taken for granted. . . . Any reader who doesn't possess the knowledge assumed in a piece (newspaper, book, computer) he or she reads will in fact be illiterate." He writes:

Too many Americans can't associate Abraham Lincoln with the American Civil War, Washington and the cherry tree, Scrooge and Christmas, the fights historical, the oceans geographical, and all the other shared materials of literate culture have become more, not less, important. The more computers we have, the more we need shared fairy tales, Greek myths, historical images. . . . That is not really the paradox it seems to be. The more specialized and technical our civilization becomes, the harder it is for non-specialists to participate in the decisions that deeply affect their lives. If we do not achieve a literate society the technicians, with their arcane specialties, will not be able to communicate with us nor we with them.[27]

This means today's and tomorrow's students will need to study the humanities, social sciences, natural sciences, and various career disciplines. Every student will need adequate reading, math, and thinking abilities that deliver a critical mass of specific information to function better throughout life and in the workplace.

Whatever new career education program your local community adopts, it will need to pass muster on the following basic criteria:

1. A reduction in only preparing students for entry-level, dead-end jobs

2. A reduction in preparing students for promotion up only one career ladder

3. Readying more students for a career of different jobs, not just one job

4. Linking school and work as mutually motivating experiences

5. Preparing students for a lifetime of learning

There are many useful career transition activities to help this process (see Figure 8-4). They need to begin early in a student's school experience and continue into the postsecondary education level (see Figure 8-5).

By drawing on this career education "tool kit" we will equip all students with (1) a broad and strong elementary and secondary education; (2) good work habits; (3) a personally meaningful set of work values; (4) career decision-making skills; (5) job-seeking, job-getting, and job-holding skills; and (6) specific career(s) skill knowledge. As students acquire this knowledge, they will be prepared for job changes and career mobility over a lifetime.[28]

There is nothing in the career education concept that only serves students who plan to work immediately after high school. These programs focus on the very areas that will make for a more valid college education: exploration of career possibilities and interests, active learning, and guided hands-on career experiences outside the classroom. In fact, college-bound students may discover that internships

Definition of School-to-Work Transition Activities	
In-School Real World Connection:	In support of a student's career awareness, career exploration, personal planning, and personal development, representatives from employers/community agencies may participate in developing skills, acting as role models, visiting classes, demonstrating projects, organizing hands-on projects, conducting lectures, and providing explanations of equipment design and use.
Tours:	Structured and meaningful visits to work sites to observe the workplace and workplace skills in action.
Tutoring:	Specific help on academic skills.
Mentoring:	A trusted coach, guide, confidant, either in or outside of the workplace, who, over a period of time, supports the student in mastering systems, processes, behaviors, and skills.
Community Service:	Unpaid or volunteer experience for students to: build understanding of the public sector, non-profit organizations or community agencies; contribute their skills to community service; and develop the skills, behaviors, and values required by community service organizations.
Youth Advocates:	A full-time professional adopts 25–30 middle school students and works with them intensively for four to five years to help students become successful as students, employees, and citizens. The advocate focuses the resources of family, school, work site, heath, church, and community for students. *(continues)*

Figure 8-4 Career Education Tool Kit

Source: Adapted from Rochester City School District and the National Center on Education and the Economy, 1994

Job "Shadowing":	A student spends time during the workday with an expert of a certain trade, craft, or profession, observing the expert's work site skills and behaviors.
Structured Job:	A part-time, paid, structured work experience that is designed to enhance a young person's understanding of the work site, work site skills and behaviors, and the links between school and work. Helping the student is a mentor who supports the student in mastering systems, processes, behavior, and skills.
Internship:	As part of a work site learning experience of several weeks or months, a student works on a specific task or project in order to become familiar with the work site, work site skills and behaviors and their application to academics (or vice versa).
Youth Work Study course and Co-op:	Paid work experience related to students' of study for credit where students learn and perform occupational skills on the job.
Youth Apprenticeship:	A strategy that combines supervised, structured on-the-job training in a bonafide and documented employment setting with related theoretical instruction. It is sponsored by employers and labor management groups that have the ability to hire and train. This education and training strategy leads to the youth apprentice's high school graduation and counts toward advancement in an apprenticeship program and/or a post-secondary certificate or associate's degree program.
College and Specialized Training:	Post-secondary courses of study and training necessary to pursue a particular career path.

Figure 8-4 (Continued)

School-to-Work Activities

	Elementary							Middle School			High School					
	Pre-K	K	1	2	3	4	5	6	7	8	9	10	11	12	13	14
In-school Real World Connections																
Tours																
Tutoring																
Mentoring																
Community Service																
Youth Advocates																
Job Shadowing																
Structured Job																
Internship																
Youth Work Study & Co-Op																
Youth Apprenticeship																
College and Specialized Training																

Curriculum

Career Development

Support Network

Structured Work Experience

Technical Training

High Recommendation

Medium Recommendation

Low Recommendation

Figure 8-5 School-to-Work Transition Activities
Source: Adapted from Rochester City School District and the National Center on Education and the Economy, 1994

and other on-the-job venues are being adopted in many degree programs as part of their required college curriculum.

Career Skill Standards

According to Motorola's Gary Tooker, "In the skill standards area, as business leaders, we either drive the train or get run over."[29] That is one reason why more than 240 state and local business coalitions nationwide are promoting standards-based education reform in their own communities.

Career skill standards define what workers should know and be able to do. They supply a common language for employers, employees, educators, and trainers. The United States has 16 broad clusters of occupations appropriate for developing career skill standards.

By the mid-1990s more than 70 industry trade associations were developing national voluntary skills standards. The job clusters include agricultural production and natural resource management; mining and extraction operations; construction; manufacturing; installation and repair; energy and utilities; transportation; communications; wholesale/retail sales; hospitality and tourism; financial services; health and social services; education and training services; public administration; legal and protective services; business and administrative services; property management and building maintenance; and research, development, and technical services.

An example of their work is *Raising the Standard*, written by the Electronic Industries Foundation (1994). This manual covers the education requirements for entry-level electronic technicians (see Figure 8-6).

The work of these industry groups has been directed by the National Skills Standards Board (NSSB), created as part of the Federal Goals 2000 legislation. This voluntary business-led independent commission includes 28 members drawn from business, labor, education, state/local government, and community groups. Its mission is to help establish a national framework of portable career-education skills and credentials across the U.S. workplace. The NSSB will not actually set rigid skill standards, but rather suggest guidelines for endorsing standards created by voluntary industry partnerships.[30]

According to Eunice Askov, a professor at Penn State University, "The skill standards movement is being driven by the business

Electronic Industries Foundation Skill Manual

Technical Skills

Equipment and materials for electronics training can be expensive. Companies should become involved in technical education at the policy, planning, and budgeting levels to validate needs and act as advocates for the schools and school systems. Companies should try to provide equipment and materials or allow access to theirs.

A. General

Estimated training time: 50 to 70 hours

A.01 Demonstrate an understanding of proper safety techniques for all types of circuits and components (DC circuits, AC circuits, analog circuits, digital circuits, discrete solid-state circuits, microprocessors)

A.02 Demonstrate an understanding of and comply with relevant OSHA safety standards

A.03 Demonstrate an understanding of proper troubleshooting techniques

A.04 Demonstrate an understanding of basic assembly skills using hand and power tools

A.05 Demonstrate an understanding of acceptable soldering/desoldering techniques, including through-hole and surface mount devices

A.06 Demonstrate an understanding of proper solderless connections

A.07 Demonstrate an understanding of use of data books and cross reference/technical manuals to specify and requisition electronic components

A.08 Demonstrate an understanding of the interpretation and creation of electronic schematics, technical drawings, and flow diagrams

A.09 Demonstrate an understanding of design curves, tables, graphs, and recording of data

A.10 Demonstrate an understanding of color codes and other component descriptors

A.11 Demonstrate an understanding of site electrical and environmental survey

A.12 Demonstrate the use of listening skills or assistive devices to assess signs and symptoms of malfunctions

B. DC Circuits

Estimated training time: 150 to 200 hours

B.01 Demonstrate an understanding of sources of electricity in DC circuits

B.02 Demonstrate an understanding of principles and operation of batteries

B.03 Demonstrate an understanding of the meaning of and relationships among and between voltage, current, resistance and power in DC

Figure 8-6 Manual Excerpt

Source: Adapted from Electronic Industries Foundation, 1994

community with governmental support. Twenty-two industry trade organizations were funded by the federal government to develop occupational skill standards for their industry." The hope is that by 2005 the nation will have developed a comprehensive set of voluntary standards for most jobs.[31] What's behind this push by the U.S. business community?

There are several very compelling reasons for establishing a skills certification system in the United States. Such a system will help local community leaders evaluate the quality of different career-education programs. If employers use a certification system, it will guide the content and validity of career-education programs and provide students with incentives for learning the required knowledge. Skill certificates will also help to overcome the objections of employers who currently do not hire high-school graduates into career track positions offering training, advancement, job security, and better wages.

Such a system will encourage employers and employees to invest more in workforce education. Employees will have more confidence that accepting a lower training wage will lead to a better-paying job. Employers will be less fearful of losing trained employees if they know they can hire from a pool of certified workers who have already been substantially educated and are ready to work.

One of the strongest cases to be made for a U.S. career certification system has been the success of our foreign competitors. As we saw in the last chapter, a variety of successful career education programs flourish overseas. Whether in Germany or Japan, England or Malaysia, all of these efforts to better educate more young people for the future workplace are based on some skill-standards system. For the past decade more and more representatives from U.S. businesses have been traveling abroad and studying how these systems work, and how they can be adapted to what works for statisfying local needs. Multinational U.S. companies such as Hewlett-Packard, Motorola, Intel, Ford, and many others already are active business partners in the career education/skill standards programs of many foreign countries.

Whatever career standards are eventually written, businesses in each of the 50 states must participate in adapting them to more than work for local needs. The National Alliance of Business Task Force on Student Standards (which includes representation from Apple Computer, Federal Express, Bell South, Honeywell, IBM, Motorola, Siemens, TRW, Boeing, and other Fortune 500 companies) has reduced all the rhetoric to nine principles that serve as a guide for the business community on this process:

1. All student education should be based on challenging academic subject-matter calibrated against the best international education standards. America needs to compete in a world marketplace. Local communities need to gear up their schools to compete in this global skill war.

2. Career education is for everyone. The United States has done a good job preparing individuals for professional careers. For the twenty-first century the labor market figures show we need to do just as good of a job in other technical and service career areas.

3. All students must have a common core of skills. Everyone needs higher grade-levels of educational fluency. As we have seen, there is little room in this high-performance world for an accountant who cannot write clearly and speak intelligibly or a technician who cannot perform algebraic equations.

4. Every student's education must reflect "real world" requirements. According to many experts, the average student faces five to six job changes, if not complete career changes, over a lifetime in the workplace. Unless we equip our students to have agile minds, America will lack the human resources in the global battle for greater competitiveness.

5. Career-education programs must be voluntary. Even the vaunted German Dual-System is actually voluntary. In the United States one size does not fit all. Local control of voluntary career education is the only realistic goal for a nation with such geographical breadth and community diversity as the United States.

6. Career-education programs must continually be updated to correspond with dynamic career occupational developments. Any educational program that we can conceive of in career preparation or in lifelong learning standards will need constant updates and modification to accommodate rapid techno/market changes and local business conditions. This is a principal failure of our current educational system which simply cannot respond fast enough to changing labor-market require-

ments. On one issue most business gurus agree—if you think that technology has dramatically altered the world in the last 20 years, "you ain't seen nothin' yet!"

7. Career-education programs must include a way to measure and certify acceptable levels of student performance. Local labor-market boards, workforce committees, or some other impartial career quality-control board must be established to measure and certify people for career entry.

8. Business people need to be at the table to make this work. A local coalition of union, education, political, and community leaders need to join with local business to establish and maintain an effective local career education pathway for students.

9. Parents and the general public must also be educated to understand what is at stake and support the needed legal and tax-structure changes to make a career education system work in their local community.[32]

Union Apprenticeship Education

America's unions have a major role to play in support of career-education standards and the entire concept of improving work-based learning. AFL-CIO president John Sweeny says, "The career education movement I envision is about offering working Americans a stronger voice so that they can improve their lives and livelihoods, their companies, their communities and their country."

The Executive Council of the AFL-CIO has urged all of their 45,000 local union affiliates to participate directly in career education programs. They have outlined what these local unions can contribute to this process (see Figure 8-7). Union leadership supports the concept of career education combining high academic and occupational standards that will better prepare more students for employment and postsecondary studies.

A major area of union expertise is in quality work-based learning, modeled after the time-honored apprenticeship concept. In the United States close to 1,000 occupations in the building trades, the manufacturing and industrial sectors, and the medical and service sectors are recognized as apprenticeable occupations.

Unions can contribute valuable networks and workplace knowledge by	Unions can give young people unique learning opportunities by	Unions can help with STW system-building by
Using direct links to thousands of private- and public-sector employers.	Teaching youth about what workplaces look like and how workers help define workplace processes.	Providing access to and recruiting unionized employers to participate in STW activities.
Using established links and communication mechanisms to 14 million unionized workers.	Working with educators on school-based and work-based career awareness activities.	Providing program models for serving youth from diverse backgrounds, linking young women with non-traditional work, and serving youth with disabilities.
Sharing their long history of working with employers on training and skill-upgrading initiatives.	Giving students and teachers opportunities to learn about the current labor movement and labor history.	Contributing knowledge about work-based learning.
Leading the effort to ensure safe and healthful workplaces.	Teaching youth how workers and unions shape and maintain fair labor standards, bring about safe workplaces, and build the middle class.	Provide models for integrating academic and vocational education.
Applying understanding of workplace dynamics, work and technology, workplace change, and all aspects of industry.	Making students aware of their rights and responsibilities in the workplace.	Helping STW systems focus on career paths with strong employment potential.
	Teaching youth about labor laws, labor-management relations, and problem-solving skills and abilities.	Ensuring that STW initiatives comply with all labor laws and all workers are protected in the STW Act.
	Recruiting and training STW mentors.	Helping to bridge the communication gap between educators and employers.
	Giving front-line shadowing opportunities to students and teachers.	
	Recruiting and training workers to work with specific teachers and schools.	
	Using union-run training programs and apprentice-ship centers to provide hands-on learning opportunities.	

Figure 8-7 What Unions Can Contribute to School-to-Work (STW) Systems

Source: Adapted from Human Resource Development Institute AFL-CIO, 1997

Not all career-education programs will result in a student participating in a paid apprenticeship. However, rather than creating a separate and lesser youth apprenticeship system, new career education initiatives should seek to build closer links with existing registered union apprenticeship systems. This will require flexibility on the part of all the collaborating parties. Unions have a great deal of expertise to share. In many instances students who benefit from higher levels of union educational programming will later become members. Certainly teachers and craft apprenticeship trainers who belong to local unions can learn to work together in expanding youth career-education opportunities. During the early part of the twentieth century in the United States, vocational high schools saw that model work.[33]

Expanding apprenticeship opportunities and collaboratively sharing educational preparation will be major challenges for America's unions. For many decades unions have been the only significant players in providing Americans with a quality technical education. By sharing some of this responsibility with other community representatives, as is done by unions throughout much of Europe, American labor will make its valuable presence felt in an expanded U.S. career education system.

What's Happening: State by State

In the past several decades many states and localities have worked to develop new educational approaches that will better prepare students to enter a fast-changing economy and society. Let's review the highlights of how some schools across the United States are now promoting high academic standards in a context of career education.

As we stated earlier, only two states, Oregon and Kentucky, have made career education a main part of public education law. In 1991 Oregon landmark career-education-reform legislation:

- Created employer incentives to take on youth apprentices
- Established career development programs that outline specific learning activities for students in elementary, middle, and high schools
- Defined six areas of career concentration
- Agreed to the transferability of high-school career majors credits for admission to colleges and universities

- Provided ongoing technical assistance to local business–education partnerships

To date Oregon law provides the most comprehensive example of how to achieve a statewide career-education program as part of a state's educational reformation efforts.

In Kentucky a 1990 Education Reform Act established various career-education awareness activities that are age-appropriate for each grade level throughout elementary and high school. For example, students in sixth through eighth grade receive 30 hours of focused career education that includes individual career assessments, career days and fairs, and the development of a personal career portfolio. The Kentucky program uses performance-based assessments that focus on a student's personal career knowledge.[34]

Seventeen states have designated specific career majors in high school and are organizing their curricula around these majors (see Figure 8-8). Almost all of these states are offering students a career-education program in business or health care. Other major occupational areas include engineering, science, and communications.[35]

Here is a brief wrap-up on ten solid career-education programs currently operating across the United States.

California	
1. School:	Health and Bioscience Academy, Oakland Technical High School
2. Career Area(s):	Health Care
3. Year Began:	1985
4. Description:	Offers both job-ready and college-ready career education. Includes a "2+2" program that links students' last two years at the academy with two years at a community college or technical college. Features paid summer internships in which students get hands-on experience working with health professionals.
5. Information Contact:	510/879-3050[36]

Arizona	Art/humanities/communications; business systems; engineering/industrial systems; family/human services; health services, natural resources.
Colorado	Health and related services; art, humanities and communications, engineering and industrial technology; human services; natural resources; and business, marketing, and finance.
Hawaii	Health services; business management technology; natural resources; human resources.
Idaho	Arts and communications; business and management; health services; human resources; industrial and engineering; natural resources.
Maine	Arts and entertainment; science and research; agriculture and natural resources; law enforcement/security; mechanics and engineering; industry and manufacturing; business operations and management; sales and promotion; health and human services; customer and personal services; education and public administration; sports and physical performance.
Maryland	Consumer service, hospitality and tourism; health and bioscience; business management and finances; arts, media, and communication; environmental and natural resources systems; manufacturing; engineering and technology; transportation technologies; construction and development.
Michigan	Business services technology; child and adult care; public safety/protective services; manufacturing technology; agriscience and natural resources; construction and building maintenance; transportation; marketing; visual imaging; electromechanical; drafting/design; hospitality; health.
New Jersey	Heath careers; business and finance.
New York	Art/humanities; business/information systems; engineering; human services; natural and agricultural science.
North Carolina	Arts and humanities; biotechnology; business/marketing; construction technology; electronics; engineering; environmental sciences; health and medical care; manufacturing technology; human services; tele-communications; travel and tourism; hospitality.
Ohio	Arts and communication; business; health services; human resources; industrial and engineering systems; environmental and agricultural systems.
Oklahoma	Manufacturing; business; personal service; education; sales and marketing; construction; transportation; repairers and mechanics; agriculture; health; social science; design/communication/art; science.
Oregon	Arts; business/management; health service; industrial and engineering; natural resources; human resources.
Pennsylvania	Agriculture/natural resources; transportation; engineering; consumer services; construction; mechanics/repairers, production industries; communications; health care; business/information processing.
Utah	Science, business/marketing; information technology.
West Virginia	Health/human services; business/marketing; science/natural resources; engineering/technical; fine art/humanities.
Wisconsin	Agriculture; arts; business; communication; education; energy; engineering; government; health care; industrial; marketing; natural

Figure 8-8 State Career-Education Programs (High School Career Majors)
Source: Adapted from School-to-Work Report, 1996

Florida

1.	School:	William Turner Technical High School, Miami
2.	Career Area(s):	Service Career Academics
3.	Students Served:	2,100 (69 percent Black, 27 percent Latino, 4 percent White)
4.	Description:	Students can earn a traditional diploma for college admission, or receive a state certificate for a specific career-related field. Turner's seven career academies are partnered with a specific business that loans equipment and offer internships such as: Industrial Technology Academy/Metra Dade Transit; Residential Construction Academy/Building Industry Assoc. of South Florida and the Latin Builders Assoc.; Finance Academy/Federal National Mortgage Assoc. (Fannie Mae). The other career academies include: argoscience, applied business technology, health, and public service television production. As juniors and seniors, students receive field experience through internships, apprenticeships, field trips, job shadowing, and by teaming with adult mentors.
5.	Information Contact:	305/691-8324[37]

Illinois

1.	School:	West Side Technical Institute (City Colleges of Chicago)
2.	Career Area(s):	12 Vocational Certificates
3.	Students Served:	1,200
4.	Year Began:	1996
5.	Description:	175,000 square foot facility offering young adults a postsecondary work-based educational experience leading to 12

vocational certificates in: building maintenance, computer-aided design and manufacturing, dietary aide, home health aide, horticulture, industrial maintenance, materials management, medical office technology, nurse assistant, occupational rehabilitation aide, office technology, and precision metalworking. An interesting innovation is that Chicago's Electricians Union Local 134 offers the first year of its five-year apprenticeship training program at this location. This eventually leads to a job as a journeyman wireman. This shows how unions and school can effectively contribute to a common goal.

6.   Information Contact: 773/843-4500[38]

Massachusetts

---

1.   School: Ridge School of Technical Arts (RSTA), Cambridge

2.   Career Area(s):   Electronics, instrumentation, building crafts, teaching

3.   Students Served: 280

4.   Year Began: 1991

5.   Description: RSTA is part of the only public high school in Cambridge. It is the second-oldest vocational program in the United States committed to 100 percent integration of academics and career studies. All students are enrolled in science, social science, math, and English courses. Beginning in ninth grade students receive a brief overview of all the career areas offered, then three-week exploratories. In the 11th grade students are offered paid apprenticeships ($7.49/hour) at Polaroid Corporation and work 2-hour shifts. Alternatively, other junior interns three

mornings a week are driven to nearby Lesley College, an 83-year-old teacher-training institution. On the other mornings they work in local elementary schools. For all these students classroom courses continue along with their career apprenticeship or internship positions. Several other Cambridge companies are interested in setting up similar work-study career projects.

6. Information Contact: 617/349-6751[39]

	New York
1. School:	Rochester City School District
2. Career Area(s):	Skilled trades, financial services, health care, manufacturing
3. Students Served:	300
4. Year Began:	1993
5. Description:	School-to-Work Transition System, Rochester Business Education Alliance (RBEA), National Center on Education and the Economy, and the Rochester Public School District in conjunction with the several local business groups are engaged in a comprehensive career education system from the elementary to community-college level. "School Is Work" and "Articulated Career Guidance" programs begin with students in elementary school. Partnerships providing career transition activities are in place with 350 city businesses, including Bausch and Lomb, IBM, Eastman Kodak Company, Xerox, and many smaller organizations. Apprenticeships start in high school and continue in the local community college.
6. Information Contact:	202/783-3668[40]

North Carolina

1.	School:	Guilford Technical Community College, Greensboro
2.	Career Area(s):	More than 50 fields, including metal-working, transportation, financial, furniture, textile and chemical industries
3.	Students Served:	10,000
4.	Year Began:	1994 (Current Business Collaborative Program)
5.	Description:	First begun as a high-school/higher education apprenticeship program; one industry after another through a Greensboro Chamber of Commerce group has expanded specific career-education programs. Business–school collaborations have led to the building of specific facilities by business in support of these education programs, including a transportation complex (Volvo, GM, and Ford); manufacturing center (Konica Film Corp. of Japan); pharmaceutical program (Banner Pharmacaps, Inc., a Dutch company); and apprenticeship training programs, such as with Dow Corning Corp.
6.	Information Contact:	336/334-4822[41]

Ohio

1.	School:	Great Oaks Institute of Technology and Career Development (36 Cincinnati area school districts outside the city)
2.	Career Area(s):	More than 50 career programs
3.	Students Served:	2,900
4.	Description:	The institute has four primary centers throughout the region with 10 satellite offices. Ninety-six percent of its 1995 graduates

found jobs or pursued further education. About 10 percent enrolled as full or part-time students at post-secondary schools. The Institute has a program specially designed for truant students, school dropouts, or those who wish to earn a GED and vocational certificate.

5. Information Contact: 513/771-8840[42]

Oklahoma

---

1. School: Tulsa Technology Center

2. Career Area(s):   About 75 career programs in automotive technology, metal work/machinery, aviation maintenance, and health sciences

3. Students Served: 1,800

4. Year Began: 1992

5. Description: Tulsa Tech offers many four-year career programs: two years in high school, two years at Tulsa Tech, and an apprenticeship/internship job training component. Largely begun by the local Chamber of Commerce, Tulsa Tech business collaborators include American Airlines, Rockwell International, Banker Oil Tools, Hilton International, General Motors, and Chrysler, to name a few. Tulsa Tech is part of the Training for Industry Program (TIP) operated by the state's Department of Vocational and Technical Education. Customized industrial/management training to meet the specific needs of business is provided through 29 schools at 40 sites statewide.

6. Information Contact: 918/828-5051[43]

Oregon

1. School:	David Douglas High School, Portland
2. Career Area(s):	Seven career areas
3. Students Served:	1996: 450 students; 1999: 1,000 students
4. Year Began:	1993
5. Description:	The Oregon Business Council, a coalition of the state's 40 largest companies, including Nike, Intel Corp., Tektronix, and Sequent Computer Systems, teamed up with the school to focus on seven career-education "pathway" areas: arts and communication; business and management; health sciences; hospitality, tourism, and recreation; industrial and engineering systems; natural resources; and social and human services. Eighth graders take career education to explore possible careers. They select a high-school pathway before graduating. As mandated by Oregon state law, freshmen and sophomores work on a Certificate of Initial Mastery in English, social studies, math, science, health, personal finance, and technology. Freshmen are "adopted" by a company to observe the variety of potential careers found in a business. In junior and senior years, students are enrolled in work-based courses, mostly as interns. Health sciences classes, for instance, might be held at a hospital or other health facility. Also, the school invites businesses to the campus to offer intern-like experiences. The last two years of this career program are devoted to working within a major area of study toward a Certificate of Advanced Mastery.
6. Information Contact:	503/252-2900[44]

Pennsylvania

1.	School:	Philadelphia High School Academics, Inc.
2.	Career Area(s):	Eleven career areas
3.	Students Served:	6,000
4.	Year Began:	1969
5.	Description:	The nation's first career academy in a secondary school was the electrical science academy at Thomas Edison High school in 1969. This applied electrical science academy was formed with a partnership among the Philadelphia Electric Co., the school district, and Philadelphia's Urban Coalition. They established an independent educational foundation supported by the business community to operate schools as career academies. These academies gradually grew to 28 sites enrolling about a fourth of the city's high-school student population in the following 11 career areas: automotive sciences; aviation and aerospace; business; communications; electrical science; environmental technology; fitness, sports education, and health promotion; health; horticulture; hotel, restaurant and tourism; law, criminal justice; and public administration. Among the 200 participants acting as partners are smaller local businesses as well as larger corporations such as United Airlines, Pep Boys, SIGNA, Rohm & Haas, and Federal Reserve Bank of Philadelphia.
6.	Information Contact:	215/546-6300[45]

Business-Led Initiatives

The incentive for career-education programs can also come directly from individual companies large or small. According to one recent survey on the U.S. business community's growing role in this effort (1997), about one of every four employers now takes part in a career-education program.[46]

This should come as no surprise, since such business advisory groups as the National Alliance of Business (NAB), U.S. Chamber of Commerce, the Business Roundtable, National Association of Manufacturers, and many other business organizations are researching and disseminating to the business community career-education "best practices."

The National Academy Foundation, begun in 1982, has teamed more than 1,000 corporations and small businesses with more than 200 local high-school academies in 30 states. By 1995, 2,328 students through their school's finance, travel and tourism, or public services academies interned at 918 companies and earned more than $3.6 million.[47]

Some businesses have become real leaders in career education for specific communities scattered across America. These include the Eastman Kodak Company, General Motors, Motorola, Siemens, UNUM Insurance, Marriott Corporation, and McDonald's, to mention only a few. Let's take a more detailed look at what people in the business community are doing at the local level to prepare the next generation of knowledge workers.

Investing in People

1. Pro Tech Health Care (Boston, Massachusetts)

Pro Tech is an industry-driven program designed by seven local hospitals, in collaboration with the Boston Public Schools, to meet their institutional needs. The program combines classroom learning, clinical internships, and paid work experiences. This youth apprenticeship model links the last two years of high school with two years at a local community college. The hospitals provide staff, appropriate space, and the resources for the hospital-based instruction delivered during clinical rotations and apprenticeships. Pro Tech helps the participating hospitals to develop a cadre of now-scarce new entry-level medical workers at advanced educational levels.[48]

2. The Boeing Company (Seattle, Washington, and Other Sites)

Boeing has begun offering paid apprenticeships or sponsoring local "tech-prep" programs for high-school students in communities where their operations are located across the United States. "To get the best possible product, we need to do what we can to help the schools prepare kids for the workplace," says Barbara Scott, education-relations manager for Boeing in Wichita, Kansas. Starting in their junior year, high-school students work on the Wichita assembly lines for two summers as trainees. They then have a good chance at a permanent plant technician job. In the Seattle area about 75 student interns spend four to six weeks over the course of three summers doing progressively more complex work. Of the first 100 students to complete the Boeing program in 1996, more than 70 have been offered jobs with the company paying between $27,000 and $29,000. The Boeing internships are part of a larger Puget Sound "tech prep" program. Begun in 1993, the Manufacturing Technology Advisory Group (MTAG) is a coalition of 20 area employers. In collaboration with local labor unions, schools, and government, MTAG by the summer of 1997 had offered internships to 259.[49]

3. Siemens Corporation

In 1992 Siemens introduced apprenticeships to its American operations. The company now trains about 13,000 apprentices in 20 countries, including 25 programs at 19 sites across the United States. A solid academic curriculum is combined with hands-on practical training. During the last two years of attendance at East Wake High School in Wendell, North Carolina, students couple a rigorous, applied learning curriculum with paid part-time work at Siemens. Then they spend two years at a local community college, again working half-time in paid positions at Siemens. With 40 factories in the United States, Siemens began their apprenticeship programs in Kentucky and North Carolina. They intend to extend them to California and to all their other locations. Apprenticeship as a stepping stone to a career at Siemens is part of the corporate culture. Over 40 percent of its upper management graduated from Siemens' apprenticeship programs, including president and CEO Albert Hoser.[50]

4. Intel Corporation (New Mexico and Other Sites)

Hands-on science centers developed by Intel were so successful with students that the New Mexico State Department of Education adopted them as a model for schools. Intel has also introduced high-school computer-technology classes and workplace learning opportunities for students and teachers. More than 1,500 students have continued in this career program at the postsecondary level in an Intel-developed technology degree program offered through two technical colleges (the Albuquerque Technical Vocational Institute and Pierce College, Lake Wood Washington), four community colleges, and at one private college. Intel's Manufacturing Technology Program offers associate degrees with a concentration in semiconductor manufacturing and additional courses in ceramics, plastics, and general manufacturing.[51]

Bottom-Line Arguments

Business participates in work-based learning programs when they produce bottom-line results. "Firms not currently involved in career-education programs need more bottom-line arguments to convince them to join up," concluded a 1998 survey of more than 600 employers conducted by Columbia University. Employee retention is one powerful argument. The findings of a U.S. Census Bureau study (1998) that surveyed more than 5,000 employers across the country found that companies participating in career education often experienced a much lower turnover rate among their younger workers. About a third of the organizations studied were small businesses.

Businesses that had a career-education program with a local school had a youth-worker (ages 18 to 26) turnover rate of 25 percent, compared with 50 percent for employers who don't participate in career education. Robert Zemsky, director of the University of Pennsylvania's Institute for Research on Higher Education, which developed the study, suggests that organizations who participate in such programs do a lot less "trial and error" hiring: they are more familiar with the education young people in a community are receiving, so they can do a better job selecting career-education applicants who will be a good fit. What this study means is there is an actual business advantage for school–business career-education collaborations. Other contemporary economic and political conditions are changing the business environment to give more U.S. businesses real incentives to participate in these programs.[52]

In 1997 Colorado became the first state to offer business tax credits for those involved in work-based learning. This tax incentive offers a 10 percent state income tax credit on all funds invested in these programs. This includes wages, workers' compensation, unemployment insurance, and training expenses.[53]

Michigan offers a $2,000 annual tax credit for each high-school student a company enrolls in a federally registered apprenticeship program. Wisconsin offers businesses cash incentives. This state gives a $500 to $1,500 incentive a year per student in a business-sponsored apprenticeship program. Other states are now seriously considering similar tax or cash incentives or have already enacted them.

A new federal tax credit may also spur employers' involvement. The Work Opportunities Tax Credit that took effect October 1, 1997, offers employers a credit whenever they hire individuals from disadvantaged groups. Companies can receive a 25 percent credit on the first $6,000 of wages. Employers also may receive a 35 percent credit on the first $10,000 of wages for the long-term disadvantaged. A small tax credit is available for youth hired for summer jobs. The credit provides an incentive to recruit disadvantaged youth into work-based-learning transition programs.[54]

Business will increase its career-education involvement if states amend liability, wage, and insurance rules that can pose obstacles to participation. The trend is now moving in that direction, with many states making or proposing new policies covering issues from work permits and safety training to new, low-cost options for liability insurance. Some examples include:

- *New Hampshire* The state's work-based accredited insurance program includes policies for 2,000 to 3,000 career education students.

- *Maine* The Maine Technical College manages payroll, tax, and insurance issues for the entire state's youth apprenticeship programs.

- *Florida* The St. Johns River Partnership pays for liability insurance to reduce the financial risk posed by students in the workplace.

- *Kansas* Local career-education partnerships create nonprofit corporations to deal with wage and liability issues.[55]

The decentralized nature of U.S. society gives states and communities more flexibility to design innovative career-education systems that better meet local economic needs. This was the role played by the Tulsa, Oklahoma, Chamber of Commerce as it helped expand business involvement in areawide career education. Local chambers of commerce are already in place across America. They could function as industry–education councils that bring together many individual players (i.e., employers, unions, schools, and government). The chambers can effectively lobby for new state education and tax laws. They can also supply the ongoing supporting implementation infrastructure needed if career education is to grow on a mass scale. In other communities, a local community foundation, such as the Philadelphia Career Academy or the education foundation in Austin, Texas, has assumed such an intermediary role.

These industry–education councils lend a formal structure and support to carry out this mission. They would help local businesses integrate their resources with education in four critical areas:

- Ongoing educator staff development in all subject areas, including career development

- Facilitation of joint curriculum development and constant revisions

- More relevant instructional materials and state-of-the-art equipment upgrades

- Collaborative educational management practices

An industry–education council is not an advisory board, but a structural community nonprofit service organization. The main challenge in each community, according to Donald Clark, president of the National Association of Industry/Education Cooperation, "is finding those individuals and organizations with the wherewithal to make it happen."[56]

Business support of career education will only succeed if parents and educators are assured that these programs offer all students a rigorous, liberal arts education and career classroom education linked to appropriate work-based learning experiences. Widespread local business collaboration is essential in each community to disseminate current and future labor-market needs that can be tied to career opportunities for children.

Education to a career means preparing a child for potentially multiple careers and job changes over a lifetime. We need to allay the real fears of some parents and educators that career education translates only into narrow technical training tied to a specific job for life.

These fears are based on the negative images of nineteenth-century vocational and trade schools. These so-called "factory schools" did much to eliminate the liberal arts from the high-school curriculum, as businesses largely demanded workers who would conform to rote mass-production methods, not people who could think and innovate. Historian Richard Hofstadler tells the story of a Massachusetts wool manufacturer who rejected too much education for the children of working men on the grounds that he could not run his mill with algebra![57]

By the 1990s these business fundamentals have changed across America. The high-performance workplace has turned basic worker educational requirements on their heads. In order to compete, most organizations endlessly search for the so-called "skilled worker." Business now expects the next generation of employees to spread innovation and creativity throughout the organization at every level.

The career-education programs we have reviewed show how individual communities or states have motivated their constituents to collaborate and overcome the major roadblocks to change. They have hammered out local coalitions that address the confusing array of potential solutions, the low skills of many students, and the provision of career information and experiences relevant to current and future jobs.

They recognize that we cannot turn back the clock to an earlier age based on a low-tech, mass-production economy. Nor can America retain its current position of world leadership by throwing away its computer-based technologies or trying to shut out the global forces of free trade. We need to prepare students for a lifetime of learning through tougher academic standards along with education to careers.

Career education holds the promise of offering more Americans more relevant knowledge and a better life in the twenty-first century. These new education programs demonstrate that earning a college degree is no longer the only entry-level ticket to "the American way of life" (i.e., entering or remaining part of the middle class). Whatever your role in the local community, isn't it time to get involved?

CHAPTER

9

A Kick in the Butt

The person who wants to lead the orchestra must turn their backs on the crowd.

JAMES CROOK

We live in a world where every business must adapt to new technologies and sources of competition or die. Entrepreneurs now use money, technology, communication, management, and labor located anywhere in the world to make things or support services and sell them worldwide. As one major communications company puts it, "In a world of communications, people make the difference." It has become more necessary than ever for employers to invest in better skills so that their people sparkle with new ideas. Yet this is not happening inside most organizations.

Training is getting killed off in the current marketplace because it hasn't been able to stand up to the line manager and say, "Make me a full business partner." Outspoken software developer Roger Schank agrees. "I think management really isn't interested in training despite the fact that they say they are. . . . They're focused on quarterly profits and they don't want to start investing massive amounts of money in something that may pay off five years from now."[1] The American Society for Training and Development (ASTD) reports (September 1996) that total business training expenditures have risen by nearly 20 percent since 1983, to $55.3 billion (1995). However, the number of workers has risen by 24 percent during that same period. Result: The amount spent per worker has declined. This is not a strong endorsement by senior management of training and development in general or the corporate university in particular. Even more ominously, ASTD warns that smaller companies are reducing their training budgets.

Unfortunately, for the foreseeable future these companies will be the source of major new job growth in the United States. How do we alter their negative perceptions of workplace training?

What's Training Worth?

Almost every firm has now experienced at least one "reengineering process" (i.e., how are we going to do more with less?). As in most periods of economic uncertainty, training and development is often undergoing significant downsizing. Granted, every department in a business is now subject to intense new scrutiny by management and is being called upon to justify its cost-to-benefit ratio. Too often, though, the learning organization has become the "cheap organization."

Since most business people consider training the soft side of the business, most management has not seriously considered the issue of training's return-on-investment (ROI). Jack Philips, a leading international expert on ROI and editor of the ASTD book *In Action: Return on Investment*, Vols. I and II, thinks that this is unfortunate.

"In my work with many organizations, we are able to determine a realistic ROI model, track the results and sell the training ROI to senior management," he says. However, Phillips cautions that you must select ROI measures that are meaningful for your particular company.

The key to ROI success in training is to do your homework (i.e., link specific company problems to potential training outcomes), compile detailed results, and make sure that the CEO takes the time to understand them. With all the current available information on ROI (see Chapters 2, 3, and 4), training directors and management no longer have any good excuse for not using ROI as part of their game plan to grow their performance-improvement programs.

Fight "Solution of the Month"

Another problem is that too many companies belong to the "solution of the month club." Trainers are constantly being asked to change priorities. Ian Rose, president of IBR Consulting Services Ltd. in Vancouver, Canada, recently completed a survey of 39 leading-edge organizations in the United States, Canada, the United Kingdom, Australia, and South Africa. What he found was that "more often than not, training departments are being kept busy helping their organizations implement one or more types of solutions, and pay little attention to identifying and agreeing upon the problems." In most businesses, few managers want to deal with the real business issues that the training is supposed to be addressing.

Unless an education program improves business operations and moves a company closer to its strategic objectives, the need for the so-called corporate university cannot be sustained. If we are to overcome the resistance to change within your business, the corporate university must become far more strategic, far more long-term in its focus than in the past. For too long, training has been stalled at the level of programs offering "behavior tricks" that are to be quickly learned and just as soon forgotten. Instead we must provide education for people that supports better ways of learning critical competencies and fosters workplace innovation. High-performance workplaces require changing management thinking, not just management behavior.[2]

Operate a Business

The corporate university's first goal should be to secure management support for its new role as a business center that helps make the company's profit. To do this, corporate university managers need to speak the language of business, not just training. Most training organizations are still seen as cost centers as opposed to profit centers. Training is still seen as a part of human resources' many other nonsynergistic functions. HR "polices" the business—it never drives it.

To change this mindset, the corporate university must sever its ties to human resources. The senior training professional must think and act as the "chief development officer" (CDO) and not simply as a technical learning expert. This change has already occurred at Sprint University, Xerox Document University, General Electric, General Motors, and Coopers and Lybrand. The CDO must have the same elevated perspective on development that the CFO has on finance. The CDO's organization must be held accountable as a resource and a vehicle that drives business strategy and values and contributes to business profit.

If corporate universities cannot do these things, they may find themselves out of work during the next five years. Many corporations in which the learning organizations are weak will move toward outsourcing the entire training function. More than one senior executive has expressed the opinion to me that because of cost pressures, businesses many someday expect employees to get the education they need from sources other than the corporate training department. The message is clear: Either the corporate university grows strategically in the organization, or it may disappear from it.

But this leaves several big questions unanswered. How do you continuously train people, without diverting them from their everyday job of making the business profitable? How do you train people to be successful elsewhere, while still encouraging them to make big commitments to your own firm? How do you get your newly liberated employees to spend their time on ideas that create value, and not simply on those they enjoy?

For many, "corporate universities" bring to mind only big businesses—Motorola, McDonald's, IBM. In contemporary American business, however, the word "university" increasingly refers to an effort by any company, regardless of size, to collectively organize the delivery of information and learning to every employee.

The corporate university is, in fact, a new rendition of an old standard: business's recognition of the critical link between education and economic prosperity.

The Evolution of Corporate Universities

The desire for a well-educated workforce is not new. Between 1895 and 1920, businesses in the United States upheld general learning for all Americans by supporting the nationwide effort that established universal, tax-supported, public education. A highly literate workforce was seen as an asset in most workplaces, especially those adopting assembly-line manufacturing based on Frederick Taylor's principles of scientific management.

During World War I (1914–1918), business took education a step further into the workplace by adopting Charles R. Allen's "four-step method" (show, tell, do, and check) as the standard method for on-the-job training (OJT) that supported burgeoning assembly-line war industries.

World War II (1941–1945) sparked an expansion of workplace education. Job Instructor Training (JIT) was designed as a train-the-trainer system for first-line and second-line supervisors to support the vast expansion of assembly-line production in the U.S. defense industry. More that two million employees received corporate training in JIT, job methods, and human relations.

For the first time in American history, the Engineering, Science and Management War Training Program (ESMWT), established during World War II, and the GI Bill exposed millions of adults to college courses on almost every aspect of management, technology, psychology, and education. The idea of the corporate university was not far behind, for by the mid-1950s, these newly educated managers formalized the use of in-house training and education programs. These early corporate universities were built around the concepts of "management behavior" and managing human resource development (HRD).

By the mid-1980s the Carnegie Foundation reported that business had invested over $40 billion in employee-education efforts, reaching almost eight million employees annually. This encompassed a wide range of in-house education programs, seminars, and institutes teaching everything from computer skills and management techniques to sales and customer service. In addition, there was a growing emphasis on basic skills training.

As the idea of offering a diversity of educational programs to a broad array of employees gained acceptance, American companies began to formally build corporate university facilities. The Xerox Center in Virginia, the RCA Campus in New Jersey, the Holiday Inn University in Mississippi, and the Motorola, Arthur Andersen, and McDonald's facilities in Illinois began to look very much like traditional college campuses, with classrooms, dormitories, and recreational facilities. The growth of these facilities, and their relative impact on overall American business culture, began to establish the idea that employee education meant something far more than just narrow training. By 1988, eight corporations purported to offer about 20 college-level degree programs! The U.S. corporate university existed—both as a broad educational concept and as an accredited, degree-granting institution.

Creating the Learning Organization

Today, corporate universities of all sizes and types operate throughout the country, from Procter & Gamble College to IRS University. Yet all share a common mission: to transform the department, corporation, agency, or institution into a "learning organization."

Just visualizing this concept of learning in a business environment is an enormous problem. So, let us reduce it to concrete reality. Calvert, Mobley, and Marshall provide a useful blueprint for putting the theory of a learning organization—and corporate university—into practice (see Box 9-1).

Wabash National in Lafayette, Indiana, shows how the concept works in real life. In 1985, working from a card table and three folding chairs in a downtown office, Donald J. Ehrlich began Wabash National to build truck trailers. This company's managers, besides calling on suppliers they already knew for orders, also called on Purdue University's management department for training. "The philosophy was that the people at Wabash were either going to make it or break it," explained Chuck Fish, vice president of human relations, in a front-page story in *The Wall Street Journal* (September 7, 1995).

They began classes for workers who wanted to be welders and for recent immigrants to learn English. A worker complained to Ehrlich that he was wasting his profit-sharing (part of the company's participatory motivational culture) on parking lot improvements. Ehrlich added a course in business basics. Now everyone can learn the difference between a capitalized expense (paving parking lots), and an operating expense (a load of parts). This formed part of a series of classes in business economics, statistical process control, the just-in-time inventory system, and team building.

All workers and managers have the opportunity to improve their skills (to comprehend the message), to receive training in basic business systems, and to be educated in the problem-solving, decision-making, and the team-building process. Wabash depends on its workers learning how a company makes a profit and how rapid growth and constant change will keep it profitable. Ehrlich says that at Wabash, "We're trying to get workers to think about building trailers."

Wabash National offers all employees basic skill classes in reading, math, writing, and English as a Second Language (ESL). By improving these comprehension levels the business can make maximum use of high-tech innovations that enhance employee productivity and company profit.

Over the past two years, workers have participated in 164 practical teams, such as the air brake stroke and the free-play adjustment team.

What do learning organizations learn that other organizations do not? Learning organizations learn
- to use learning to reach their goals
- to help people value the effects of their learning on their organizations
- to avoid making the same mistakes again (and again)
- to share information in ways that prompts appropriate action
- to link individual performance with organizational performance
- to tie rewards to key measures of performance
- to take in a lot of environmental information at all times
- to create structures and procedures that support the learning process
- to foster ongoing and orderly dialogues
- to make it safe for people to share openly and take risks

What does a learning organization look like? A learning organization
- learns collaboratively, openly, and across boundaries
- values *how* it learns as well as *what* it learns
- invests in staying ahead of the learning curve in its industry
- gains a competitive edge by learning faster and smarter than competitors
- turns data into useful knowledge quickly and at the right time and place
- enables every employee to feel that every experience provides him or her a chance to learn something potentially useful, even if only for leveraging future learning
- exhibits little fear and defensiveness; rewards and learns from what goes wrong ("failure" learning) and right ("success" learning)
- takes risks but avoids jeopardizing basic security of the organization
- invests in experimental and seemingly tangential learning
- supports people and teams who want to pursue action-learning projects
- depoliticizes learning by not penalizing individuals or groups for sharing information and conclusions

How does a learning organization evolve? What are the first steps to becoming a learning organization? A budding learning organization can begin by
- questioning current assumptions about learning
- getting an outside perspective
- tying the goal of becoming a learning organization to its organization vision
- finding or creating a champion in top management
- looking for the "pain" in the organization—the place where more effective learning could help
- articulating learning–organization ideas plainly
- rewarding group as well as individual learning success and failure
- finding an external enemy to spur greater cooperative learning
- finding ways to collaborate internally in and unhampered by boundaries

Box 9-1 Anatomy of a Learning Organization
Source: Calvert, Gene, Sandra Mobley, and Lisa Marshall,
"Grasping the Learning Organization," *Training & Development*, 48(June 1994), p. 41.

These groups have saved the company hundreds of thousands of dollars through practical, thoughtful production innovations.

Does Wabash support a "corporate university"? At Wabash, Jerry Ehrlich says, "three Einsteins would be no match" for a factory full of workers attending classes and contributing ideas. This is the essence of the learning organization/corporate university concept.

American business is at the end of an era in which only managers controlled people, information, and ideas. Victor Hugo was right: "Nothing in the world is as powerful as an idea whose time has come." We have entered the era of the corporate-university concept for every organization, large or small.

The corporate-university philosophy will become more pervasive in business with each passing year. Some say the next step will be a "virtual university" where workers will select from courses offered in-house, or by private seminars and educational institutions. Distance learning or "education on tap" cannot satisfy every employee educational need. However, the mixed use of high-performance, computer-assisted learning and face-to-face instruction will continue to grow steadily throughout the corporate classroom, putting large and small business players on a far more equal information/learning footing.

Enter the "virtual training organization" (VTO). This "learning university" approach offers a varied menu of learning methods, including interactive computer technology, self-directed learning tools, and customized packages of print materials. The VTO university may feature self-paced workbooks, self-study courses, CD-ROM instructional packages, and a formal mentoring/coaching process.

In the Silicon Valley, National Semiconductor University is both global and virtual. It networks various academic institutions, business learners, training suppliers, and customers on three continents. This university's goal is to spread a learning vision and philosophy that develops intellectual capital for future change.

U.S. business has passed from an era of large corporate bureaucracies to a new period in which even bigger businesses are trying to organize around small work units. Technical invention will continue to accelerate. Yet, increasing value will be placed on fostering personal creativity and innovation. The "learning job" of any business, whether a multinational corporation, a mid-sized company of 500 people, or a small family business, is to develop its human capital through a lifelong learning process. This is the ultimate goal of the corporate-university philosophy, and the ultimate challenge for U.S. business culture.

Corporate University Review has offered detailed business case studies that answer these questions and shows why it makes fundamental economic sense for many companies to develop their own people for the long term. Whether the corporate culture calls it a learning alliance, training center, campus, resource center, or a university, *Corporate University Review* has given up-to-date information on the growing array of means for delivering learning profitably. Companies representing a broad spectrum of U.S. business have been profiled in case studies (see Box 9-2 and Figure 9-1), including:

- Burger King University
- Dana University
- Disney University
- Eddie Bauer University
- Eli Lilly's Global Learning Alliance
- Ford's Fairlane Training and Development Center (FTDC)
- General Motors University
- IBM Global Campus (virtual university)
- Land Rover University
- Reebok Training Resources
- Saturn University
- Southwest Airline's University for People
- Volvo University

Needed: A Kick in the Butt

Today we know more ways to develop employee knowledge more rapidly than ever before. The diversity of America's response to doing business in the twenty-first century means there will remain organizations with short-sighted vision looking no further than the next quarterly dividend. By starving their investment in people, these businesses in the long term increase the risk of appearing as an "obituary" in *The Wall Street Journal*. These companies need a kick in the butt,

The Land Rover Way
Culture, values, and teamwork

☐ **Create the Magic**
Initial Center training

☐ **4×4ward Program**
Teambuilding/"Magic" refresher

☐ **Dipped in Green**
Intro to Land Rover

☐ **Leadership Institute**
Center management

Off-Road Techniques
Application and adventure

☐ **ASCENT (Levels 1–3)**
Off-road driving certification

☐ **TReK Challenge**
Retailer competition

☐ **Camel Trophy**
U.S. teams/trails selection

☐ **Driving School/Events**
The Equinox Driving Academy
Creek guides, dealer meetings

Support the Sell
Skills and product knowledge

☐ **Selling the Land Rover Way**
Basics of selling

☐ **4×4 Authority**
Product and competitive info

☐ **New Model Introduction**
Product launch training

☐ **In-Retailer Support**
In-store visit
All point bulletins
Hot topics sales meetings
Other material

☐ **Skills Enhancement**
F&I, used car marketing
Business management

Support the Product

☐ **For Technicians**
Introduction to Land Rover Products
V-8 engine overhaul
Engine management systems
Transfer gearbox overhaul
Manual transmission overhaul
Automatic transmission overaul
Axles/Swivels/Differentials
Chassis Systems
HVAC/climate control
Electrical troubleshooting I and II
Operation Pride 7 Cities

☐ **For Parts Personnel**
The Land Rover Parts Professional
The Land Rover Parts Manager

☐ **For Warranty Personnel**
Warranty administrator

☐ **For Service Advisers**
Service adviser training

☐ **Other**
RSOV U.S. Army Ranger vehicle training

Box 9-2 Land Rover University Curriculum

Source: Corporate University Review, November/December 1997

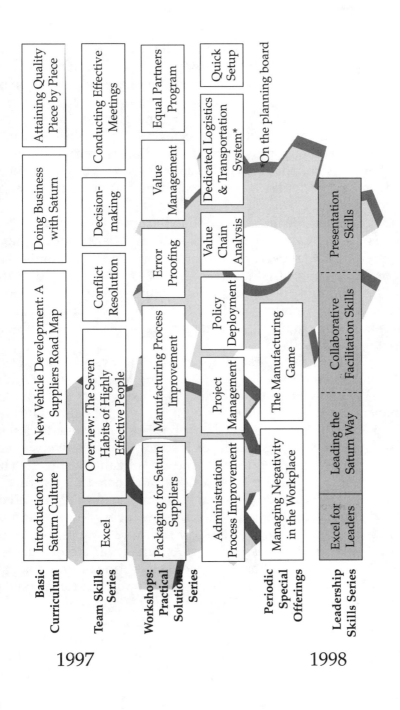

Figure 9-1 Saturn University 1997 and 1998 Curriculum
Source: Courtesy of Corporate University Review

269

for they are being left far behind by the agile entrepreneur who wants not just to survive, but to thrive by sprinting ahead of the pack with new and better products and services and other innovations driven by increasing human capital.

Investing in human capital is not something to be done lightly. Those managers who invest their energies in the development of a "knowledge workforce" must have reliable measurement tools to confirm that decision. The Human Capital Scoreboard (see Chapter 5) is one example of a realistic management-measurement system to achieve this goal.

Management also needs to subscribe to this guiding principle: "All Training Is Not Created Equal!" As several recent studies have pointed out (A. T. Kearney, 1994), 80 percent of company training is of such poor quality that it is never used back on-the-job by the employee. Why? Because behavior-based training needs to be largely replaced by a more cognitive, critical-competency approach that activates personal innovation and change-management abilities. Training is for dogs—education is for people.

Investing in human capital is not a one-shot event. Unfocused, least-common-denominator, generic training will usually yield a lower ROI. We know that a thoughtfully planned, sequentially driven performance-improvement program will achieve a better ROI over time. By using the latest design advances in employee education, business can achieve higher levels of learning that positively affect personal performance, productivity, and organizational profit. The bottom-line result: increasing knowledge means increasing profit.

The history of the United States has been the story of the pursuit of new knowledge in applications that improve everyday life. Rapid globalization and advancing technology continue to raise the "education bar" for every business. Today the pursuit of knowledge has never been more important for everyone. Call it pride or pragmatism, the United States was founded and still stands upon this fundamental belief—that Americans need not be the victims of ignorance.

10

Investing in Human Capital: A Blueprint for the 21st Century

In a global economy it is education, not location that determines the standard of living.

ALBERT HOSER, PRESIDENT, SIEMENS CORPORATION

In 1997 the American Management Association reported that a Fortune 100 conglomerate needed to replace one-third of its 10,000 technical people due to retirement in the next few years. This is the same story that I have heard repeatedly from companies across the United States. What are corporate leaders going to do as they compete for an ever-shrinking pool of "knowledge workers"?

The Pepsi company's chief executive officer, Roger Enrico, offers one innovative answer. He donated his 1998 salary. Except for $1, his salary will provide scholarships for children of employees making less than $60,000. Enrico, who grew up in a blue-collar family, persuaded his board of directors to contribute $1 million to the company's scholarship fund. This fund can now be used by what Enrico calls the company's "front line" for tuition at two-year technical and vocational schools, or four-year colleges. In the past scholarships were only offered to students attending traditional four-year schools. Enrico is donating his annual salary of $900,000 "for the foreseeable future" because like many other CEOs, he understands that American business needs new thinking for a new era.

The twenty-first century will be a marked contrast to the twentieth century. The old century has seen crisis after crisis: the "War to End All Wars" (World War I), the Great Depression, the Second World War, and the Cold War. The United States came out on top every time, making the twentieth century the "American Century." The next crisis—the "Skill Wars"—might have a different ending.

At the dawn of the twenty-first century the "information age" may be at an end. The "knowledge age" has begun. You will not succeed in business unless you can create new knowledge (i.e., the skills, hunches, and insights of your workforce). The driving force behind the "Skill Wars" is a global economy that is virtually unregulated, powered by space-age technology and an ocean of money. It is creating an unrelenting demand for high-skilled labor. The jobs will be there. Will the educated workers be there?

As we have already noted, at least one-fifth of American workers are not able to participate fully in this new knowledge "war" (U.S. Census Bureau, 1995). Coopers & Lybrand (1997) reported that CEOs of the fastest-growing high-tech firms have lowered growth expectations for their own shops because of this skilled worker shortage. Also, nearly seven of ten employers say high-school graduates lack the skills to succeed at work (1998 New York Public Agenda). The National Association of Manufacturers (1998) agreed when they reported that 40 percent of all 17 year-olds do not have the math skills,

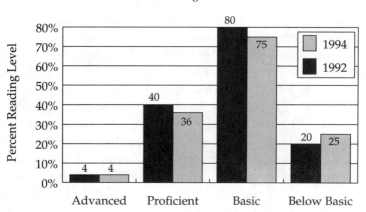

Grade 12 Reading Performance 1992–1994

Figure 10-1 National Assessment of Education Progress
Source: Adapted from U.S. Department of Education, Office of Educational Research and Improvement, National Center for Educational Statistics, "NAEP 1994 Reading Report Card for the Nation and the States," January 1996.

and 60 percent of 17 year-olds lack the reading skills, to hold down a production job at a manufacturing company.

These gloomy surveys point to the basic reasons for the unrelenting countrywide competition for skilled labor. Even if the next recession offers momentary labor market relief, from top to bottom the U.S. educational establishment is failing the knowledge litmus test for the twenty-first century.

The National Assessment of Educational Progress (NAEP) showed continued declines in the reading performance of U.S. high-school students (see Figure 10-1). Only about 40 percent of high-school seniors were reading at or above their grade level. Also, the results of a mathematics and science test (1998) of 12th graders in many countries showed the United States to be among the least knowledgeable (see Figure 10-2). Earlier in the 1990s a similar series of tests showed the lowest 25 percent of 8th graders in Japan and South Korea could outperform the average U.S. student.[1]

What is more disturbing is that the American Council on Education (ACE) reported that at least 13 percent of the nation's undergraduates were enrolled in at least one remedial course (1993). Also, 98 percent of

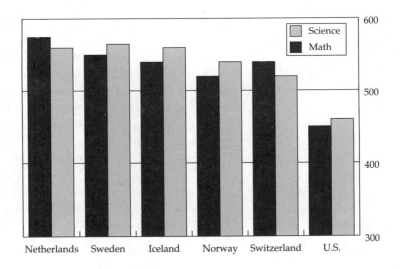

Figure 10-2 International Test Comparisons
Source: Adapted from Third International Mathematics and Science Study; compiled by Rick Santos and Tricia Ford/*Los Angeles Times.*

America's colleges allow remedial reading, writing, and math students to take regular courses at the same time. Twenty-three percent of these colleges even award degree credit for remedial courses!

As a result, Frederic L. Pryor of Swarthmore College and David Schaffer of Haverford College in *Who's Not Working and Why* found that it was not just possession of a college degree that determined a graduate's employment or salary, but his or her level of functional literacy. It is the skills college grads possess that determine their job-level readiness. "The shortage of qualified college graduates is real" says Pryor, "but the key word is 'qualified.'"[2]

This "people paradox" of having "too few" properly educated workers for "too many" sophisticated technology-driven jobs was predicated a long time ago by a noted economist:

We are suffering not from the rheumatic of old age, but from the growing pains of over-rapid changes—from the painfulness of readjustment between one economic period and another. The increase of technical efficiency has been taking place faster than we can deal with the problem of labor absorption.

John Maynard Keynes, 1930

Since 1900 millions of manual-labor jobs have been replaced by technology. Yet over the same period the number of jobs has grown almost continuously, and with it the real incomes of most people in the United States. America is now entering a new watershed era. We are leaving the age of the wrench and entering the age of the robot and the advanced computer. This rapid rate of technological change increases the need for almost all new entry-level workers to be better educated. There is also a growing demand for the continuous educational improvement of the current workforce that will have an impact on personal performance and the productivity of almost every organization (see Figure 10-3).

If Peter Drucker is right and knowledge is the "only meaningful economic resource," here is an answer for what a business can do with their own workers who lack education or who need to be retrained for the next generation of technology. Business can make these workers more adaptable by investing in performance-improvement programs that can be applied to everyday business needs.[3]

But what drives manufacturers crazy is getting these people trained so they can work in today's manufacturing environment. "We

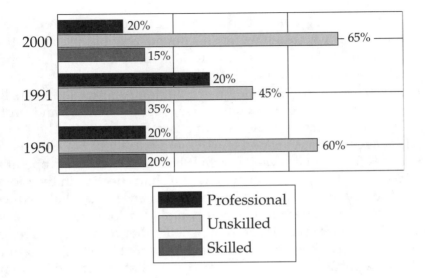

Figure 10-3 Demand for Skilled Labor
Source: Adapted from U.S. Bureau of Labor Statistics

are doing more with fewer people today. Education is the component that we need to improve," says Robert W. Crandall, a senior fellow at the Washington-based Brookings Institution, in his study "Manufacturing on the Move" (1993). I have heard almost exactly the same words countless times from managers in virtually every business sector from coast-to-coast.

The truth is that this business strategy is not being followed, and a disturbingly large share of American workers are hopelessly lost in the knowledge-driven global economy. The gap between so-called "knowledge workers" and low-skilled workers is widening at an alarming rate. It now appears that this gulf will continue to grow as global business expands. Why?

Because too many businesses are engaged in an act of financial levitation, trying to make bigger and bigger stacks of money from companies that are barely growing. Their magic act centers on cost-cutting, squeezing staffs, slashing training, eliminating everything except their "core business operations." The predominant American management philosophy of the 1990s has been that business exists only to drive up stock prices and enrich shareholders. This is the philosophy as stated by its strongest advocate Albert Dunlap, CEO of Sunbeam Corporation, known as "Chainsaw Al" for his downsizing of the corporations he has headed: "The point of business is to make a profit. The responsibility of the CEO is to deliver shareholder value. Period."[4]

Between 1987 and 1996 more than 5 million American workers lost their jobs due to this downsizing binge, yet productivity and profits for many businesses remained anemic (see Figure 10-4). The American Management Association (AMA) in a survey of 547 downsized businesses found that fewer than half had improved their operating profits and that 77 percent experienced a sharp decline in the morale of the "survivors." Even more to the point, fewer than half reduced their costs; only 22 percent realized hoped for productivity improvements; less than 25 percent accomplished either improved cash flow or increased shareholder's return-on-investment; only 15 percent reduced bureaucracy; and fewer than 10 percent improved customer satisfaction or product quality.[5]

Joseph and Jimmie Boyett write in *Beyond Workplace 2000* (1995) that the reason these downsizing restructurings often fail is, "Rarely do senior executives contemplate changing the basic processes and behaviors by which a company operates." Downsizing is a lazy form of management for a quick buck. It is not a good substitute for long-term strategic planning. Mike Useen at the Wharton School of Management thinks that many managers "screwed up by believing that

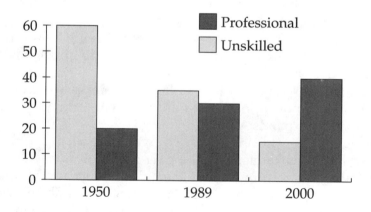

Figure 10-4 U.S. Workforce Changes
Source: Adapted from National School-to-Work Team.

downsizing could masquerade as a corporate strategy." Dana Mead, Tenneco, Inc.'s chief executive, agrees. "We need a viable alternative to the slash-and-burn mentality that prevails in too many board-rooms. You can't downsize your way to prosperity. You need to build a company to achieve value."[6]

According to a provocative survey by the New-York-based Confer-ence Board, prior to 1980 almost all business leaders saw themselves as "serving the community in the broader sense." In the 1950s we be-lieved, "What's good for General Motors is good for America." By the 1990s this sense of wider responsibility has vanished. Each person is out for himself. There exists an equal disdain among many male and female managers for broader community concerns.

Why is this happening? Competition? Technology? No personal ideology seems to be driving this management behavior. Executives do have choices. What many are doing now is just the simplest and the easiest thing: treating people like disposable parts, instruments, objects. It is also supported by the dominant "triumph of material-ism," "greed is good" ideology.

The functioning of any business is based on a set of mutual obliga-tions and responsibilities among all its employees. A growing dispar-ity now exists between the bottom line and this ethical arrangement. The popular business rhetoric of teams is often no longer supported by employee real-life experiences. People sense they need to continu-ally grow and learn in order to keep up, yet real learning opportuni-ties are being eliminated. Many employees are angry over this hypocrisy—they feel betrayed, and employee loyalty is falling.

CEOs are dependent on the effort of their company teams. They are not just individuals acting alone. They will squander their company's human capital by constantly failing to replenish it. Employees today will not follow leaders unless they believe in their programs and in-tegrity. If they don't, their leaders' actual power to lead is gone.[7]

Peter Drucker, one of the fathers of modern management theory, keys in on this flagrant neglect of human capital. He argues that what is now believed on the street and being taught in MBA programs about knowledge management is either wrong or seriously out of date. One widely held errant belief is that management's job is to run the business rather than to concentrate on developing people's critical competencies to check on what's going on outside the business. In-stead, management needs to focus, ". . . especially on how to organize the supply of a type of information that is totally absent today for executives—information about the world outside the company. By that I mean such information as the economic chain of which your business is a small part, the market, the environment, the society, the world economy."[8]

Therefore, the "core business idea" in a high-performance workplace is really not only providing easy access to information, but also constantly building up the individual's knowledge capacity to process, understand, and apply it, making problem solving/analytical thinking educational competencies more relevant for applied, day-to-day business innovations.

Stretching the Limits of Innovation

What is innovation? The magic formula of innovation includes obsession with products/services, long-term vision, listening to customers, firm leadership, and benchmarking. But one key element is lacking. The employee's well-educated abilities to comprehend the message! Without this, executives find their business can't compete. It's kaput.

If employees are to prosper in this turbulent era, they must first and foremost "learn how to learn"—how to actively acquire new skills as their old ones lose value and fade away in the marketplace. The new economy rewards passion, agility, creativity, initiative, and independent thinking—qualities too many businesses discourage by withholding continuous education from employees.

Such renowned "management gurus" as Tom Peters, Stephen Covey, and Rosabeth Moss Kanter are espousing a new pact: "Give employees continuous learning through training and work experiences and in exchange earn their commitment and trust."[9]

Yet adoption of this management wisdom seems slow. Most companies seem to suffer from a bad case of arrested development, lacking clearly defined plans to implement employee initiatives to make the concept viable. A Development Dimensions International (DDI) survey of 232 organizations in 16 countries shows that many important business practices are not being supported by company training (see Figure 10-5).

As we previously reviewed, of the money now invested annually by U.S. business (1998, estimated $60+ billion), too much is spent on managers, professionals, and salespeople (over 66 percent), and too

Program	Australia/ New Zealand	US/ Canada	United Kingdom	Pacific Rim	South Africa	Japan	France
Technical skill development	81	75	83	65	52	45	36
Interpersonal and communication skills	31	37	33	33	26	27	20
Group/team decision-making or problem-solving skills	25	39	42	26	16	31	18
Individual planning and organizing skills	25	14	25	17	10	13	27
Team building skills	13	28	33	30	13	10	18
Leadership skills	13	7	25	19	13	19	18
Quality/statistical analysis	6	22	17	14	7	16	27
Mentoring or coaching programs	0	0	0	12	3	6	18
Career or personal development planning	13	12	8	19	0	28	18
Understanding the business	0	8	25	9	13	3	18
Company-sanctioned formal education	0	14	8	10	6	27	

Percentage of Organizations Offering the Program to Most, Almost All, or All Employees

Figure 10-5 International Training Comparison
Source: *Training & Development*, September 1998

little on the people who need the most development (see Figure 10-5). According to a U.S. Labor Department Survey (1996), less than 3 percent of American businesses offer basic-skills training to their workers.

The educational neglect of both our current and future workforce is so woeful it almost defies description. As we have seen through a host of international comparisons, the achievement of U.S. students is at the middle (in reading) or the bottom (in science, math, geography) of these rankings in test after test, year after year. To put it truthfully, there is now a great domestic education vacuum in the lives of our children and employees from all walks of life and across every region of the United States. The question is not, "How profitable will it be for business to change this?" It is, "How are we as corporate leaders going to avert a long-term, general structural melt-down in America's standard of living?"

The Second American Education Revolution

As the United States begins a new century, America needs a "Second American Education Revolution." Employees and students need a higher level of academic, technical, communication, and information-processing skills in order to function effectively in society. Public education needs to be reinvented, rather than reformed. We need a greater diversity of local, small community schools in which students receive better education-to-careers.

As you read this, the "Second American Education Revolution" is gathering momentum across the United States. Its "timeline" may extend out to 2020 to get the job done (see Figure 10-6).

Much of what now drives the Second American Education Revolution is parental dissatisfaction with local schools. Many of these parents are business people, but all parents are concerned about future jobs for their children. It is becoming ever more apparent that what schooling should do best—giving all students a solid liberal arts education and some preparation for real-world careers—is now waning at every level of education. Why? Because change has happened faster than local communities can respond to rethink the educational requirements of the twenty-first century.

During the twentieth century, we have erected artificial barriers to "protect" education from the capitalist world of business. This

Phase One (1983–1984)

A Nation at Risk begins a period of criticism and general dissatisfaction with America's schools.

Phase Two (1985–1988)

The Carnegie Commission and other think tanks issue reforms centered on more of the same, ideas that only tinker with the system: spend more money, reform curriculum, change teacher training, establish local school councils, etc.

Phase Three (1989–1990)

Individual states, cities, or civic groups initiate radically different educational programs that depart from past contemporary schools: the state of Minnesota's Choice Program, Wisconsin's voucher system for Milwaukee's disadvantaged children.

Phase Four (1991–1998)

Revisionist educators, and business leaders research and apply selected new educational models and publish their successful results. Career education/school-to-work, more charter schools, career education programs begin. Public awareness and support increase for adopting broad systemic change. (*America 2000*, The SCANS Report, etc.)

Phase Five (1998–2005)

Political, business, union, and educational leaders begin backing new education models that have earned popular acceptance with local communities. New state/federal legislation establishes significant new school model programs. Business begins to seriously adopt lifelong learning. The U.S. Supreme Court redefines "public education."

Phase Six (2005–2010?)

More professional educators begin supporting these new school initiatives. Education for all employees spreads to more businesses linked to performance and productivity.

Phase Seven (2010–2020?)

Local, radically changed community school programs are available across the United States. Organizations perceive life-long education as part of its business culture that drives competitiveness and profit.

**Figure 10-6 The Time-Line for the
Second American Education Revolution**

attempt at "purity," we thought, was essential to keep most education purely theoretical, rather than thrusting teachers and their students into the front lines of working America. As a result, business people and educators were largely divided into two very different ideological camps. This worked well because technical and societal change happened more slowly.

The times have changed. The useful educational half-life of engineers, psychologists, electricians, and most managers is often ten years. Company-sponsored continuing professional development, corporate universities, or technical training programs are often coming up short. It now appears that educators must become more practical at applying what they teach. Business people are beginning to participate in "writing the curriculum." Managers are beginning to catch on to the fact that sitting down next to the professors and teachers and telling them what current and future jobs demand in education, skills, training, and thinking abilities is not just a good community service; it's also vital to company profits and the long-term survival of their business.

As we have seen, the artificial barriers between business and education are now coming down in many states. Collaboration, listening, talking a common language are now skills that business people and educators are struggling to master in order to have a meaningful dialogue (see Figure 10-7). If our chief foreign competitors in Europe and Asia have mastered these new business tactics, why can't we? However, no country has a "lock" on the right institutions or policies. What works in one period or country may not work in another.

No matter what the eventual scenario of the Second American Education Revolution, it will not reach completion overnight. Even drastically improved public education is incapable by itself of supporting America's industrial competitiveness. Of equal importance is quickly establishing a corporate policy that expands the role of lifelong employee education within all businesses, both large and small.

Senior managers must understand that planning for better performance and improved productivity means investing in employee workforce education through expanded company training and development programs. This will raise the overall level of employee strategic competencies that make the high-performance workplace click. The realization of these twin strategic objectives—a national education revolution and local company investment in human capital development programs—will help America regain lost productivity

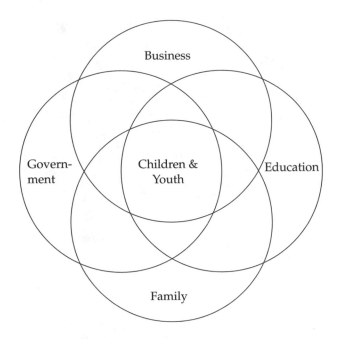

Figure 10-7 Community Collaboration Model

and international competitive advantage in almost every business sector. Let us now consider each of the key issues of the Second American Education Revolution and the role of the business community.[10]

Issue #1: Educational Choice

Bureaucracy defends the status quo long past the time when the quo has lost its status. (Laurence J. Peter)

Q. Why do we need educational choice?
A. Despite the fact that public per-pupil spending now averages over $7,000, it seems that too many students' achievement doesn't add up (see Figure 10-8). The last straw for Maryland State Delegate Tony E. Fulton came when he tried to buy venetian blinds at Linen World in Baltimore. Not only was the store worker, a recent high school graduate, unable to convert measurements in feet to inches,

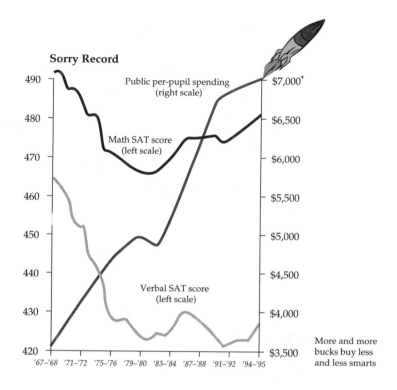

Figure 10-8 U.S. Education: Spending/Test Scores
Source: Adapted from *College Entrance Examination Board;*
U.S. Department of Education.

but Fulton was also unable to interest either the employee or the store manager in the importance of being able to do such a calculation.[11]

Contemporary school reform's overall dismal results have failed to catch up to the harsh realities of making a living at the beginning of the twenty-first century. The American public is beginning to grasp the fact that the fundamental social changes occurring across the world require complementary changes in the structure of many basic American institutions, including the public schools (see Figure 10-9). Across America staggering numbers of adults and children are poorly educated because too many local public and private schools have enshrined outdated curricula and bureaucratic form over the necessary educational substance required for life in the new millennium. America's schools need a new social contract.

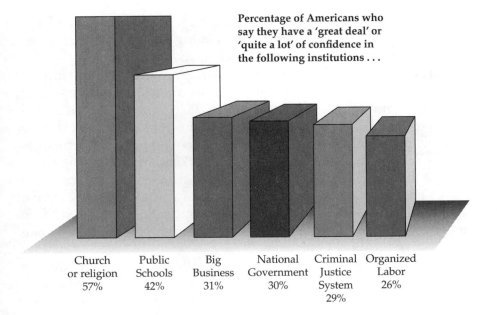

Percentage of Americans who
say they have a 'great deal' or
'quite a lot' of confidence in
the following institutions . . .

| Church or religion 57% | Public Schools 42% | Big Business 31% | National Government 30% | Criminal Justice System 29% | Organized Labor 26% |

Figure 10-9 Confidence Building
Source: Adapted from 1998 Gallup Poll

Q. Are there any models of choice systems that have worked in the past or present?

A. Charles O'Malley, former Director of Private Education for the U.S. Department of Education and a national educational choice expert, points out that in the early 1800s, well before public schools took root in our country, New England and the Mid-Atlantic states often offered interested parents the option of choosing any local schools and the state paid all or part of the tuition. This practice only ended after the individual states established the tax-supported public-school system.

One of the crown jewels of post-World War II liberalism, the 1944 GI Bill, was actually an educational choice program for higher education. The law was a staggering success. Between 1944 and 1949 more than half of 15 million veterans exercised their educational choice: 2.2 million attended college and 3.5 million, trade schools. Returning veterans went to Notre Dame, Southern Methodist University, or Penn

State. No one seemed to see this choice program as a sinister scheme to undermine the U.S. Constitution by violating the separation of church and state or enriching any denominational church.

This original GI educational choice program was overwhelmingly successful. At a cost of $5.5 billion it produced 450,000 engineers, 240,000 accountants, 238,000 teachers, 67,000 doctors, 22,000 dentists, and tens of thousands of skilled technicians and craftsmen who fueled the postwar boom in America. They flooded factories, farms, and offices with highly skilled knowledge workers, triggering the explosion of the American middle class and our successful consumer economy. The Veterans Administration reports that the government eventually collected almost eight times as much in income taxes from these veterans as the $70 billion paid out under the original and later GI choice educational programs.[12]

The GI Bill spawned a diversity of colleges and universities in American that is unrivaled in the world. Surprisingly, in 1944 leaders in public education proclaimed their fear that the choices offered through the GI bill might signal their death knell, as everyone would choose to go to a private college. Yet 50 years of experience proved otherwise. At its inception in 1944, 80 percent of all higher-education students were enrolled in private institutions, only 20 percent in public. Today these percentages are reversed![13]

No other country in the world invests more money in higher education than the United States. Publicly funded Pell Grants, the Federal Child Care Bill, and other state and federal financial programs are available to students who wish to attend public or private colleges and universities. The top 20 percent of our society are well educated through America's social contract for higher education. But what about the other 80 percent of Americans who will never graduate from any college?

A partial answer was the recent passage of the "Workforce Investment Act of 1998." Unemployed workers will be given "individual training accounts" that will allow them to choose from public or private educational programs. These providers will be required to have certification that their educational programs will help workers find new jobs. These programs, which have been characterized as a "GI Bill for America's Workers," offer adults educational choice by consolidating dozens of marginal public training programs and relying more on the private sector.[14]

Q. What is educational choice?

A. Educational choice is essentially a new funding policy. It is not a conservative right-wing conspiracy to destroy the nation's public schools, nor is it a sinister liberal plot to take over religious schools through the gradual encroachment of the federal government. Endless political rhetoric swirls around the issues of school funding, vouchers, local control versus national education standards, public versus private schools, teacher rights versus parent rights, charter schools, etc. A very divisive atmosphere has been driven by numerous special interest groups who seem to be willing to endlessly defend the status quo.

Educational choice seeks to reinvent America's public education system, not abolish or weaken it through promoting greater diversity in local community schools and in the ways professional educators produce results. It seeks to create additional options—a wider variety of local schools organized and run by teacher cooperatives, parent associations, nonprofit corporations, community-based organizations, and religious institutions—and to revitalize every community's public schools. Parents would be free to match their children to the school that best meets their needs. Improving learning is the issue here. Such a new public school system would create a new regulatory environment requiring less bureaucracy, and the state's role would no longer be based on the proposition that schools must be centrally managed according to a single formula.[15]

Parents should have the legal right to select from any local school that provides a well-thought-out program of instruction and that offers career-education opportunities, ample occasions for parental involvement, reasonable discipline, and dedicated professional staff unencumbered by educational bureaucracy.[16]

Schools should be free to differ from one another because there is no single instructional approach that is right for everyone. If you support the concept that the state-run "common school" is the only institution capable of inculcating American traditions, culture, and democracy, I can understand your ideals. But your view of what our current public schools offer is far too narrow in our modern pluralistic society.

But what happens to the public school student with problems in school, and parents who are indifferent regarding choice, learning, or schools in general? Many sincere public school educators believe that school choice programs will not only drain off public funds, but also leave these forgotten students in underfunded, miserable schools. How do we satisfy these legitimate concerns?

Educational choice must offer a new funding policy for *every* student in *every* school. We need to revitalize our present schools whether they are public or private, not just establish new schools. Ultimately, it is the responsibility of each state to guarantee a free and appropriate education to every child. Right now "appropriate education" translates into the lowest common denominator education for all. This must change. This will cost money.

When in 1944 the GI Bill started the flow of billions of dollars into higher education, everyone profited. A rising tide of funding raised all boats and brought about a Renaissance for U.S. colleges and universities that continues to this day.

We now need to apply this same "rebirth" mentality to elementary and high-school education. The crux of choice is really not just redistributing school funds, but in mobilizing the American people into realizing that *all* children need much better educational preparation for life and into putting their money where their mouth is. For too long America has earned an international reputation of supporting general education for all, but not quality education for all. America's time has run out as the clock of history moves from the twentieth to the twenty-first century.

I find it hard to believe that any state legislature will craft a choice program that would educationally hamstring large numbers of students in dysfunctional schools. However, sometimes politicians follow the path of least resistance and do what is popular for the moment rather than right for the long-term. Indeed it even took some states up to 1918 to recognize that all children had a right to public tax-supported education. Today, let individual state legislatures be forewarned that if they attempt to hide behind the choice issue and use it to deny equal access to improve educational programs, people and businesses will vote with their feet and simply leave those reactionary states that don't really want to improve education but to demean it.

I believe that the vast majority of all parents across America, regardless of ethnic or economic background, will always seek the best educational alternative for their children. We cannot hold all children hostage in our current outdated schools under the banner that the indifference of a few necessitates mediocrity for the many.

Consider this perspective. The people who run and attend private schools, both religious and secular, are Americans just like you. If their vision of values and how they teach them works well in our current public tax-supported system of higher education, then why not offer the same approach in elementary and secondary schools?[17]

Q. What about the constitutionality of elementary/secondary school choice?

A. In June 1998 the Wisconsin Supreme Court upheld the Milwaukee Parental Choice Program, which allows about 6,000 mostly African-American inner-city children to use $4,900 in grants at 80 private schools (about 60 with a religious affiliation). The program works in the same way as Pell Grants (federal college-tuition assistance), the GI Bill, or federal day-care preschool vouchers. The money goes directly to the student, whose parents designate the institution that will receive it. There is no state subsidy of any religious institution. Just as a graduate student can choose to use her Pell Grant at Notre Dame, Yeshiva University, or Ohio State, or a toddler's parents can use a federal day-care voucher to choose between a local Baptist or public school preschool program, about 15,000 children from low-income families in Milwaukee can now choose to send their child wherever they want.

The Wisconsin Supreme Court upheld the choice program for Milwaukee and ruled that it did not violate the First Amendment's ban on laws respecting "an establishment of religion" because state funds are distributed based on "neutral, secular criteria that neither favor nor disfavor religion." This case was immediately appealed to the U.S. Supreme Court.

The following November (1998), the Supreme Court ruled by an 8–1 vote to let stand the Wisconsin Supreme Court decision. However, the justices did so without issuing a written ruling. This means until such time as they do so, the Wisconsin high court's decision is the most definitive statement of the law on school choice.

Over the past decade the U.S. Supreme Court has moved away from the legal doctrine of strict separation. In other recent rulings it has allowed some public funding to go to parochial schools, such as allowing federally funded tutors to teach in parochial schools. The court sees this as constitutional as long as the key educational choices are being made by students and parents—not by public officials—and as long as the state's aid is not seen as endorsing any particular religion. The next legal battle grounds are likely to be in Ohio, Texas, Florida,

Pennsylvania, and Michigan. All these states have active choice movements and receptive local political climates.

If school choice ultimately is ruled unconstitutional, we will still need to find new ways to both refocus and refinance U.S. elementary and secondary education. This issue is not just going to go away. However, today there exists little overall public support for massive new investment in our current public/private school systems, unless we show parents how to change dramatically the ultimate outcome: preparing more students for high-pay/high-skill lifetime careers. We need whole new ways of thinking about what it will take to create a "well-educated person" for the third millennium.

The problem is in the minds of many Americans. We tend to think of a "good education" in terms of the way we were educated. "If it was good enough for our generation, then what's wrong with it now?" remains the attitude of many business people. But that is the central problem. Only about 25 percent of our generation got a really good education. The rest didn't. Too many people are functionally illiterate for the careers of the twenty-first century. We need real change. We need an education revolution.

Until this happens, a host of private scholarship programs and a few pilot public choice programs will continue to give poorer families the same educational opportunities for their children that many other Americans already have (see Figure 10-10). Theodore Forstmann, a New York financier, and John T. Walton, a director of Wal-Mart Stores, Inc., established a $200 million national scholarship fund for low-income families—the Children's Scholarship Fund. They join a long list of other foundations and funds that have helped local groups across America support private choice programs.

Two major reasons lead these groups to believe that school choice will happen in America. The first is its success in other countries. Many industrial nations—Canada, Sweden, Denmark, Germany, Israel, Australia, New Zealand, the United Kingdom, and Holland, among others—have already established school choice alternatives that have improved academic quality and promoted class, racial, and religious equity. Interestingly, in many of these nations the struggle for school choice has been led by trade unions and labor parties representing the needs and interests of their members.

Many of the dire consequences that some predict school choice will bring in America have simply not occurred in other countries. There

Private Voucher Programs Number of Scholarships Awarded					
City	1992–93	1993–94	1994–95	1995–96	1996–97
Albany, N.Y.	0	25	25	105	90
Atlanta	200	160	160	128	128
Austin, Tex	0	46	69	78	83
Battle Creek, Mich	53	116	180	118	178
Bridgeport, Conn	0	0	0	125	123
Buffalo, N.Y.	0	0	0	150	400
Dallas	0	0	100	235	335
Denver	0	42	74	78	49
Detroit/Lansing	0	8	3	159	330
Fort Worth, Tex	0	0	23	36	41
Houston	0	0	91	196	305
Indianapolis	895	1,075	984	1,013	1,014
Jackson, Miss	0	0	0	155	152
Jersey City, N.J.	0	0	0	42	42
Knoxville, Tenn	0	0	0	13	18
Little Rock, Ark	0	17	17	391	387
Los Angeles	0	0	775	775	776
Midland, Tex	0	8	5	1	4
Milwaukee	2,089	2,450	2,699	4,465	4,127
Oakland, Calif	0	0	169	250	250
Oklahoma City	0	0	0	117	106
Orlando, Fla	0	0	0	196	225
Philadelphia	0	0	0	0	100
Phoenix	0	57	60	41	100
Pittsburgh	0	0	0	0	38
San Antonio	930	950	902	940	955
Seattle	0	0	0	0	6
Washington, D.C.	0	57	175	180	225
Total	4,167	5,011	6,511	9,987	10,587

Source: CEO America

Figure 10-10 Private Choice Programs

has been no mass exodus from government schools. No religious denominations have come to control any country's educational system. And no free-market hucksters have succeeded in establishing profit-making schools in any of the nations that offer school choice.[18]

A good example is the United Kingdom, where some church schools, particularly in inner-city areas, tend to be popular with families of all nationalities and religions. The Church of England now provides one in four elementary schools and one in 20 secondary schools, about 5,000 in all. However, of their 900,000 pupils (1997), only about 679,000 are church-affiliated.[19]

The second source of encouragement that choice will eventually become national educational funding policy is the fact that it already exists in some form across the United States (see Figure 10-11). Some states offer only public school choice within some or all school districts. Other states permit public school choice throughout the state. A few even offer publicly sponsored full school choice. This is in addition to the private sector scholarship programs already mentioned.

Q. When school choice is declared as a constitutional education alternative, what must be done to make it work?

A. State school choice programs must address the following issues:

1. Provide sufficient educational options so parents truly have a choice.

2. Develop an ongoing, pervasive, public information program so that all parents in each local community are aware that they have an educational choice and are apprised of what their choices are.

3. Public transportation must be provided for all students if the school selected is not in the local neighborhood or served by public transportation.

4. School choice must serve as a catalyst for engaging business, parents, and educators to offer innovative new curricula; reduction of bureaucratic controls; ongoing teacher professional education; career-education programs; better coordination of special education and social services; increased local business community involvement; and more parental participation. Unless these and other systemic changes take place, choice will become only another passing fad.[20]

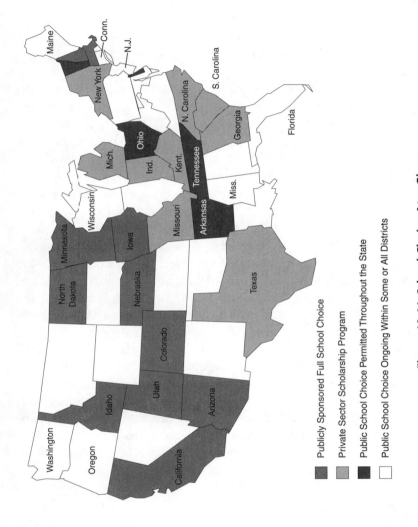

Figure 10-11 School Choice At-a-Glance

Source: Adapted from Center for Education Reform 202/822-9000, Institute for Justice 202/457–4240

Publicly Sponsored Full School Choice

Private Sector Scholarship Program

Public School Choice Permitted Throughout the State

Public School Choice Ongoing Within Some or All Districts

Issue #2: Welfare-to-Work

The continuing falling national unemployment rate has perked the interest of more businesses in hiring the "hard-core" unemployed. The changes made by the Federal Personal Responsibility and Work Opportunity Reconciliation Act passed by Congress in 1996 eliminates entitlement to many benefits. Over time, it phases in dramatic changes that require welfare recipients to engage in work activities.

Recent corporate welfare-to-work programs that have risen to the challenge of using these workers to fill entry-level positions include those at Sprint Corp., United Parcel Service (UPS), United Airlines, Borg-Warner Security Corporation, Intel, American Airlines, and The Limited. These are among the 2,500 companies that have similarly pledged to hire and train workers from the welfare rolls.

This is all to the good, but significant problems persist. After 6 to 12 months many programs discover that only 40 percent of these new employees are left on-the-job. Welfare-to-work experts speak of 20–60–20 breakdown, which estimates that one-fifth of welfare recipients have the skills and experience needed to get and hold a job without major assistance (see Figure 10-12); another fifth have great difficulty earning a living because of significant educational shortcomings, disabilities, and other problems. The 60-percent balance is the primary focus for corporate welfare-to-work strategies.

Carolyn J. Heinrich at the University of Chicago studied the results of a successful job program for the residents of Ford Heights, Chicago's most depressed suburban community. She found that, to keep people from losing their new jobs, this welfare-to-work program had to address several factors: limited work histories or no prior job connections; poor technical skills; child-care problems; going to work as an unknown or threatening experience; and few role models to teach them the behavior patterns necessary to succeed in jobs.

A "Job Support Toolbox" is needed to overcome these problems. Many of these useful ideas are suggested in "'Learn to Earn' Issues Surrounding Adult Education, Training and Work in Welfare Reform," by Suzanne Knell, the executive director of the Illinois Literacy Resource Development Center. (The study was funded by the National Institute for Literacy.) Programs need to feature a holistic service approach that sequentially or concurrently provides for all necessary employment, training, and supportive services. The intent

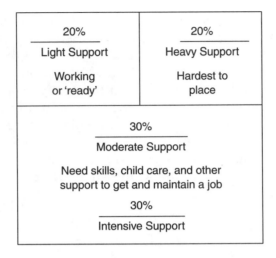

Figure 10-12 Welfare-to-Work People Profile

of this service approach is to emphasize longer-term education, intensive personal coaching, and job-specific, customized training that promotes long-term job retention.

The main objective of the coaching activity is to help all job trainees identify and work through any problems they may encounter during the training period. This means frequent contacts and a very "hands-on" approach, with a coach making phone calls or house calls after hours to ensure that trainees are attending class or fulfilling job responsibilities.

Trainees may also need assistance through role-playing and mock interviews, vocabulary development, guidance on hygiene and personal presentation, motivational sessions, and assistance with the development of a résumé. Additional Job Support Toolbox services might include meals, uniforms, shoes, equipment, books, child care, point-to-point job transportation, medical care, and even crisis services that include family counseling.

Success Prep, an Omaha, Nebraska-based nonprofit firm, has developed such a transition-to-work 40-hour training toolbox, "Preparing Youth to Excel in the Workplace." In a series of eight modules, it delivers to trainees and their coaches alike dramatic, real-life advice on how to motivate, communicate, and resolve conflicts and develop positive personal attitudes for job success in the workplace. "We've been very pleased with our Success Prep graduates. They do a fine job in readying the candidate for the workplace," says Charlene Meyer, a vice-president at Security National Bank.

However, all these educational and supportive service activities will be of little importance unless they are built around one major foundation: concurrent, effective on-the-job training. With unemployment at a 25-year record low, business needs to use these strategies when turning to the large pool of long-term unemployed workers in order to shape them into the productive knowledge workers of tomorrow.

Issue #3: Workforce 2020

Look around you. How many other baby boomers can you see in your office? Back in the late 1980s, Workplace 2000 predicted that a shortage of people in the labor market was coming. Many scoffed at this notion. No longer. With the labor force projected to grow by only 11 percent between 1996 and 2006, companies will have difficulty filling job openings.

Let's examine the latest numbers from the Bureau of Labor Statistics (see Figure 10-13). There are big changes underway in the age makeup of the U.S. labor force. In the ten years 1986–1996, more than 9 percent of all workers were in the 35–44 age group, which has been considered by many managers as the most productive years for employees.

Between 1996 and 2006, the size of this age group will shrink by about 1 percent; those 45 to 54 years of age increase by over 8 percent; and, more significantly, those 55 to 64 increase by over 6 percent! This means a major rethinking of the old practice of laying off or retiring people in these age groups as "less productive" because they can't or won't be retrained.

American business has little choice in this regard. Unless we find successful ways to "reprocess" older employees' knowledge acquisition, we just won't have enough people to go around. As one Midwest senior railroad executive told me, "I just don't know where I am going to find the skilled people to run this railroad!" This is a lament I have heard with increasing frequency from top managers across the

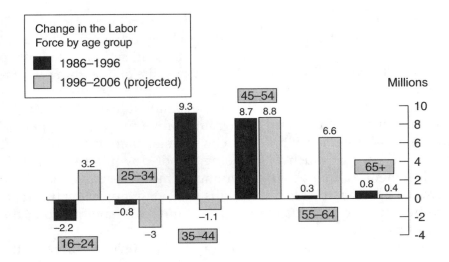

Figure 10-13 The Future Workforce
Source: Bureau of Labor Statistics

United States and in most professional/service/production business sectors.

But are older adults (40–65) trainable? We have already looked at how the critical competencies for any business are being trained more effectively within many organizations. Warner Sclaire, director of Penn State University's Gerontology Center in University Park, Pennsylvania, has been studying aging and brain function since 1956 among thousands of adults in an HMO organization in Washington State. Dr. Sclaire's studies show that, with training, people even in their 70s or 80s can still sharpen their mental skills, such as abstract reasoning or spatial skills for technical areas.

These results aren't just wishful thinking, says Arnold Scherbel, director of the Brain Research Institute at UCLA. With proper life-long training these skills can be maintained or even increased because "it's wired into our brain cells." Proper training serves to activate those parts of the brain that control competencies critical to any high-performance business.[21]

Fifty years ago, even 20 years ago, it was preposterous to talk about "teaching intelligence," particularly for older adults. Everyone presumed that intelligence was the fixed score on an IQ test. A person's intelligence never really changed. If it did, only children might benefit from advances in learning theory and teaching techniques. This point of view discouraged management from making serious attempts to offer employees, particularly older workers, lifelong learning opportunities in the corporate classroom.

Frederick Goodwin, a director of the National Institute of Mental Health, believes that training programs cannot make a 70 IQ person into a 120 IQ person, "but you can change their IQ in different ways, perhaps as much as 20 points up or down, based on their environment." Older as well as younger employees have many underdeveloped abstract learning skills not being tapped by the average business because of the artificial limits we have put on "the learning organization."

During the first decade of the twenty-first century, maximizing the critical competencies of older workers will emerge as a major, necessary business goal. We know how. We know who. We know why. Let's do it.[22]

Issue #4: Information Technology in the Schools

Much of the technology available in today's schools does little to advance student learning. The reason: 60 percent of schools have outdated, inadequate hardware and software, according to a 1997 study by the CEO Forum on Education and Technology, a business–education alliance.

The number of computers in schools has grown enormously from fewer than 50,000 in 1983 to 5.5 million in 1994. Ninety-eight percent of schools now use computers for some instruction. However, that tells only part of the story. The opportunity for a typical student to have access to a computer for any significant length of time is still very limited. In 1994 the ratio of students to computers across all grades was 14 to 1. Many students have more access to a computer at home than at school.[23]

The greater difficulty is that the industry that makes the equipment and software and the educators who want it usually have no clue about how to use it. Jane Healy, author of *Failure to Connect: How Computers Affect Our Children's Minds—For Better and Worse* (1998) and a longtime advocate of the educational potential of digital technologies, spent two years visiting classrooms across the United States. This is what she found.

I am sorry to report that I was both discouraged and dismayed by what I saw—too many ill-informed software choices; inadequate teacher preparation; children engaging in idle clicking, game-playing, and silly surfing; lack of relevance to curriculum; expensive equipment obsolete or ill used—to name just a few.

We know that what is right for a 15-year-old is not necessarily right—and may be outright damaging—to a 5-year-old. Where did we get this preposterous notion that very young children need computers lest they somehow fall behind? Several responsible educators she interviewed deemed up to 85 percent of current education software not only "worthless" but possibly damaging.[24]

If teachers don't know how to use information technology, and if they do not demand better software that integrates with the curriculum, computers in schools will largely go to waste. Though U.S. schools spent more than $5 billion on IT in 1997, a federal study (1995) found that states put roughly 15 percent of their edutech budgets toward staff development (see Figure 10-14).[25]

As a result, Henry Becker, a professor at the University of California, Irvine, estimates that only 5 percent of computer-using teachers know how to use IT as a tool to teach problem solving or to create a term paper, rather than as a reward for completing other work or for mindless drill activities. (This is regardless of the fact that most teachers don't even use IT as a teaching tool at all.)[26]

Many educators agree that standard computer literacy doesn't necessarily generate the literacy that counts in reading, writing, and math. Too often students use the technology not to gather and understand information, but to design nifty graphics. Indeed, the Internet may breed a kind of intellectual laziness. "The Net's ability to find and list mountains of data," says Sherry Turkle of MIT, "is no substitute for figuring out how to organize that information."[27]

For the business community, these are serious issues. Not only do we need more workers receiving a working knowledge of IT from their basic education—we need them at higher levels of literacy to interpret and manipulate the information that drives these technologies. Unless U.S. schools do a better job making IT education a successful learning tool, how will the average business be able to use

Percentage of Teachers with at Least Minimal—Nine Hours—
of Technology Training, by State:

Alabama	2%	Louisiana	11%	Ohio	8%
Alaska	21%	Maine	14%	Oklahoma	8%
Arizona	13%	Maryland	15%	Oregon	15%
Arkansas	10%	Massachusetts	15%	Pennsylvania	10%
California	15%	Michigan	10%	Rhode Island	11%
Colorado	20%	Minnesota	15%	South Carolina	11%
Connecticut	15%	Mississippi	11%	South Dakota	21%
Delaware	10%	Missouri	10%	Tennessee	18%
Florida	20%	Montana	18%	Texas	18%
Georgia	18%	Nebraska	15%	Utah	20%
Hawaii	23%	Nevada	15%	Vermont	18%
Idaho	15%	New Hampshire	14%	Virginia	14%
Illinois	10%	New Jersey	11%	Washington	28%
Indiana	13%	New Mexico	10%	West Virginia	17%
Iowa	15%	New York	15%	Wisconsin	16%
Kansas	15%	North Carolina	22%	Wyoming	20%
Kentucky	28%	North Dakota	17%	**National average**	**15%**

Figure 10-14 Technology Training for Teachers
Source: U.S. Department of Education, 1993–94 Schools and Staffing Survey

the technology of a high-performance workplace to boost productivity successfully?

Issue #5: Updating the Teaching Profession

It is ludicrous to expect teachers to teach science, math, or any other
subject if they haven't seriously studied the subject themselves.
According to the National Commission on Teaching and America's
Future, nearly a quarter of all high-school teachers do not even have

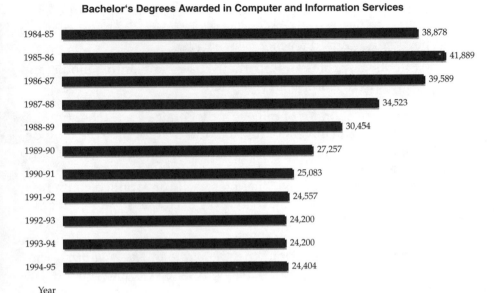

Bachelor's Degrees Awarded in Computer and Information Services

Year

Figure 10-15 Workplace Snapshot: Computer Graduates
Source: U.S. Department of Education

the equivalent of a college minor in their subjects. The proportion is even higher for math and science teachers.[28] This is a major contributing cause to the steady decline in degrees awarded in computer and information sciences (see Figure 10-15). We need excellently prepared teachers motivating more students to pursue IT careers.

How can we change the schools and offer more appropriate career programs for the twenty-first century if we lack the algebra and physics teachers who are needed in larger numbers in every high school across America?

A 600-teacher survey by the Council for Basic Education offered recommendations for change in stronger language than most school reform advocates generally use:

- Require all teachers to know the content of the subjects they teach.
- Train people to teach in the context of the subject content.

- Offer prospective new teachers internship, apprenticeship school-based training experiences before you allow them to become a licensed teacher.

- Get college professors off their chairs and into schools and businesses to learn what is needed.[29]

A long-time collaborator of mine is Judy Ponticell, a teacher training expert at Texas Tech University in Lubbock. Both of us have long decried the reluctance of professors in education or other disciplines to go out into their community, into schools and businesses, and learn firsthand what is happening. Call it "field research" or "applied continuing professional education"—we have long believed that not enough academics are willing to test their theories with the realities of the classroom and marketplace. We agree with Don Sneed, a professor of journalism at the University of Mississippi, when he wrote in *The Wall Street Journal* that "All too many professors cloister themselves, not even interacting with colleagues across campus. To overcome institutional inertia of doing business as usual is as great a challenge as getting professors to work outside the protective cocoon known as the classroom."[30]

Some of these changes are already beginning because of the business community. Representatives of trade associations, employers, and educational institutions are talking about how to better prepare more adults to fill the technology jobs going begging across the United States. And they are acting. In California, there are Joint Venture and the Silicon Valley Network. In Nebraska, the National Science Foundation, private industry, and the state government are mobilizing an institute to direct the changes needed in college instruction. In Illinois, the Illinois Coalition and the Chicago Software Association (encouraged by the Illinois Board of Higher Education) are moving to introduce new curricula for Illinois colleges and universities developed through consultation between professors and employers. These efforts will provide fast and focused education that fits the job specs for a new wave of workers. The college education revolution has begun. Let's drive it into our elementary and high-school teacher training programs as well.[31]

At Motorola, since 1992 public-school principals, superintendents and school-board members have been enrolled in the company's "leadership institutes." These classes teach how to cope with changes in education and the uses of technology. Six states now receive these institutes: Texas, Illinois, Massachusetts, Iowa, New Mexico and Arizona.

Other high-tech firms like Motorola tend to offer educators programs in the communities where many of their employees live. In 1995 IBM began a three-year online advice program on a variety of classroom topics for teachers in 21 school districts. Other businesses need to offer similar outreach educational programs to educators in their local communities.

Issue #6: You Get What You Pay For

Part of America's Second Education Revolution is not only to better prepare more people to teach diverse curriculums at smaller, local schools, but to motivate them to stay in teaching as a lifetime career. One of the principal reasons why the United States faces a critical shortage of math, science, and master career educators is that too much money is spent on administration in our elementary schools, secondary schools, and colleges/universities. National figures vary, but this represents 30 to 40 percent of our education investment. This is too high.

One of its consequences is that many teachers leave the profession for higher salaries. Why should a high-school chemistry teacher earn only $32,000 annually when industry might offer more than double that wage? Over the past 20 years the average annual salary of most educators has remained fairly static, with some states doing better than others (see Figures 10-16 and 10-17).

Even if the United States invests a great deal in education in absolute terms, compared to other industrialized nations our expenditures are just about average when examined as a percentage of our gross domestic product (OECD, 1998). More significantly, the United States devotes a smaller percentage of its national income to teachers' salaries than do other countries.[32]

Let's be honest with each other. Most Americans look down on teaching as a low-status, low-pay profession. Undoubtedly, any education revolution must adjust the proportion of our education budgets invested in finding and keeping better classroom teachers in all subject areas. If we wish to motivate more young people to begin and continue teaching careers in math/science as well as other subjects, we are going to have to make new investments in teaching careers. Why should the typical high-school math teacher

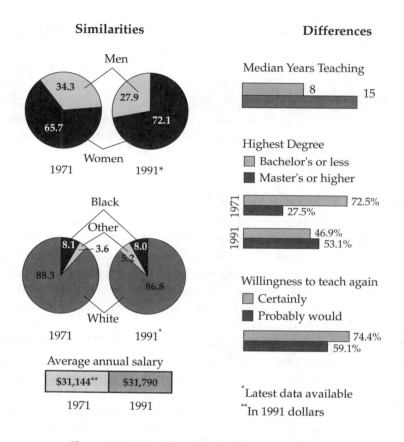

Figure 10-16 Profile of United States Teachers

in Germany be paid over $60,000 each year and our teachers be given only 50 percent of these wages? Do we wish our children and future employees to learn only 50 percent of the math learned by our German competitors?

If local businesses want a highly skilled, well-prepared entry-level workforce, we must be prepared to pay for it. Changing the manner in which the schools are administered, designing the curriculum for careers, offering parental choice—all these changes will mean nothing unless we can attract and keep a larger share of America's brightest minds and employ them teaching our children in every local community school.

High	Moderate	Low
Alaska	Arizona	Alabama
Arkansas	California	Georgia
Colorado	Florida	Illinois
Connecticut	Idaho	Louisiana
Delaware	Iowa	Maine
Hawaii	Kentucky	Massachusetts
Indiana	Maryland	New Hampshire
Kansas	Michigan	New Jersey
Minnesota	Mississippi	New Mexico
Missouri	Nevada	New York
Montana	Oklahoma	North Carolina
Nebraska	Pennsylvania	Tennessee
North Dakota	Rhode Island	Utah
Ohio	South Carolina	Washington
Oregon	Texas	West Virginia
South Dakota	Virginia	
Vermont		
Wisconsin		
Wyoming		

Figure 10-17 Growth in Relative Teaching Salaries
Source: Adapted from Dale Ballou & Michael Podgursky, *Teacher Pay and Teacher Quality,* W. E. Upjohn Institute for Employment Research, 1997.

The Bottom-Line Answer: Investing Now for a Better Tomorrow

We already know how the skill wars will come out. There is a certain inevitability to the outcome. The mass-production era yielded to the information age. There is an inevitable sort of justice that the future "knowledge age" will be controlled by those businesses and nations who are able to make the most practical use of it. Society must progress. But which businesses will progress faster in the twenty-first century?

U.S. business has largely dominated most industries in the second half of the twentieth century as a legacy of winning the Second World

War. But times have changed. As we enter the knowledge age, the U.S. business community must now decide whether to stay in its current mode of "operating on the cheap" by focusing almost exclusively on short-term profit for the few, or change directions by carefully investing in long-term knowledge development, producing profit for many.

The prime moving factor in the future of America will be how well our people can use their knowledge in practical applications of advanced technologies. Brains have replaced brawn. For business, more knowledge, and the understanding of it, will mean more profit. This outcome is inevitable.

Throughout the 1990s, many experts, including this writer, have advocated business investment in a wide range of human-capital-productivity strategies. But until now, many companies were too worried about controlling costs to think about any major investments in long-term training and education programs for current or future employees.

With profits hitting 40-year highs, more organizations now can begin to take a longer view and devote more resources to workforce education. Also, the low unemployment rate and current labor market demographics give corporate America powerful incentives to lift the skill levels of current workers as well as hiring marginal workers who need retraining. Paul Alleire, chairman and CEO of Xerox Corporation and chairman of the Council on Competitiveness, tells his peers that "Competitiveness depends on lifelong learning."

Riding the Third Wave

We are now experiencing the third wave of the industrial revolution. In its first and second waves the revolution didn't stop with the introduction of the steam engine (early 1800s) or electricity (early 1900s), but went on to overhaul business, government, education, and the sciences. Look at the roster of the 100 largest U.S. companies at the beginning of the 1900s. You'll find that only 15 are still in existence.

During our twentieth century, the basic fabric of society has changed forever, and with it the way people think, work, and live. The second wave of the industrial revolution created the modern factory, and with it, the hierarchical business and a bureaucratic society. All these things are now being replaced. Consider *Fortune* magazine's

1956 list of America's top 500 companies. By 1992 only 29 of the first 100 firms remain in the top echelons of business.

One reason is that the information revolution set off shock waves throughout the United States and the world. The semiconductor integrated circuit has become the steam engine of the next millennium, sweeping aside many of society's business, political, and educational structures. Yet this "information revolution" is now yielding to the even more powerful forces of a "knowledge revolution." In a recent interview Tracy Kidder, author of *The Soul of a New Machine*, explains why.

I think computers are simply tools. What makes them seem different to us is that they are allied with intellectual work, but that doesn't make them intellectual things themselves. . . .

There are all kinds of things that are wrong with computers as far as writing and thinking go. From doing a little editing once at New England Monthly, *I remember a guy who did a story and I was trying to get him to fix it. All he would do in his rewrites was move stuff around. . . . That ability to move stuff around is a real impediment to the development of consecutive thinking. Because it gives you the illusion of doing something. It's absurd.*

I also think that for math children should learn how to add, subtract, divide, and multiply because they ought to understand what those things are *[emphasis added] rather than* summoning a machine to do them. At some point, you create a bunch of people so stupid they wouldn't know what addition was.[33]

In reality, organizations are not just machines filled with technology that are supposed to do the same tasks over and over again. Instead they are brains holding and refining their human capital—the collected wisdom, the critical competencies, of everyone associated with the business. Winning the skill wars means negotiating the transition of your human capital from stressing mass and bulk to emphasizing knowledge and understanding. Harvesting knowledge will always be more profitable than harvesting wheat or soybeans.

Reengineering gurus Michael Hammer and James Champy, authors of *Re-Engineering the Corporation*, also see the need to push against this leadership inertia and radically change management thinking.

I tell companies they need to quadruple their investment in education. Training is about skills; education is about understanding broad knowledge. Everybody who works in a company needs to understand the business. . . . We want workers to make decisions, and they can't do that without a knowledge about the business context.[34]

The Silent Revolution

At the beginning of America's twenty-first century, market forces will be a main source of progress and prosperity in American social democracy. However, government (with a small "g") will remain as a safeguard for the greatest good for the greatest number.[35]

The continued rapid pace of change has made the old command-and-control management model obsolete. The United States will no longer be run only from Washington, but also from the state and local community levels. A silent revolution is occurring as the whole decision-making process is being reorganized. Organizations are no longer going to be driven from boardrooms, but from empowered knowledge workers in the trenches.

Theresa Welborne, a professor in the Industrial Labor School at Cornell University, singled out companies that invested in workforce education and in other ways developed their human capital as strategic assets. In her study of 136 companies that went public after 1988, 92 percent of these human-capital companies survived (1993), compared to only 36 percent of the companies that focused on short-term profits. The former companies also gained 87 percent in the stock market while the latter organizations lost 18 percent of their market value.[36]

As a study by the Harvard School of Business points out, this "stakeholder" form of corporate governance could mark a major change in America's business culture. Human-capital investment is the necessary cornerstone that will help begin a major commitment by business to the long-term skills, training, and education needed by the American workforce.[37]

Into the Future . . .

Americans have always been fascinated with images of the future. Perhaps this has contributed to the remarkable popularity of the *Star Trek/Star Wars* phenomenon. These films offer us compelling representations of future centuries. Everyone in the world of *Star Trek* is well educated. The number of managers and professionals appears rather limited. However, savvy technicians abound. America's continued economic prosperity many very well hinge on how well we can balance the technology and skills in a new world where no one has gone before.

The decisive moment is at hand for all Americans to come together and recognize that our current Band-Aid approach to school reform isn't working. We must reinvent our schools through systemic change for a future far different from our twentieth-century past. All 50 states have a basic constitutional responsibility to shape a new education social contract that will more realistically address the livelihood of twenty-first-century generations to come.

Yet to win the skill wars, neither the market, nor government, nor technology alone will provide these answers by themselves. Unlike the other dangers in this century that the United States has overcome, this national challenge is not an external threat so much as it is within ourselves. It calls for each of us to in some way alter our own perspectives and support lifelong education in the workplace and more diverse educational preparation in the classrooms of America. Only this long-term investment by American society and business will strengthen our capacity to compete in a twenty-first-century global society, and to find workable strategies to win the skill wars for most Americans.

I believe that this populist message of workforce education will be embraced across America once it is more widely understood. *Skill Wars* makes the case to business management, union leaders, and the American public. Its compelling vision of workforce education provides America with a sound scenario that improves career opportunities for the current workforce as well as future generations who are waiting in the wings to make the next 100 years another great "American century."

Notes

Chapter 1 Notes

1. Jon Bigness, "Machine Shops Go from Grimy to Shiny with High-Tech Tools," *Chicago Tribune*, September 10, 1998, sec. 3, p. 3.

2. Paul Salopek, "Good Old Days Gone, U.S. Manufacturing Technology Adapts," *Chicago Tribune*, September 7, 1996, sec. 1, p. 1.

3. Robert L. Rose, "Hard Driving," *Wall Street Journal*, September 7, 1995, p. A1.

4. Murray Weidenbaum, "American Isolationism in a Global Economy," *Management Review*, December 1995, p. 45.

5. R.C. Longworth, "The Painful Cost of the Economic Revolution," *Chicago Tribune*, October 6, 1996, p. 1.

6. "Survey: The World Economy," *The Economist*, September 28, 1996.

7. Joseph H. Boyett and Henry P. Conn, *Workplace 2000*, New York: Dutton, 1991.

8. Raju Narisetti, "Job Paradox," *Wall Street Journal*, September 9, 1995. p. A1.

9. Joseph H. Boyett and Jimmie T. Boyett, *Beyond Workplace 2000*, New York: Dutton, 1995, p. xv.

10. *Skill Standards in Action*. National Alliance of Business, Vol. 1, no. 1, May 1996.

11. Haynes Johnson, "The War That Changed America," *Milwaukee Journal Standard*, August 13, 1995, sec. J, p. 1.

12. E.E. Gordon, R.R. Morgan, J.A. Ponticell, *FutureWork, The Revolution Reshaping American Business*, Westport, CT: Praeger, 1994, pp. 1–8, 193–212.

Chapter 2 Notes

1. T.T. Baldwin, K.J. Ford, "Transfer of Training: A Review and Direction for Future Research," *Personal Psychology*, March, 1988, pp. 63–105.

   Mary L. Broad and J.W. Newstrom, *Transfer of Training: Action Packed Strategies to Assure High Payoff from Training Investments*. Reading, Massachusetts: Addison-Wesley, 1992.

   J.K. Ford and D.H. Weissbein, "Transfer of Training: An Updated Review and Analysis," *Performance Improvement Quarterly*, February 2, 1997, pp. 22–41.

2. Brian Hackett, *The Value of Training is the Era of Intellectual Capital*. New York: The Conference Board, 1997, p. 17.

   Terri Bergman, "Training: The Case for Increased Investment," *Employment Relations News*, December 22, 1994, p. 381.

3. Polly LaBarre, "The Rush on Knowledge," *Industry Week*, February 19, 1996, p. 53.

4. Leif Edvinsson and Michael S. Malone, *Intellectual Capital*. New York: Harper Business, 1977, pp. 22, 139–144.

5. "A Star to Sail By?" *The Economist*, August 2, 1997, p. 53.

6. Jack J. Phillips, editor *Measuring Return on Investment*, Vol. 1 (1994), Vol. 2 (1997), American Society for Training and Development.

7. Interview with Robert Klein, Sales Education Manager, Nabisco, on his published ROI case study. "The New Case for Continuous Sales Training," *Corporate University Review*, July/August 1996.

8. John Tobin, presentation at the *National Employer Leadership Conference*, March 1988.

9. *Workforce Economics*, National Alliance of Business, April 1997, p. 5.

10. Edward E. Gordon and Boyd Owens, "Measuring the Impact of Basic Skills Training: Otto Engineering," in *Measuring Return on Investment*, Vol. 2, Alexandria, VA: American Society for Training & Development, 1997, pp. 267–282.

11. Edward E. Gordon, "Training, Time and Profit," Training and Development Forum in *Management Review*, December 1996.

12. Edward E. Gordon, "Training Investments: The Global Perspective," *Technical and Skills Training* (ASTD), July 1996.

13. "Investing in People," *The Economist*, March 26, 1994, p. 92.

14. Kevin Hollenbeck, *Classrooms in the Workplace*. Kalamazoo, MI: W.E. Upjohn Institute for Employment Research, 1993.

15. Jacob Mincer, "Job Training: Costs, Returns and Wage Profiles." Cambridge, MA: National Bureau of Economic Research, December 1989, Workpaper #3208, pp. 15–39.

16. Brian Hackett, *The Value of Training*, p. 5.

Chapter 3 Notes

1. Edward E. Gordon, "Investing in Human Capital: Solving the ROI Dilemma," *Corporate University Review*, March/April 1997, pp. 36–39.

2. Riel Miller and Gregory Wurzburg, "Investing in Human Capital," *The International Organization for Economic Cooperation and Development Observer*, April/May 1995, pp. 16–18.

Chapter 4 Notes

1. Lowell L. Bryan, "Stocks Overvalued? Not in the New Economy," *Wall Street Journal*, November 3, 1997, p. A24.

2. Edward E. Gordon, "Investing in Human Capital: Tax and Accounting Issues" *Corporate University Review*, May/June 1997, pp. 50–51.

3. Edward E. Gordon, "Investing in Human Capital: Lip Service or Reality?" *Corporate University Review*, July/August 1997, pp. 51–52.

Chapter 5 Notes

1. Interview with Richard T. Quinn.

     Anthony J. Rucci, Steven P. Kirn and Richard T. Quinn, "The Employee–Customer–Profit Chain at Sears," *Harvard Business Review*, January–February 1998, pp. 83–87.

2. Hedrick Smith, *Rethinking America*, New York: Random House, 1995, pp. 218–221.

3. Timothy J. Gilfoyle, "Making History," *Chicago History*, Summer 1996, pp. 61–63.

4. Robert Falvin as quoted in Smith, *Rethinking America*, p. 334.

5. Oren Harari, "When Intelligence Rules, The Manager's Job Changes," *Management Review*, July 1994, p. 34.

6. Joseph H. Boyett and Henry P. Conn, *Workplace 2000*, New York: Dutton, 1991.

7. Virginia Postrel, "The Work Ethic, Redefined," *Wall Street Journal*, September 4, 1998, p. A10.

8. Ronald Kotulak, "Making the Connection," *Chicago Tribune*, February 26, 1998, sec. 1, p. 1.

9. Thomas Petzinger, Jr., "The Front Lines, A Plant Manager Keeps Reinventing His Production Line," *Wall Street Journal*, September 19, 1997, p. B1.

10. Edward E. Gordon, Ronald R. Morgan, and Judith A. Ponticell, *Future-Work, The Revolution Reshaping American Business*, Westport, CT: Praeger, 1994.

    R.R. Morgan, J.A. Ponticell, E.E. Gordon, *Enhancing Learning in Training and Adult Education*, Westport, CT: Greenwood, 1998.

Chapter 6 Notes

1. Charles N. Darrah, *Learning and Work*. New York: Garland Publishing, 1996, pp. 52–53, 96–98, 102–103, 161–172.

    Calhoun Wire and Cable and Techno Industries are pseudonyms for the actual corporation whose work practices were studied by the author as part of a Stanford University research team.

2. *Benchmarks of Excellence*. National Alliance of Business, Washington, D.C., April 1994.

3. Eunice Askov, *Framework for Developing Skill Standards for Workplace Literacy*, National Institute for Literacy, Washington, D.C., 1997.

4. *Maintenance/Repair Technician, The Industry Skills Standards Project*, St. Joseph County, IN: Connect, 1996.

5. Mike Royko, "Illiteracy Knows No Bounds in Land of Opportunities," *Chicago Tribune*, February 9, 1996, sec. 1, p. 3.

6. Tom Burke, "How Do You Spell Quality," *Wall Street Journal*, April 8, 1996, p. A18.

7. William H. Davidson and Michael S. Malone, *The Virtual Corporation*, New York: Harper Business, 1992, pp. 187–189.

8. T & D Extra, "Is Live Training Dead?," *Training & Development*, November 11, 1998.

9. E.E. Gordon, J. Ponticell, R. Morgan, *Closing the Literacy Gap in American Business*, New York: Quorum 1991, pp. 111–116.

———, *FutureWork, The Revolution Reshaping American Business*, Westport, CT: Praeger, 1994, pp. 39–72.

10. Suzanne Knell, *Learning That Works: Basic Skills Programs in Illinois Corporations*, Campaign, IL: Illinois Literacy Resource Development Center, 1993.

11. Hank O'Roark, "Basic Skills Get a Boost," *Technical Training*, American Society for Training and Development, July/August 1998, pp. 10–13.

12. "Former Rover Chairman Sees Illiteracy Throughout English-Speaking World," *Report on Literacy Programs*, June 22, 1995, p. 101.

13. Constance Casey, "If Schools Don't Train Workers, Companies Find They Must," *Newhouse News Service*, March 22, 1996.

14. "The Employer's Decision to Train Low-Wage Workers," University of Washington, 1992, Grant Number: 99-0-1897-75-104-02 National Technical Information Service, Springfield, VA 22151, 703/487-4650.

15. Stan Davis and Jim Botkin, "The Company of Knowledge-Based Business," *Harvard Business Review*, September/October, 1994, pp. 165–170.

Chapter 7 Notes

1. Edward E. Gordon, Judith A. Ponticell, Ronald R. Morgan, *Closing the Literacy Gap in American Business*, New York: Quorum, 1991, p. 133.

2. Betsy A. Bowen, "Four Puzzles in Adult Literacy: Reflections on the National Adult Literacy Survey," *Journal of Adolescent & Adult Literacy*, December 1998/January, 1999, pp. 315–316.

3. Edward E. Gordon, "Meeting the International Workplace Education Challenge," *Workforce Training News*, March 1995, p. 30.

4. *The Single Market*, Office for Official Publications of the European Communities, Brussels/Luxembourg, 1995.

5. "International Star," *The Economist*, April 11, 1998, p. 17.

6. Grant Thornton, "European Business Survey," International Business Strategies, Ltd., Spring 1995.

7.   "Education in Germany, the Next Generation," *The Economist*, August 20, 1996, p. 44.

8.   Hedrick Smith, *Rethinking America*, New York: Random House, 1995, pp. 137, 140.

9.   Wilfried Preno, "The Sorcery of Apprenticeship," *Wall Street Journal*, February 12, 1993, p. A22

10. Interview by author with Helmut Schaible, Oberstudiendirektor (Director), Robert-Bosch Schule (School), Ulm, Germany, October 16, 1995.

11. Edward E. Gordon, "The German Dual System Model: Does It Pay in America?" *Workforce Training News*, April 1995, p. 17.

12. Edward E. Gordon, "The British Lion Wakes Up," *Workforce Training News*, May 1995, p. 28.

13. Chris Hasluck, "Modern Apprenticeships—A Success Story," *Skills and Enterprise Briefing*, Department for Education and Employment, August 1997, p. 1.

     Fiona Frank, Lancaster University, Paper and Interview presented at the Winter Institute on Workplace Training, Georgia Tech University, Atlanta, January 1998.

14. "The Training Set," *Briefing on Britain*, Vol. 2, Issue 3, p. 16.

15. "High-Tech Scotland," *Briefing on Britain*, Vol. 1, Issue 4, p. 18.

     Interview by author with Gail Longmore, Vice Counsel for Economic Development, British Consulate-General, Chicago, April 20, 1995.

16. Christina Barron, "Calling Ireland," *Europe*, July/August 1995, pp. 16–17.

     "A Gaelic Boom," *The Economist*, April 26, 1996, p. 58.

17. Mary McCain, "Apprenticeship Lessons from Europe," *Training and Development*, November 1994, pp. 38–41.

     Robert Rothman, "In Denmark, Remembering the `Forgotten Half'," *Education Week*, June 12, 1996, pp. 40–42.

     "Report on the International Federation of Training & Development Organization Conference," Dublin, Ireland, *Association of Human Resource Development On-Line Newsletter*, July 1998.

18. Dana Milbank, "Signs of Vitality," *Wall Street Journal*, February 14, 1995, p. A2.

    "Education, the Advanced Training Campaign," *Business Guide to Switzerland*, The Economist Intelligence Unit, August/September 1995, p. 39.

    Samuel Halperin, "School-to-Work, Employers, and Personal Values," *Education Week*, March 12, 1997, pp. 38, 52.

19. Edward E. Gordon, "Training's New World Order: Lessons from the Pacific Rim," *Workforce Training News,* July/August 1995, p. 28.

20. William J. Holstein, "Korea," *Business Week*, July 31, 1995, pp. 56–63.

21. Paul Kennedy, *Preparing for the Twenty-First Century*, New York: Vintage Books, 1993, p. 140.

22. Hedrick Smith, *Rethinking America*, New York: Random House, 1995, pp. 141–145.

23. Stephen F. Hamilton, "Youth Apprenticeship Systems," *Educational Researcher*, Vol. 22, no. 3, April 1993, pp. 11–12.

Chapter 8 Notes

1. Edward E. Gordon, "Work-Based Learning in America: Solutions for a New Century," *Corporate University Review*, November/December 1997, pp. 36–37.

2. Clifford Adelman, "Turning College 'Access' into 'Participation'" *Education Week*, October 22, 1997, p. 40.

   "World Is Doing Better at Graduating Students," *Chicago Tribune*, November 24, 1998, sec. 1, p. 23.

3. Interview with Dr. Kenneth B. Hoyt, Kansas State University, July 1995.

4. Tom Kean interview with Hendrick Smith, October 15, 1993, for *Rethinking America*, New York: Random House, 1995.

5. Nina Munk, "You've Come Too Far Baby," *Forbes*, July 28, 1997, pp. 39–40.

6. Lynn Olson, "The Career Game," *Education Week*, October 2, 1996, pp. 31–32.

7. Stephen Hamilton, "Prospects for an American Style Youth Apprenticeship System," *Educational Researcher*, April 1993, pp. 12–17.

8. *Training Strategies: Preparing Non-College Youth for Employment in the U.S. and Foreign Countries.* Washington, D.C.: United States General Accounting Office, 1990, p. 24.

9. *The Skilled Workforce Shortage: A Growing Challenge to the Future Competitiveness of American Manufacturing.* Washington, D.C.: National Association of Manufacturing, 1998.

10. Marc Tucker, "A School-to-Work Transition System for the United States," Washington, D.C.: National Center on Education and the Economy, 1998, p. 6.

11. Frank Levy and Richard J. Murane, *Teaching the New Basic Skills: Principles for Educating Children to Thrive in a Changing Economy.* New York: The Free Press, 1997.

12. "Regional Voc Ed Program May Serve As National Model," *Vocational Training News*, December 19, 1996, p. 1.

13. Kristina J. Shelly, "The Future of Jobs for College Graduates," MLR, *Monthly Labor Review*, July 1992, pp. 13–19.

14. C. Douglas Marsh, "The People Crunch," *Solid State Technology*, September 1996, p. 164.

15. Meg Sommerfeld, "Big Wheels," *Education Week*, August 7, 1996, p. 54.

16. Andrew Zajac, "Nerds Get Their Resume as Tech Jobs Go Begging," *Chicago Tribune*, July 19, 1998, sec. 1, p. 1.

17. David Barringer, "The Standby Generation," *American Bar Association Journal*, June 1996, pp. 80–81.

18. Hans A. Schieser, "Educating America's Labor Force to Meet a Global Competition," *Training Today*, February 1987, p. 8.

19. Robert J. Sternberg, "What Should We Ask About Intelligence?" *Network News and Views*, May 1996, p. 25.

20. Evans Clincky, "Who Is Out of Step with Whom?" *Education Week*, February 4, 1998, p. 48.

21. David Lubinski and Camilla P. Benbow, "Optimal Development of Talent," *Network News and Views*, October 1995, pp. 26–35.

22. Edward E. Gordon, "Work-Based Learning," pp. 36–37.

23. Paul E. Barton, *Cooperative Education in High School: Promise and Neglect*, Princeton, NJ: Educational Testing Service, 1996, pp. 1, 4.

24. "A High-Skills Workforce—The Employer's Options," *Youth Research*, Youth Policy Institute, Washington, D.C. December 31, 1996, p. 20.

School-to-Work, Washington, D.C.: U.S. Departments of Labor and Education, National School-to-Work Office, October 1996.

Foundations for Life, Washington, D.C.: National School-to-Work Office, National Alliance of Business, 1998.

25. Donald Clark, "Recent International Development in School-to-Work Policy," *National Association for Industry–Education Cooperation Newsletter*, February/March 1997, p.1.

26. Kenneth B. Hoyt, *Career Education and Transition from Schooling to Employment*, Manhattan, KS: Kansas State University Press, 1998.

27. E.D. Hirsch, Jr., *Cultural Literacy, What Every American Needs to Know*, New York: Vintage Books, 1987, pp. 11, 13, 31.

28. Kenneth Hoyt, *Refining the Career Education Concept*, Washington, D.C.: U.S. Department of Health, Education and Welfare, 1976, p. 28.

29. *Benchmarks of Excellence*, Washington, D.C.: National Alliance of Business, 1996, p. 5.

30. "Board Sets Job Areas for Skill Standards," *School-to-Work Report*, February 1997, p. 10.

"Job Standards Board Sets Skill Guidelines," *Vocational Training News*, December 5, 1996, p. 1.

31. Eunice N. Askov, *Framework for Developing Skill Standards for Workplace Literacy*, Washington, D.C.: National Institute for Literacy, 1996.

32. *The Challenge of Change*, Washington, D.C.: National Alliance of Business, January 1995.

33. Gail Kinney, *Involving Unions in School-to-Work Initiatives*, Washington, D.C.: Human Resources Development Institute AFL-CIO, 1997, pp. 6, 32, 34, 53, 59.

34. "School-to-Work Systems Slow to Show Results," *Vocational Training News*, May 29, 1997, pp. 1, 3.

35. "States Encourage Students to Select Career Majors," *School-to-Work Report*, May 1996, p. 36.

36. "Getting a Head Start on a Career," *Update*, Association for Supervisor and Curriculum Development, October 1994, pp. 1–3.

37. "Miami High School Prepares Students for Two Paths," *Vocational Training News*, October 3, 1996, pp. 10–12.

38. Building an Educated Workforce," *Crain's Chicago Business*, October 7, 1996, p. 9.

39. "Ridge School of Technical Arts in Cambridge Mass: Using the Community to Develop Student Talents," in *Hands and Minds: Redefining Success in Vocational Education*, Washington, D.C.: Education Writers Association, 1992, pp. 26–31.

40. *1994 Annual Report*, Rochester, NY: Rochester Business Education Alliance, National Center on Education and the Economy, 1994.

41. Fred R. Bleakley, "Ready to Work," *Wall Street Journal*, November 26, 1996, p. A1.

42. "Businesses Are the Boss in Biggest Voc Ed District," *Vocational Training News*, December 12, 1996, pp. 1–2.

43. Interview with Jan Keim, Director of Marketing Communications, Tulsa Technology Center, August 12, 1998.

   Mary Ann Zehr, "Driven to Succeed," *Education Week*, February 18, 1998, pp. 32-35.

44. Interview with Marybeth Steiner, David Douglas High School, January 6, 1997.

45. Interview with Connie Majka, Philadelphia High School Academics, Inc., August 14, 1998.

   "Business Partners Making Philadelphia Academics Click," *Vocational Training News*, October 9, 1997, pp. 5–6.

46. *Work Based Learning Survey*, Washington, D.C.: U.S. Census Bureau, and The National Center on the Education Quality of the Workforce, 1997.

47. Interview with Bonnie Silvers, National Academy Foundation, New York, January 19, 1997.

48. The *Health Care Industry—School-to-Work Transition*, Washington, D.C.: The National Alliance of Business, 1997.

49. Joetta L. Sack, "Boeing Program Moves Vocational Education to a New Plane," *Education Week*, September 10, 1997, pp. 1, 12.

   Brandon Copple and Louise Lee, "Labor Squeeze Forces Corporate America Back to High School," *Wall Street Journal*, July 22, 1998, pp. A2, A9.

50. "At Siemens, Learning and Earning Go Hand in Hand," *Work America*, Washington, D.C.: National Alliance of Business, October 1996, pp. 1, 4–5.

   "President and CEO of Siemens Corporation Albert Hoser" (Interview), *Europe*, no. 328, July/August 1993, p. 20.

51. Michele Johnson, "Mobilizing Community Resources to Facilitate Intel's Move to Washington State," Presentation at the League for Innovation Annual Conference, Los Angeles, CA, February 17, 1997.

   "Worker Shortage Requires School-to-Work Links," *School-to-Work Report*, June 1998, p. 47.

52. Eleena DeLisser, "Size May Not Matter Under New Federal Safety Rules," *Wall Street Journal*, November 24, 1998, p. B2.

53. "Colorado Firms Get Tax Credit for School-to-Work Efforts," *Vocational Training News*, July 3, 1997, p. 1.

54. "Trends and Forecasts," *School-to-Work Report*, January 1998, p. 1.

55. "States Ease Liability Concerns in School-to-Work Programs," *School-to-Work Report*, November 1997, p. 85.

56. Donald M. Clark, "How Business/Education Collaboration Should Work," *Technical Training* (ASTD), September/October 1998, p. 56.

57. Richard Hofstadler, *Anti-Intellectualism in American Life*, New York: Vintage Books, 1962, pp. 257, 264.

Chapter 9 Notes

1. Theresa Minton-Eversole, "Roger Schank Talks Training," *Technical Training*, May/June 1998, p. 10.

2. Ian Rose, "Improving the Effectiveness of Corporate Training," IBR Consulting Services Ltd. Report, Vancouver, Canada, 1996.

Chapter 10 Notes

1. Paul L. Williams, *1994 NAEP Reading: A First Look*, Washington, D.C.: Office of Educational Research and Improvement, U.S. Department of Education, 1996.

2. Gene Koretz, "The Sheep Skin Paradox," *Business Week*, October 6, 1997, p. 30.

3. Peter Drucker, *The Knowledge Creating Company*, New York: Oxford University Press, 1995.

4. R. C. Longworth, "Global Squeeze," *Chicago Tribune*, October 9, 1996, sec. 1, p. 1.

5. Robert M. Tomasko, "Restructuring: Getting It Right," *Management Review*, April 1992, pp. 10–15.

6. "And Now, Upsizing," *The Economist*, June 8, 1996, p. 72.

7. "Backlash," *Across the Board*, July/August 1996, pp. 24–39.

8. Peter F. Drucker, "Management's New Paradigms," *Forbes*, October 5, 1998, pp. 23–27.

9. Bibi S. Watson, "Colloquy at Brush Wellman on the New Social Contract," *Forum on Training*, American Management Association, September 1995, p. 1.

10. Edward E. Gordon, Ronald R. Morgan, Judith A. Ponticell, *FutureWork, The Revolution Reshaping American Business*, Westport, CT: Praeger, 1994, pp. 204–207.

11. Millicent Lawton, "Promote or Retain? Pendulum for Students Swings Back Again," *Education Week*, June 11, 1997, p. 1.

12. Michael E. Young, "How the GI Bill Changed America," *Chicago Tribune*, April 2, 1995, sec. 1, pp. 1, 18.

13. David W. Kirkpatrick, *School Choice: An Idea That Can't Be Conquered*, Indianapolis, IN: Milton & Rose D. Friedman Foundation: 1997, p. 4.

14. Sarah Brookhart, "Job Training Reform Enacted," *The Industrial–Organizational Psychologist*, October 1998, pp. 102–103.

15. Chester E. Finn, Jr., "Different Schools for a Better Future," *Network News & Views*, October 1996, p. 91.

16. Douglas W. Kmiec, "School Choice: Why Hasn't Its Time Come?" *Chicago Tribune*, August 25, 1997, sec. 1, p. 13.

17. Marshall J. Breger, Robert A. Destro, "Is Parochial School Choice Unconstitutional?" *Wall Street Journal*, February 27, 1996, p. A18.

18. "Other Major Cases May Rise to the Docket," *USA Today*, October 2, 1998, p. 13A.

Amy Stuart Wells, Stuart Biegel, "Public Funds for Private Schools: Political and First Amendment Considerations," *Network News & Views*, June 1993, pp. 1–17.

19. "Parent Power," *The Economist*, Vol. 331, no. 7862, May 7, 1994, p. 83.

John S. Gardner, "The Best Choice . . ." *Network News & Views*, June 1995, pp. 53–54.

Quentin L. Quade, "Two Ghastly Specters Confront America's Parents," *Network News & Views*, December 1996, pp. 96–103.

20. Susan Uchitelle, *School Choice: Issues and Answers*, Bloomington, IN: Phi Delta Kappa Educational Foundation, 1993, pp. 31–33.

21. Marilyn Chase, "Feed Your Brain, and It May Thrive in Old Age," *Wall Street Journal*, November 21, 1994, p. B1.

22. Edward E. Gordon, Ronald R. Morgan, and Judith A. Ponticell, *Future-Work, The Revolution Reshaping American Business*, Westport, CT: Praeger, 1994, pp. 9, 125–126.

23. Howard D. Mehlinger, "School Reform in the Information Age," *Phi Delta Kappan*, February 1996, p. 403.

24. Jane M. Healy, "The 'Name' That Ate Childhood," *Education Week*, October 7, 1998, pp. 37, 56.

25. Mary Ann Zehr, "Teaching the Teachers," *Education Week*, November 10, 1997, p. 24.

26. Debra Viadero, "A Tool for Learning," *Education Week*, November 10, 1997, pp. 12–18.

27. David A. Kaplan and Adam Rogers, "The Silicon Classroom," *Newsweek*, April 22, 1996, pp. 60–61.

28. Mike Dorning, "Teachers Fall Short, Study Says," *Chicago Tribune*, September 13, 1996, sec. 1, p. 10.

29. Diana Wyllie Rigden, "How Teachers Would Change Teacher Education," *Education Week*, December 11, 1996, pp. 48, 64.

30. Don Sneed, "Getting Profs Off Their Chairs," *Wall Street Journal*, March 29, 1996, p. 12.

31. Len Strazewski, "Training Workers to Fill the Jobs of the 21st Century," *Chicago Tribune*, June 10, 1997, sec. 6, p. 1.

32. *Human Resources Competitiveness Profile*, Washington, D.C.: Council on Competitiveness, 1995.

33. "Computers and Classrooms," *Chicago Tribune*, August 24, 1997, sec. 14, p. 3.

34. Hal Lancaster, "Managers Beware: You're Not Ready for Tomorrow's Jobs," *Wall Street Journal*, June 24, 1995, p. B1.

35. Robert Samuelson, *The Good Life and Its Discontents: The American Dream in the Age of Entitlement 1945–1995*, New York: Time Books, 1996.

36. "Worker Friendly," *Chicago Tribune*, April 21, 1996, sec. 5, p. 7.

37. Hedrick Smith, *Rethinking America*, New York: Random House, 1995, p. 417.

Index

Butterworth-Heinemann Business Books . . . for Transforming Business

Cultivating Common Ground: Releasing the Power of Relationships at Work
      Daniel S. Hanson, 0-7506-9832-2

Diversity Success Strategies
      Norma Carr-Ruffino, 0-7506-7102-5

5th Generation Management, Co-creating Through Virtual Enterprising, Dynamic Teaming, and Knowledge Networking, Revised Edition
      Charles M. Savage, 0-7506-9701-6

Flight of the Phoenix: Soaring to Success in the 21st Century
      John Whiteside and Sandra Egli, 0-7506-9798-9

From Chaos to Coherence: Advancing Individual and Organizational Intelligence Through Inner Quality Management®
      Bruce Cryer and Doc Childre, 0-75067007-X

Getting a Grip on Tomorrow: Your Guide to Survival and Success in the Changed World of Work
      Mike Johnson, 0-7506-9758-X

Infinite Wealth: A New World of Collaboration and Abundance in the Knowledge Era
      Barry C. Carter, 0-7506-7184-X

Innovation Strategy for the Knowledge Economy: The Ken Awakening
      Debra M. Amidon, 0-7506-9841-1

The Hidden Intelligence: Innovation Through Intuition
      Sandra Weintraub, 0-7506-9937-X

The Intelligence Advantage: Organizing for Complexity
      Michael D. McMaster, 0-7506-9792-X

The Knowledge Evolution: Expanding Organizational Intelligence
      Verna Allee, 0-7506-9842-X

Leadership in a Challenging World: A Sacred Journey
      Barbara Shipka, 0-7506-9750-4

Leading Consciously: A Pilgrimage Toward Self-Mastery
      Debashis Chatterjee, 0-7506-9864-0

Leading from the Heart: Choosing Courage over Fear in the Workplace
      Kay Gilley, 0-7506-9835-7

Learning to Read the Signs: Reclaiming Pragmatism in Business
      F. Byron Nahser, 0-7506-9901-9

Leveraging People and Profit: The Hard Work of Soft Management
      Bernard A. Nagle and Perry Pascarella, 0-7506-9961-2

Liberating the Corporate Soul: Building A Visionary Organization
    Richard Barrett, 0-7506-7071-1

Life Work Transitions.Com: Putting Your Spirit Online
    Deborah L. Knox and Sandra S. Butzel, 0-7506-7160-2

A Little Knowledge Is A Dangerous Thing: Understanding Our Global Knowledge Economy
    Dale Neef, 0-7506-7061-4

Marketing Plans that Work: Targeting Growth and Profitability
    Malcolm H.B. McDonald and Warren J. Keegan, 0-7506-9828-4

Navigating Cross-Cultural Ethics: What Global Managers Do Right to Keep From Going Wrong
    Eileen Morgan, 0-7506-9915-9

A Place to Shine: Emerging from the Shadows at Work
    Daniel S. Hanson, 0-7506-9738-5

Power Partnering: A Strategy for Business Excellence in the 21st Century
    Sean Gadman, 0-7506-9809-8

Putting Emotional Intelligence to Work; Successful Leadership Is More Than IQ
    David Ryback, 0-7506-9956-6

Quantum Leaps: 7 Skills for Workplace ReCreation
    Charlotte A. Shelton, 0-7506-7077-0

Resources for the Knowledge-Based Economy Series

Knowledge Management and Organizational Design
    Paul S. Myers, 0-7506-9749-0

Knowledge Management Tools
    Rudy L. Ruggles, III, 0-7506-9849-7

Knowledge in Organizations
    Laurence Prusak, 0-7506-9718-0

The Strategic Management of Intellectual Capital
    David A. Klein, 0-7506-9850-0

Rise of the Knowledge Worker
    James W. Cortada, 0-7506-7058-4

The Knowledge Economy
    Dale Neef, 0-7506-9936-1

The Economic Impact of Knowledge
Dale Neef, G. Anthony Seisfeld, Jacquelyn Cefola, 0-7506-7009-6

Knowledge and Special Libraries
James A. Matarazzo and Suzanne D. Connolly, 0-7506-7084-3

Knowledge and Strategy
Michael Zack, 0-7506-7088-6

Knowledge, Groupware and the Internet
David E. Smith, 0-7506-7111-4

The Rhythm of Business: The Key to Building and Running Successful Companies
David Shuman, 0-7506-9991-4

Setting the PACE® in Product Development: A Guide to Product And Cycle-time Excellence
Michael E. McGrath, 0-7506-9789-X

Skill Wars: Winning the Battle for Productivity and Profit
Edward E. Gordon, 0-7506-7027-2

Synchronicity: The Entrepreneur's Edge
Jessika Satori, 0-7506-9925-6

Systems Thinking Managing Chaos and Complexity: A Platform for Designing Business Architecture
Jamshid Gharajedaghi, 0-7506-7163-7

Time to Take Control: The Impact of Change on Corporate Computer Systems
Tony Johnson, 0-7506-9863-2

The Transformation of Management
Mike Davidson, 0-7506-9814-4

What Is The Emperor Wearing: Truth-Telling in Business Relationships
Laurie Weiss, 0-7506-9872-1

Who We Could Be at Work, Revised Edition
Margaret A. Lulic, 0-7506-9739-3

Working from Your Core: Personal and Corporate Wisdom in a World of Change
Sharon Seivert, 0-7506-9930-2

To purchase a copy of any Butterworth-Heinemann Business title, please visit your local bookstore or call 1-800-366-2665.